THE
EVERYTHING®
REAL ESTATE
INVESTING
BOOK

How to get started and make the
most of your money

Janet Wickell

Adams Media
Avon, Massachusetts

W9-AUA-521

For my parents, Earnest Lloyd Armstrong and Thelma Lyons
Armstrong, who are never far from my thoughts.

An Everything® Series Book.
Everything® and everything.com® are registered trademarks of F+W Publications, Inc.

Published by Adams Media, an F+W Publications Company
57 Littlefield Street, Avon, MA 02322 U.S.A.
www.adamsmedia.com

ISBN: 1-59337-131-4
Printed in the United States of America.

J I H G F E D C B A

Library of Congress Cataloging-in-Publication Data
Wickell, Janet.
The everything real estate investing book / Janet Wickell.
p.   cm.
ISBN 1-59337-131-4
1. Real estate investment. 2. Real estate investment–Finance. 3. Real estate management.
I. Title: Real estate investing book. II. Title. III. Series: Everything series.

HD1382.5.W515 2004
332.63'24–dc22

2004008569

This book is available at quantity discounts for bulk purchases.
For information, call 1-800-872-5627.

Contents

Acknowledgments

Many thanks to Barb Doyen and the staff at Adams Media for their support and patience during a period filled with personal challenges. To my coworkers at Brevard Realty Team—thanks for being there when I couldn't. And, as always, thanks to my family for their constant support.

Top Ten Ways to Prepare
for a Real-Estate Investment Career

1. Get your finances in order. Don't miss out on a fantastic property because you are short of cash or have bad credit.

2. Become familiar with your local real-estate market. You won't know a good purchase unless you're in tune with what's available.

3. Network with friends, relatives, and other people you see on a daily basis. Tell everyone you are interested in buying real estate.

4. Take a real-estate licensing class, just for the information that it offers.

5. Find a mentor, someone who has already achieved success in the field. The advice will be invaluable.

6. Develop a professional relationship with at least one good real-estate agent. Agents are a wonderful source of information about your local real estate.

7. Talk to a tax professional to determine how you should progress with your business.

8. Find a local attorney who practices real-estate law.

9. Become familiar with the methods used to find public documents that are recorded online or at your county courthouse. Real-estate purchases and sales require a good deal of research, so it's important to learn how to find what you need.

10. Talk to locals who are already part of the local real-estate community.

Introduction

▶ Welcome to *The Everything® Real Estate Investing Book*. Are you ready to begin exploring the world of real-estate investing? You've come to the right place, and you might be surprised to learn that the topic can take you down many different pathways. There's a real-estate specialty to suit just about everyone.

You've no doubt heard people say, "I wish I had invested in real estate thirty years ago." Well, thirty years from now, people will still be making that comment. There's no time like the present to get started. The longer you wait, the higher real-estate prices will be—that's one reason real estate is such a wonderful place to invest your money. It's one of the most stable investments you'll ever find. The worst mistake you can make is *not* buying the "wrong" property—it's not buying anything at all.

Many real-estate investors find that residential properties are the perfect place to start—they're a safe investment and, when you choose wisely, not too difficult to turn around in a hurry. Whether you stick to that path or branch off to another is up to you. There's plenty to choose from, including commercial real estate, land development, or owning and managing a large apartment complex or strip mall—perhaps one of those specialties is more appealing to you.

You'll become a good detective as you learn to research properties and locate their owners. The real-estate negotiation process will help you improve your people skills because it forces you to interact with home-buyers, home-sellers, tenants, agents, and other members of the real-estate community. The knowledge you'll acquire will help you buy and sell personal residences, too. You'll even get to practice your home repair and maintenance talents as you remodel and care for your investment properties—and who among us can't use those skills every day?

Get ready to discover how much fun it is to buy a piece of real estate that everyone else thinks is a disaster and to use your creativity and knowledge of the market to turn it into a property that's in high demand. Success takes a good bit of imagination—including the ability to see beyond chipped paint and outdated decorating—and it requires dedication and a willingness to get your hands dirty once in a while. It's definitely worth the effort—a successful real-estate investment career can put money in your pocket today and help secure your future wealth.

This book offers a step-by-step analysis of the process of buying, selling, and renting real estate. It's essential for you to understand the details that must be considered before you initiate any type of real-estate transaction, and this book offers a solid background to help you do just that.

Some deals are risky—others are a sure thing. More risk usually equals more potential gains (and losses), but many of us can still do without the stress involved in *those* transactions. Not to worry, because there's a spot for everyone, and finding it can be an exciting adventure when you have the background you need to feel confident about your decisions. Use the resources on the following pages to help you find your niche—that special segment of real estate where each of us has a home. Ⓔ

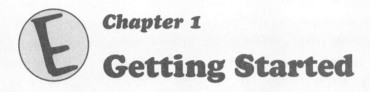

Chapter 1

Getting Started

Over time, real estate has proven to be one of the most stable investments a person can make. If you do your homework and let common sense guide you, the risks are far less than you'll encounter in the stock market, but the gains can be just as good. Real estate takes hard work and dedication, but if you're ready to roll up your sleeves and get your hands dirty, your efforts will be rewarded. Let's get started.

Is Real-Estate Investing Right for You?

Before you get involved, consider your goals and motivations. Do you want to break into real estate because you've heard that it offers quick profits with little effort? If that's the case, you may need to rethink your attitude. If investing in real estate were an easy job with instant payoffs, everyone would be doing it. Most of the people who recommend those quickie (and sometimes questionable) methods make their income from selling their books and tapes, not from working in real estate.

Dealing in real estate is hard work that requires a great deal of research before you even think of making an offer. The offer itself must be crafted carefully in order to protect your interests. Provisions must be inserted that allow you to back out with no penalties if certain conditions are not met—and you won't know what provisions to request unless you've done your homework.

After an offer is accepted, the task of getting the transaction to the closing table. That journey can be filled with an array of problems:

- The appraisal might come back low.
- An inspection could uncover structural problems that you're not willing to deal with.
- The level of radon gas might be high, requiring a mitigation system to lower it.
- Your lender might not approve the loan.

There are very few trouble-free transactions, so be prepared to deal with stressful situations, no matter what type of real-estate investments you choose. Before you get started, take some time to analyze yourself and your motivations. Going through that process will help you determine exactly where you fit in the world of real-estate investments.

Consider Where You Fit In

Finding your niche is what it's all about, isn't it? You'll be more successful in your investment career if you genuinely like what you are doing. If you don't enjoy working with people, taking on landlord duties probably isn't for you. You can still own rentals, but plan on having someone else handle the management. If you can't deal with stress, don't take on commercial properties or any property that seems extremely risky—at least not until you have plenty of extra cash and confidence in your ability to deal with all phases of a project.

Many investors start out by living in an investment property while they get it ready to sell or rent. That technique offers benefits, including the lower down-payment and interest rate that are available for owner-occupied dwellings, as well as one less mortgage payment.

Your Available Time

How much time do you have to devote to real estate? The best profits are sometimes the result of refurbishing a cosmetically challenged or true fixer-upper property. The more work you can do yourself, the more money will stay in your pocket when it's time to rent or sell.

However, if you already work sixty hours a week, you'll have to hire someone to handle every renovation task. That doesn't just lower profits—it often means it will take longer to complete the project.

Your Personal Life

Do you have a spouse, a family, or a significant other? How do they feel about sharing you with your real-estate career? A successful career in real estate takes a great deal of time and effort. Once you've made it to some degree, you can delegate responsibilities and hire help, but for most of us that takes awhile. It's easier on your home life if your loved ones are interested in being involved in some way—or are at least understanding of your goals.

Your Hands-On Expectations

You're going to get your hands dirty. At the very least, plan on doing a lot of cleaning. Painting is a given, too. How about laying tile and carpeting and taping off drywall—are you up to those chores? If not, it will limit the number of properties you should consider, unless you have someone who will do the work for you for a reasonable fee.

Your Flair for Interior and Exterior Decor

You might be surprised how many buyers can't see past dirty floors and scuffed walls. If you want to be successful in real-estate investing, you should be able to look beyond the surface and visualize what the structure will look like with a basic cleanup, then take it a step further to determine what kinds of changes would make significant improvements in its appearance and usability.

An effective way to train yourself to be able to see the potential in any property is to read decorating magazines, watch home-improvement shows, and browse the Internet for decorating ideas. The more information you're exposed to, the more likely you are to instinctively know what should be done to make immediate improvements to a property, inside and out.

Where Will You Get the Funding?

Do you have savings or access to other funds? Mortgage terms for investment properties aren't as liberal as loans for owner-occupied dwellings, and they're even stricter for commercial investments. You might be able to persuade a seller to finance all or a portion of the property, but you'll need cash or a line of credit to make updates and repairs.

It might be worthwhile to float expenses for projects you think you can turn over quickly on a credit card, but you sure don't want to be stuck with a high-interest debt for very long. High credit-card balances can also affect the way mortgage lenders analyze your credit reports and scores.

How long can you handle a negative cash flow before it hurts you financially? Your first project could go quickly, but it's more realistic to expect delays. Dealing with real-estate sales and rentals is a learning process, and it might take one or two transactions before your skills are consistent. Plan your budget to include available cash for delays and possible setbacks.

Your Comfort Level

Most importantly, consider your comfort level. How much are you willing to risk? While it's true that real-estate investing is far less risky than the stock market or most business investments, the risk factors depend on what kind of real estate you're working with. Investing in residential real estate carries less risk than commercial properties and land purchases, but some risk is still involved. If you cannot deal with any type of risk at all, real estate is not your best investment choice.

QUESTION?

Are you willing to make sacrifices?
Buying an investment property will probably take a bite out of your free money, the dollars you use to have fun. Are you willing to give that up for awhile? Fewer dinners out, fewer vacations, a general cutback on entertainment—is it worth it to you to eliminate these things while you build equity in properties?

Analyze Your Real-Estate Market

There are potential real-estate investments of every type, from single-family residences to large commercial developments. What's right for you? Some investors are content buying and selling residential properties. There's plenty of diversification in that single field because we can specialize in foreclosures, fixer-uppers, multifamily projects, or other types of residences. Every other area of real estate offers just as much variety, so there's something for everyone. The trick is finding the segment of the real-estate market that you enjoy the most.

What's in Demand Close to Home?

Unless you live in a very small town, there are probably many real-estate investment avenues to pursue. The most important thing you can do is keep your mind open to all possibilities. Look at properties from a fresh perspective, visualizing what they could be with updates or simple changes rather than focusing on their current conditions.

Most properties that are for sale are listed with real-estate agencies, so the majority of buyers go to agents when they are in the market to buy. Experienced real-estate agents can be one of your best sources of information about what buyers and renters are looking for. Develop a relationship with one or more agents who specialize in the types of properties you want to buy.

Read all of your local papers, and pick up every real-estate for-sale publication that's available in your community. Pay close attention to ads, noting prices versus features for rental homes and properties listed for sale. Take regular drives through the communities you are most interested in. Your goal is to become familiar with every aspect of the real-estate market in your town.

Look at local demographics. Is your buyer pool made up primarily of one group of people, such as senior citizens? Knowing as much as you can about the population makeup will help you with any type of real-estate investment, from selling single-family homes to finding commercial tenants that specialize in businesses and services important to your town.

National and International Opportunities

If you can't find what you're looking for locally, branch out to other areas. There's never been a better time to shop nationally or internationally—the Internet brings distant real-estate opportunities to anyone who has a computer and a Web connection.

A downside of distant investments is managing them effectively, so be prepared to hire someone to handle tenants and maintenance for you. The extra expense must be considered when you analyze the potential returns on your investment.

But before you branch out to other areas, it's important to become accustomed to your local real-estate market. Real-estate transactions are handled very differently across the United States. Worldwide, you'll see even more variations. Understanding your local process will give you more confidence and better prepare you to ask questions about the procedures in other areas.

One way to begin a real-estate investment career at a distant location is to buy a vacation home. How about an area where you like to spend a few weeks each year, or a location where you think you would like to retire? Chances are it's a spot you already know at least a little bit about, and that can be a plus when it's time to select properties.

If you have a child or grandchild away from home in college, consider buying a house or condo instead of paying rent for a dorm or apartment. The residence will fill a need during the young person's college years, and its value will appreciate for you. Make the time away from home an investment opportunity instead of paying rent for four or more years. Sell the home when your child leaves school, or continue to use it as a rental for other students.

Finding Your First Investment

Buying a single-family home is a great way to start your real-estate investment career. Why should you go with a single-family residence? Because they are generally the properties in most demand, which in turn makes them the easiest properties to sell. Let's walk through a typical scenario, in which you've researched the market in preparation to buy a single-family home.

Let's say your market research shows that senior citizens make up a large portion of the buying pool in your town. They likely want a house that's not *too* small, but not too large, either. A three-bedroom, two-bath home is perfect, something around 2,000 square feet or slightly less.

Local agents have advised you to look for a house with no steps—or just a few. Even seniors who aren't bothered by steps yet are looking for one-level living with a minimum of stairs to climb. That eliminates split-foyer homes, homes where you must climb high porches in order to enter the front door, and homes with finished living areas on two levels.

Most seniors want a house in move-in condition. They don't want to paint or make repairs. That's where you step in. Your goal is to find a house that's structurally sound and has the required features but that needs cosmetic updates. If you can't find that type of house at a bargain price, you might need to look at houses that need a little more work, but for this first purchase, steer clear of anything that involves structural repairs unless you are an experienced builder.

ALERT!

Lenders offer lower interest rates and down-payment terms for owner-occupied homes, so moving into the investment property could save you money. If you live there for two years or less, you won't even owe capital gains taxes when you sell it. Many investors move from house to house, increasing their gains with each sale.

You've talked with enough real-estate agents to know that hardwood floors are very popular and that seniors in your area prefer gas fireplaces to the wood-burning versions. If you can't find a house with those features, you plan to add them. You have a good idea of the house you want to buy, so now it's time to start looking.

Scout Out the Neighborhoods

Your ideal find is a slightly rundown house in a desirable, low-crime neighborhood close to shopping, hospitals, and other services. Ask an agent what's for sale in neighborhoods that fit that description, and get copies of multiple listing sheets so that you'll have addresses and detailed information about the homes. Don't just drive by those houses—browse other streets in the same neighborhoods to find "For Sale by Owner" (FSBO) properties that agents won't mention.

Tour the Properties

Make appointments to see the most interesting properties. Take notes about interior and exterior components. List the most desirable features of each house. What updates are required? A total kitchen revamp could be costly, but maybe you can get by with painting or staining the cabinets and adding new countertops. New flooring and paint can do wonders, and so can opening up spaces between rooms. Each home will present you with an entirely different scenario of possibilities, and it's up to you to determine which ones will bring the most return when you sell or rent the property.

Who Else Will Like the House?

Seniors may be your primary target, but they aren't the only buyers out there. Will the house appeal to other age groups—young couples or families with children? You've already looked for a location near local services, but throwing a good school district into the mix will give you more options when it's time to sell or rent.

Making an Offer

You've found a house and want to make an offer. You've already talked with a lender, and you know you can qualify for a loan before you sell the house you live in. The resources in Chapter 7 will help you determine value, and other chapters will walk you through negotiations and contracts.

Give Yourself Some Time

That brief scenario was a fast-forward version of just a few of the steps you'll take when you search for your first property. You may be looking for something entirely different, something that fits in with the needs of the buyers and renters in *your* town. You might not even make an offer on a property at the end of your search.

Don't be in too much of a hurry to buy. Sure, it's exciting and you want to find that first property *now*, but are you truly ready? Can you make an offer and negotiate a contract without letting your emotions take over? The more time you spend learning about your real-estate market, the less likely you are to make hasty decisions about any one property.

There are many things you can do to make absolutely sure you are ready to buy your first property:

- **Devote time each week to research.** That includes browsing properties on the Internet, talking to local real-estate professionals, making trips to your county courthouse to check the prices of recently sold properties, and then driving by those properties to help you judge the going rates in specific neighborhoods.

- **Do some more reading.** This book will get you started, but you might consider getting more information about specific areas of the real-estate market. There are many publications and Web sites devoted to particular aspects of the business. Getting your hands on this information could mean the difference between failure and success.

- **Consider taking a real-estate agent licensing course.** You'll get a quick introduction to the laws and customs that affect your state and local community. Taking the course doesn't mean you should become an agent. In fact, that can work against you. Agents must disclose their status to all potential sellers, and some property owners you approach will flatly refuse to deal with a real-estate agent.

- **Become involved in your community.** Join clubs and associations. Start developing a network of people who know you are interested in buying real estate. Make sure your family and friends know to contact you first when they hear about a property that sounds like a good buy.

- **Learn about home repair and construction.** Take a course at a local community college or attend weekend classes at home improvement centers. You'll be surprised how quickly you can learn to handle minor repairs and redecorating tasks. You may never learn to build a house, but you will learn more about building components—enough to help you estimate repairs and recognize a problem when you see it.

- **Learn landscaping basics.** Curb appeal is a top priority when it's time to sell or rent, and you can save a great deal of money by handling landscaping chores yourself. A nicely landscaped lot can sell a house, but it's an element that many sellers don't even consider enhancing.

Spend time driving around the area, getting to know the neighborhoods as intimately as possible. If you see a house with a "For Sale" sign, call to get the details about it, including the price. Printed materials are a good resource, but they rarely tell you where a property is located, and when you're not familiar with an area, you can't relate location to price anyway. Spending some time in neighborhoods will help you get a better feel for the differences in prices based on location, and you might just find a spot that you're certain would be the perfect choice if the right home comes on the market.

Always be on the lookout for investment opportunities. Last year you might not have paid too much attention when your friend told you about a family that needed to sell their house quickly in order to move on to a better job. This year, you'll jump on that statement and gather enough information to check out the property.

Real estate doesn't have to rule your life, but new investors usually agree that it does dominate it for a while. Once you're past the basics, you'll find yourself relaxing a little more. The details will come more naturally, and you won't stress over every decision you make. Take it slow, keep your emotions in check, and you'll find success in the real-estate market. Ⓔ

Chapter 2

Residential Properties

Real-estate investors can choose from a huge variety of properties. If you prefer to invest in residential properties, here's an overview of some of the different types of real estate available to you. It includes tips that help you recognize the types of properties you are looking at. In addition, details are provided to help you understand how the land that homes are built on often dictates the type of buildings that are constructed there and how they can be used.

Single-Family Homes

A single-family home is built to accommodate one person or group of people living together. There's usually one main entrance and only one address for the property—it's the type of house many of us think of when we hear the term "neighborhood." Single-family homes are by far the most common form of residential housing, and they are the favorite choice among the majority of people shopping for a home.

The land beneath a single-family home is nearly always part of the purchase package, but some houses are built on leased lots. You are most likely to encounter houses on leased land in resort areas, where land is expensive and hard to find, within church-owned developments, and in assisted-care facilities.

Not all single-family homes are constructed in the same way. They can be sorted into several different categories, and it is important for real-estate investors to understand the differences between them before they buy or sell.

The Site-Built House

Site-built houses are the structures most of us are familiar with. All of the elements needed to construct a home are delivered to the site, and then a builder puts the home together piece by piece. Local building codes dictate how the site-built house should be constructed. Houses in a hurricane zone might be required to have heavy-duty walls and foundations. Wood shingle roofs are sometimes banned in communities that are prone to wildfires. Building codes are designed to help builders avoid safety hazards and make sure that every house is a stable structure for the area it is in.

The builder must apply for permits to complete the house, and as building progresses, local inspectors arrive to verify that the work being done conforms to all building codes. The owner usually can't move into the house until a certificate of occupancy (CO) is issued.

Manufactured Housing

Manufactured houses were formerly called *mobile homes* or *trailers*. They are built in a factory to conform to the U.S. government's Manufactured

Home Construction and Safety Standards Code, known simply as the HUD code. Each manufactured home—or segment of a home—is labeled with a red tag that guarantees the home conforms to the HUD code.

ALERT!

Many lenders will not finance manufactured housing unless the home is on a permanent foundation—not resting only on its wheels. Always check foundation status before moving forward with a loan application.

Manufactured homes are built on a permanent steel chassis and transported to the building site on their own wheels. Sometimes the wheels are removed, but often they're still visible under the house after it is completed.

There should be a data plate inside the home stating its date of manufacture. The plate is usually on or near the main electrical panel, in a kitchen cabinet, or in a bedroom closet. The data plate is important because it gives information about the home's original heating and cooling systems, plus other appliances and components. The data plate also tells you the wind zone and snow load for which the home was built.

ESSENTIAL

Manufactured housing is sometimes more difficult to resell. New home packages that don't require a down payment are so attractive that buyers often flock to them before buying a resale. Research the area where you are buying to learn about past sales of pre-existing manufactured homes.

Buyers often purchase manufactured housing as part of a land-home package that's put together by the retailers that sell the homes. Interest rates are typically higher than the rates offered for site-built home purchases, but the packages are popular because buyers can usually move in to a house without a down payment. Manufactured housing qualifies for FHA and VA loans.

Some communities and housing developments will not allow manufactured housing. Individual deeds often contain restrictions against manufactured housing, even if there are similar homes on lots surrounding the parcel of land. It's important to make sure any home will be allowed on the land you want to place it on, so check all associated restrictions before you buy a manufactured home.

Modular Homes

Buyers are often confused about the differences between modular homes and manufactured homes. Modular homes are partially constructed in a factory, but that's where their resemblance to manufactured housing ends. Modular homes are built to conform to specific building codes at their destination. Then the segments are transported to the home site on flatbed trucks, where they are placed on a prebuilt foundation, joined, and completed by a local builder.

Modular homes have changed dramatically in recent years. At first, many of the modular homes offered by manufacturers were simple one-story ranch houses that resembled a doublewide manufactured home. They were easy to spot when you were house shopping. Now the styles are endless, and unless you are there to see a house delivered and assembled, you would probably never guess it's a modular. Manufacturers can easily draw plans to meet your specifications or make changes to customize one of their existing designs.

Lenders typically finance modular homes in the same way they finance site-built homes. An appraiser might or might not mention that a home is modular on an appraisal. Modulars are usually acceptable in developments where site-built homes are the norm. Check restrictive covenants and deed restrictions to be certain you can build a modular home on the lot you wish to buy.

QUESTION?

Are modular homes marked to help identify them?
Yes. Look inside the kitchen cabinets and bathroom vanities for a typed page that's glued to a vertical panel. It lists the modular company that built the house along with details about the components used within it.

Modulars can usually be built much faster than a site-built home. Their sections are constructed indoors with no weather delays, and the factory aspect itself helps speed production. The cost of a modular home is often less per square foot than for a similar site-built house, making them attractive to buyers, but cost can vary quite a bit by manufacturer and design.

Multifamily Dwellings

Condos, townhouses, duplexes, fourplexes—all of those structures are considered multifamily dwellings, separate homes that are housed within the same structure or group of structures. Some multifamily units are deeded differently than single-family homes. The titles for condos, townhouses, and cooperatives are often described as being a hybrid form of ownership. That's because the properties include elements of real estate that are owned by individuals as well as elements that are owned by a group of people.

Condominiums, or Condos

An individual who owns a condominium owns the condo unit only, not the land beneath it. That means condos can be stacked on top of each other. Some condominium developments have always been owner-occupied, but you'll probably encounter former apartment complexes that have been converted to condos.

All condo owners in a development share ownership of common areas, such as the land, the exterior of buildings, hallways, roofs, swimming pools—any area used by all owners. A property owners' association usually manages the condo development, collecting fees from owners in order to maintain the common areas.

Condominium owners pay property taxes only on their individual units. The association pays property taxes on the common areas.

Condominiums located in tourist destinations often have a property management company on the premises, making it easier for owners to rent their units. The agents in those offices can give you a good idea of rental potential and the fees associated with hiring the company to market and rent the property. You can act as your own property manager, but using an agency that is already set up to market rentals might bring higher returns, even after the expense of paying for their services.

Some condo and townhouse restrictive covenants do not allow you to use your unit as a rental. Learn the rules associated with each property before you make an offer to purchase it.

Townhouses, or Town Homes

Townhouses are usually a series of single or multistory units that are linked to each other horizontally by common walls. Townhouse owners own their units and the land beneath them, so townhouses cannot be stacked on top of each other. Owners of townhouses pay property taxes on their individual units and the land under them.

Common areas are owned jointly by all townhouse owners, and they are managed in the same way as condominium developments are.

How Do Cooperatives Fit In?

Cooperatives, also called co-ops, often resemble apartment buildings or condos. All property that's part of a cooperative is owned by a corporation. Buyers purchase stock in the corporation and are shareholders—not owners—of real estate. Each shareholder has a lease to his unit that runs for the life of the corporation. New cooperative shareholders must typically be approved by an administrative board.

Property taxes are paid by the corporation, and mortgages are usually held and paid by the corporation. Costs to operate the property are shared by all shareholders. Cooperative ownership is not common in most states.

Duplexes and Fourplexes

Some people make their first real-estate investment a duplex or fourplex, a structure that contains two or four residences. These structures can resemble a condo or townhouse development but with fewer units. It isn't uncommon for the building and the land it sits on to be owned by one person, but it is possible for the units to be individually owned.

This type of residence can be a great way to get started with investments. Many owners live in one unit and rent the others, letting the tenants' rent pay the mortgage and helping the owner build equity in the property.

Tackling a Residential Development

Instead of investing in existing houses, you might opt to buy a tract of land and develop it into a neighborhood for one or more of the housing options we just discussed. Going from bare land to a residential subdivision takes a great deal of research and planning. There are roads to build, utilities to bring in, restrictions to put in place to ensure a consistent community, and many other considerations you must make before you can move forward with the project.

Accessibility of Utilities

To construct a residential complex, you'll need access to electricity, phone, water, and sewer systems. How far will you have to run electric and telephone lines to get to the property? How will those tasks affect your development costs? Are water and sewer connections available to the projected lots? If not, will you develop a community system for each utility, or will property owners be responsible for installing private wells and septic systems?

Is the land suitable for individual septic systems, and if it is, how far must each system be from a well or other water source in order to avoid contamination? A septic system works like this. Liquid waste from bathrooms, the kitchen, laundry, and other areas is carried to a large storage tank. The waste begins to decompose in the tank and turns into a sludge-like liquid. When it reaches a drain at the top of the tank, the liquid flows into pipes that stretch into a network of gravel-lined trenches, called a drain field. Holes along the length of the pipes release the liquid into the trenches. The liquid seeps into the soil beneath the drain field, where bacteria and oxygen in the soil complete the neutralization process.

Land filled with rocks or clay-like soil does not drain easily, so larger drain fields—and lots—will be necessary. The minimum size of the lot depends on the types of systems used in your area, the laws that control the placement of those systems, and the topography of the land. A thorough soil evaluation should be tops on your "to do" list for this type of housing development.

An engineering study might be required to ensure your development makes best use of the land. A survey must be done to verify the development's boundaries, and each lot must be surveyed separately in order to split it off from the larger tract. Your local laws will dictate many of the tasks you must perform prior to developing the land.

Road Work

Another important task is building roads to access the lots, and it's likely that ordinances will dictate the minimum road width and how roads are constructed. If you must cross another person's land to get to your development, more ordinances will kick in to cover the right-of-way that's required to allow permanent and legal access.

Is It Worth It?

You'll have funds invested in the land and the improvements. How many lots can you realistically get from the tract? How much are similar lots selling for in your area, and what's their average time on the market? Do the math to determine if you can recover your costs *and* make a profit.

If You Work with Builders

Many people who develop land for subdivisions never build a house themselves. They prefer to stick with lot sales and let the new owners build their own homes. However, sometimes it's easier to sell a new house on a lot than it is to sell a lot that's vacant. Talk with local builders to see if any of them have an interest in working with you to build spec houses—speculation houses that are built to market to the public rather than for a specific individual. Check each builder's references, and get legal advice before embarking on a spec house project.

Smaller Developments

Smaller developments might be subject to fewer guidelines. Talk to your local planning board to find out if a tract of land can be split into two or three parcels without forcing you to follow rigid subdivision guidelines. If so, you might be able to sell larger lots to buyers who wish to have more land for privacy or other reasons, while bypassing the formal approvals that are required for subdivision development.

FACT

Even though subdivision guidelines are rigid, it's a good idea to follow them as closely as possible even if you aren't forced to. The laws were implemented for a reason, and staying within the guidelines can make your land more attractive to future buyers.

Restrictive Covenants

Restrictive covenants are deed restrictions that apply to property located within a specific development. Restrictions give the development a more standard appearance because they control the types of homes built there and some of the activities that take place within its boundaries. Restrictions are usually written by an attorney who works for the developer and who uses the developer's goals for the property to draft the wording.

When they are enforced, restrictions help protect property values. They nearly always stipulate the minimum size of residences allowed within the development, how many homes may be built on one lot, and what type of construction the homes must—or must not—be.

The following topics are usually outlined in restrictive covenants:

- Setbacks—how far structures must be from streets and lot lines
- Easements and rights-of-way, such as a pathway for power lines or future road expansion
- Assessments owners must pay for road maintenance or other fees
- Information that explains how restrictions can be changed or voided
- Rules regarding pets and other animals
- Rules that regulate in-home businesses and house rentals
- Rules that regulate tree-cutting, fencing, and other landscaping issues

In addition to those common rules, you might see clauses that attempt to reduce clutter on lots, or try to create a sense of uniformity by dictating what colors you may paint a home or which materials are banned for use in construction of new homes.

Restrictive covenants have nothing to do with zoning or governmental regulations. Those are both separate issues that you should investigate before making an offer on a property.

If you find a property that you want to place an immediate offer on, but you haven't yet read the restrictive covenants, insert a contingency in the offer that states you can back out of the contract with no penalties after reviewing the restrictions. Place a realistic time limit on your review.

Sometimes additional restrictions are recorded on deeds. Read the seller's deed to verify there are no additional restrictions that will interfere with your planned use of the property.

Easements and Rights-of-Way

An easement is the right to use another person's land for a specific purpose. It can be written so that it applies to a property in general or to a specific portion of the land. Easements can cover any issue on which the two parties agree, and they usually become a permanent part of the deeds for both parcels. A right-of-way is a special type of easement that gives someone the right to travel across property owned by another person.

An easement doesn't have to be given to an individual. It might be written to benefit a property instead. For example, Mr. Smith gives current and future owners of a neighboring piece of land the right to cross his property to access a nearby lake. The adjacent landowner might be allowed to build a roadway or simply use an existing road. Another type of easement could allow the neighboring property owner to install a private well on Mr. Smith's property, with permanent water lines leading to the adjacent parcel.

A permanent easement can also benefit a business or an organization. A utility company might have the right to erect power lines or bury utility lines on a tract of land. A housing development could be granted an easement that allows it to build and maintain a water storage facility on someone else's property.

Easements can also benefit an individual. Mr. Smith might allow a specific person to cross his property to access the lake without attaching the permission to a piece of land. This type of easement normally expires at a specific time or event or upon the death of the person who benefits from it. These easements are not usually added to a deed description.

Potential Problems

Easements can have a negative effect on property values. The landowner who grants the easement usually cannot build structures within the easement area or use fencing that would hinder access to the easement owner.

Before you purchase any property, you should know where all of the easements are located and exactly how they restrict your use of the land. Knowing the details about easements is critical for any land you purchase, whether it's residential, commercial, or industrial.

Another downside of easements is buyer perception. Potential buyers are often turned off by the fact that others have *any* type of right to use the land. If the easement is for something like high-tension power lines, the negative feelings are even stronger. Not only are those lines unattractive, many people consider them to be a health risk.

Just because an easement is not being used doesn't mean it will never be used. If an easement is a permanent part of your deed, there's always a chance that the individual who benefits from it will decide to take advantage of it. Talk with an experienced real-estate attorney to find out what steps you can take to remove an unused easement from your deed.

Boundary Surveys

A boundary survey shows you exactly where a parcel's property lines are located. The survey should be performed by an experienced, licensed surveyor. The lines surrounding the property are marked with a combination of iron pins, concrete posts, or other permanent items. By referring to landmarks such as rocks and large trees, the surveyor also cuts a path along the line, which is especially helpful for visualizing property lines in wooded areas.

FACT

Sometimes the surveyor's paths, called cut-throughs, are visible for years after a survey has been performed. Visibility depends on the topography at property lines and whether the owner has attempted to keep the pathway free of weeds and other vegetation.

In some areas, surveys are a routine occurrence whenever property is sold, but in other locations, the buyer must decide whether a survey is necessary. It's always a plus to order a survey, even if your lender doesn't require it. Don't be lulled into thinking that existing fences mark the property lines. If the fencing is old, the current owner might not know who built it and whether it conforms to property boundaries. Many sellers do not know the location of their boundary lines at all.

Make your offer to purchase dependent on your approval of the resulting boundary lines. If there are problems, such as a neighboring structure that extends onto the land you are buying, you want to find out about them before you buy. The seller should be responsible for clearing up any issues that affect your use of the property due to poorly marked boundaries.

Exceptions to the Rule

Performing a survey never hurts, but sometimes you might decide it isn't necessary. If you're buying an existing home in a development, and there are surveys on file for that development, you can very likely use them to find previous survey marks. The distance between each marker should be recorded on the survey, so you can get a very good idea whether the actual markers are positioned where they should be.

In some areas, it's typical for a seller to pay for a survey. In others, it's regarded as a buyer expense, but that doesn't mean you can't ask the seller to pay for it. The seller might not agree to pay the entire cost, but you might be able to negotiate a deal to split the expense.

Furthermore, surveys that have been done in recent years can often be updated for a lower fee than a brand-new survey. If you're paying for the survey, find out who performed it last and make inquiries about an update. Always have your survey recorded at the county courthouse or an equivalent place that houses public records. You would be surprised at how often survey copies are lost by owners. If the surveyor dies or goes out of business, you might not have access to a copy unless it's part of the public records.

Survey Markers

Surveyors generally mark property boundaries with surveyor pins—iron posts that only stick up a few inches above the ground. They become covered with leaves quite easily; if they aren't visible, you may need to use a metal detector to locate them. Surveyors also use paint to mark trees near the iron posts, or they might hang a piece of brightly covered tape from a nearby branch. Both of those methods make it easier for you to see when you are near the actual marker.

It's not common, but survey pins are sometimes secretly moved by neighboring landowners who dispute a property line. A new survey will show you where the markers should be.

Once your survey has been done, it's best to figure out a method to help you remember where markers are located. Flag the posts with brightly colored plastic tape or paint a mark on trees as surveyors do. Use any method that helps you locate your property lines quickly and easily.

Chapter 3

Commercial and Industrial Properties

Working with commercial or industrial properties offers a whole new range of possibilities for real-estate investors. Commercial properties include apartment buildings, strip malls, coin laundries, and endless other types of real estate built to accommodate businesses and services. Here's a preview of some of the types of properties you might encounter if you choose to invest in commercial real estate.

Apartment Buildings

If you're a people-person, owning and managing an apartment building might be the perfect investment for you. It can be a large complex or a building with just a few units. One thing's for sure—dealing with a variety of tenants means you'll never have a dull day, and you'll have plenty of opportunities to practice your negotiation and diplomacy skills.

Are rentals stable in your area? The rental market fluctuates, but knowing how it has performed in recent years will help you decide if an apartment building is good investment choice. What are tenants looking for? Read ads and study the rental market very closely to help you determine which features are in most demand, then set out to find a property that fits the criteria, either as-is or with updates.

How Much Is It Worth?

If you find a building of interest, you'll have to determine how much it's worth. Putting a value on an apartment building is a different process than you encounter when you buy residential real estate. Its value is tied closely to the rental income it generates. If you decide to buy it, you'll eventually have the building appraised, but a quick way to preview its value is to use the gross income multiplier method, or GM for short. The GM is a number that's determined by analyzing the average sales prices that similar apartment buildings have sold for versus the amount of rents they produce.

QUESTION?

Can I determine value by using the average asking prices of properties that are currently for sale?
The prices that sellers put on properties are usually inflated enough to allow at least a little bit of negotiation room, because buyers like to feel they are getting a bargain. It's more accurate to use actual sales prices to help you determine value, because they represent the true prices that buyers were willing to pay for similar properties. (For more information about property valuation, refer to Chapter 7.)

Let's look at an example. Consider a building with five apartments, each producing $600 per month in rent, for a total of $3,000 monthly income from the entire building. The building recently sold for $324,000. Here's how you would calculate its GM:

1. Multiply the total monthly rent by the number of months in the year to find the annual gross income: $3,000 × 12 = $36,000.
2. Divide the price the building sold for by its annual gross income to get the GM: $324,000 ÷ $36,000 = 9.

Now imagine that the building you want to buy is very similar to the building used in the example, except that its total yearly rent is a bit lower, at $30,000. Turn the equation around and multiply the GM by the building's total annual income to estimate its value.

$30,000 (INCOME) × 9 (GM) = $270,000 (ESTIMATED VALUE)

Calculate the GM for as many apartment-building sales as you can find to help you develop an understanding of the average GM for that type of property in your area. A real-estate agent who is actively involved with commercial sales can give you information about sold properties and offer an opinion of the average GM.

Improve Rental Income to Increase Property Value

Does the building have untapped potential? Updates might allow you to raise rents, resulting in an increase in income *and* property value. Do the math, and figure out how much it will cost to make the changes. Can you afford to do the work? How much can you raise rents without going over the average rental rates in your area? How long will it take to recover the cost of the improvements at the new rent levels, assuming full occupancy? If occupancy falls, so will your cash flow. Can you continue the project without harm to your finances?

If being a landlord isn't in your plans, it doesn't mean you can't invest in apartment buildings, as long as you don't mind dealing with tenants for a short time. You could buy an apartment building, make improvements, raise rents and value, and then resell the property to another investor. Find out how long it has taken similar properties to sell, and determine whether you can truly rent the property at increased prices before you decide to go that route.

Check the Seller's Documentation

When you buy an apartment building—or any building with rental tenants—you should ask to see copies of all current leases or rental agreements. It is not unreasonable to ask the seller to show you past income-tax returns and deposit slips to verify that the rentals have actually generated the amount of income that is being claimed. Most sellers are honest, but let's face it: It isn't difficult to give a potential buyer inflated income figures in the hopes that verification won't be requested. You should also review utility bills for the past few years if the building owner is responsible for paying them. If the seller is working with a real-estate agent, the agent probably has copies of the documentation you need.

At closing, all tenant security deposits should be transferred to you from the former owner. Make sure that topic is addressed in your offer to purchase any property in which security deposits are held by the current owner.

Study the leases to learn their terms and to find out when they expire. It's best if they don't all expire at once, especially if you plan to refurbish the apartments and raise rents. Your entire tenant base could move out at once, putting a crimp in your cash flow until new occupants are found. Consult a real-estate attorney if you aren't quite sure how to decipher the terms of the leases.

Office Buildings

Office space is normally rented for a specific dollar amount per square foot of space, with rates differing widely across the country and even within the same town. Rates fluctuate with the economy and with supply and demand—the more available space, the less rent you can charge. Since vacancy and rent rates can be erratic, office buildings are not usually the best option for a beginning investor who does not have reserves of cash to draw from during down times.

Like other commercial buildings, the value of an office building is tied to the amount collected from its rentals. You can use the GM method described on page 29 to determine an approximate value for a building. Take some time to study the office rental situation in the town where you plan to invest. Is there a need that hasn't been filled? Perhaps there's a demand for small suites, but most of the space currently available is for larger businesses. Can you find a building where suites could easily be created?

Be Informed

Keep up-to-date with the needs of local businesses by developing a network of contacts within the business community. The staff at your local chamber of commerce can probably give you a list of clubs and other groups made up of local businesspeople. Join a few—their members are great contacts. Attend city council meetings. Get to know the folks at your local planning board. Talk to commercial real-estate agents, those who sell and those who manage commercial properties, to find out what their rental and buyer clients are looking for. If one type of property keeps popping up on most-wanted lists, get creative—try to determine if you can provide it by making changes to an existing property.

FACT

If your downtown area is on the verge of renewal, you might be able to find buildings that can do double duty, with retail stores on the ground level and offices or residential apartments upstairs. That technique is most often used in small to mid-size towns and cities.

Buyer Beware

The ideal scenario is to find something in a good location that, with some work, can be turned into a building that's more attractive to tenants.

Your renovations will be overseen by building inspectors, and you must determine whether or not planned changes will conform to local zoning ordinances and handicapped access laws. Always protect yourself by inserting contingencies in your offer to purchase that give you time to explore your plans before you make the final commitment to close on a property. If you cannot make the changes that will put a building to its best use, there's no reason to buy it.

Many rental agreements for office space use a net lease, a lease in which tenants pay for a portion of the building maintenance. You will likely inherit leases from the former owner, so be sure that your purchase contract includes a condition that gives you the right to study those leases before you buy the property—and to back out if you don't like what you see. As with other rental buildings, all security deposits should be transferred to you at closing.

Retail Buildings

There are always many types of retail properties available for investors to purchase. What's a retail property? Think convenience and shopping—any building that houses a business where the public goes to buy a product. Typical kinds of retail properties include large and small malls and other buildings occupied by pizza parlors, restaurants, clothing stores, convenience shops, grocery stores, pharmacies—it's an endless list.

ALERT!

Check local regulations to learn the rules that apply to handicap parking for any type of commercial building you plan to buy or renovate. Make sure the parking area is large enough to include space for handicapped and other consumers.

Finding a good location for a retail building is slightly different from finding a good space to locate an office or other commercial property that the public uses in some way. If you're shopping for a pair of shoes, you expect to be able to get to the building easily and to park in a convenient and safe place. If you can't, you'll go to another shoe store.

When you visit your doctor's office, you'd like those features, but you won't necessarily change doctors just to get them. Comparing the places you like to shop with the places you avoid is a very personal way to begin evaluating retail locations.

Retail stores can exist on any level of a building, but spaces located on the building's entry level always command more rent, even if an elevator is available to take shoppers upstairs. Good parking is critical, and sometimes congested parking areas can be reworked to provide more spaces and a better flow of traffic.

Leases for Retail Buildings

Depending on their location, retail buildings might be leased or rented by the square foot or by the amount of frontage they offer along a busy street. Frontage is determined by measuring the total linear feet the building occupies along the length of its main entrance—the side of the building that's most likely to attract customers. That method is often used for popular locations in busy shopping districts, where retail space is in much demand. The square footage method is an alternative that can be used for any property.

Some landlords require retail tenants to sign a percentage lease, in which a portion of the rent is based on the tenant's gross or net income. The lease usually includes a minimum amount of rent that's due no matter what the tenant's income. You'll find that leases vary quite a bit from area to area, so you must do some research to learn which kinds are typical where you live.

Investing in Strip Malls

Large shopping malls are out of the reach of most investors, but small strip malls are often affordable. You've seen them—they're retail complexes where businesses are typically housed side by side in one long building, although L-shaped malls and other configurations are also common. For best customer traffic, a strip mall should include at least one store that appeals to a wide segment of the population, such as a clothing retailer, a grocery store, or a chain pharmacy that stocks other items in addition to pharmaceuticals. Additional tenants that can fill in the gaps are pizza shops and restaurants, florists, health-food stores, and numerous other types of specialty shops.

Having a good mix of businesses helps the mall appeal to many people, and that appeal drives traffic to the complex, benefiting every business in it. What's a good blend? That combination differs for every area. For instance, if there's a college nearby, a good mix might be businesses that appeal to college students *and* other residents. How about a bookstore, a copy shop, and perhaps a store that specializes in shipping packages?

If your plan creates a steady flow of customers, it won't take long for tenants to see positive results, and flourishing tenants means continued cash flow for your property.

Take some time to research your local market. Which strip malls in your town seem to always be rented? Have the same tenants occupied those centers for quite a while, or does there seem to be a constant turnover? Why do you think people are attracted to the popular malls? The more insight you have into a mall's success, the more likely you are to make your own venture a successful experience.

Industrial Possibilities

Industrial properties are a special type of commercial real estate. Industrial sites are not usually places where you would go to buy a product or find a service. They are often the places where products are made or distributed. Small and large factories and distribution centers for retail or wholesale products are all examples of industrial properties. Industrial properties vary, but they have one thing in common—most require a great deal of investment funds and know-how from their owners. They are best avoided until you feel certain you can tackle a large project.

Industrial buildings that have been used to make a product can be burdened by environmental issues that must be resolved before you buy. This is especially true if you plan to convert the property so that it's suitable for a different industry than it presently serves. What was manufactured there, and did the area around the building suffer from the dumping of any kind of waste?

Zoning regulations are critical, and you must work effectively with planning boards and other agencies on the local, state, and federal levels. Move slowly and carefully. Don't tackle any type of industrial project until you acquire plenty of experience, and even then seek additional advice from experts in the field.

FACT

Owning a small industrial park that involves only the distribution end of several companies is one way to enter the field of industrial real estate. Find out if mail-order companies or other types of warehouses are looking for space in your area. A location that's close to an airport and popular shipping agency locations is always a plus, and access should allow for entry and exit of large trucks.

Land Development

Developing a piece of raw land in a commercial area can be complex or simple, depending on the project you plan to undertake. In some areas, development is controlled on a local level; in others, the state is more involved. Your specific project could also be subject to federal regulations. No matter what you plan to do with the land, be sure your plans conform to all applicable laws and ordinances.

Before you make final plans for the property, you must research zoning and environmental issues in order to find out if there are limitations on land use. Even if zoning isn't an issue, deed restrictions might prevent you from using the land for specific purposes. A deed could state that the property cannot be used for industrial purposes. A deed might even prevent a specific kind of business from being built on the land. For instance, the former owner might also own a nearby lawn-and-garden center. Before selling the land, he inserts a clause stating that the land cannot be used to operate a lawn-and-garden company. It's always important to analyze a property's deed to help determine how the land can be used.

Questions about environmental issues, such as the presence of protected wetlands, are another important issue that should be resolved before you buy a tract of land.

Are there plans for new roads or widening existing roads in your area? Those improvements are often a signal that local governments are expecting growth in the area. It's worthwhile to research the reasons behind the road improvements and look at land near locations where improvements are planned.

Land Speculation

You might prefer to leave the land alone, holding on to it and reselling for a profit when its market value has increased. That type of investor is called a speculator—someone who gambles that a piece of land will go up in value at some time in the future. Whereas some are simply speculating that the value will go up based on general trends, others have inside knowledge about an upcoming project that will make the land more desirable. The risk of being a land speculator is that land value might go down instead of up, and you'll have to hold on to the property until it comes back up again.

Do your homework if you choose to buy lots and land for eventual resale. Make sure there's an active market for the type of property you plan to buy. You may be gambling that the area you invest in will grow over the long term, and that's fine—just as long as you are prepared to sit on the property until that happens.

Sometimes a lot that won't sell as undeveloped land is easy to move if a house is on it. Talk to builders about the possibility of erecting a spec house—a house built on speculation and marketed to the public. Consult an experienced real-estate attorney before signing an agreement with a builder.

Good Option for Beginners

Investing in undeveloped land is within the reach of beginning investors, but you'll need expert counsel to guide you through the many laws and regulations associated with land development. Large land tracts can be good investments if you are very familiar with the area and have a good feel for what the land might be useful for now or in the future. You can hold the investment until the per-acre market value reaches a point where it makes sense to sell, or you can move forward with some type of development

Lots for Manufactured Housing

One development option is to build lots for manufactured housing, which may be rented to people who own manufactured homes. Check local ordinances carefully before you embark on a development for manufactured housing. If you can find the right land, with utilities that are readily available, this type of development can be a lucrative investment.

Recreational Vehicle Parks

An RV campground can be a basic facility that caters to travelers who need a place to stop for a single night, or it can be a full-service park with a swimming pool, miniature golf, and any other amenity you'd like to add. Most RV parks offer concrete pads and utility connections. They can be located along a major highway or in a tourist destination. Research existing RV campgrounds to learn about the typical amenities and costs that travelers encounter in different areas. The resources in Appendix C will help you locate RV networks.

Self-Storage Centers

We all have too much *stuff*. That's probably one reason that self-storage centers are so popular. Metal buildings built on concrete slabs are the most common configuration for these popular units, and unless you wish to offer climate-controlled areas, the buildings you rent don't even have to be heated or electrified.

Collecting rents from tenants can be a headache, and some tenants who stop paying may never retrieve their goods. It isn't unusual for storage centers to auction goods left by tenants in order to cover past-due storage bills. Protect yourself with tenant deposits and a good rental agreement, and choose a great location to see excellent returns from a storage center investment.

Finding Expert Advice

This chapter has touched on only the basic details about investing in commercial properties. As you become more involved in real estate, you'll encounter many types of properties and an endless number of ideas for potential investments. No matter which ones you choose to pursue, do your homework and *always* get expert advice before moving forward with an offer.

Here are a few of the people you might contact for advice about commercial properties:

- Commercial real-estate agents can help you find comparable properties in order to determine value and can keep you informed of new listings on the market.
- Staff at your local planning board and other similar agencies are important contacts for information about land development, zoning, and many other issues.
- Staff at your county courthouse can show you how to view tax maps of land and find public information regarding the current owner's mailing address.
- Surveyors and appraisers provide services that can be critical to your success. Get to know the professionals in your area so that when you have a question, you can get it answered.
- Attorneys who specialize in real-estate transactions can help you draft an offer to purchase commercial properties and follow up with lease agreements for your tenants.
- A tax professional can offer important advice to help you structure you investments.

Commercial properties can be lucrative, but they are riskier and require more funds than investing in a single-family home you intend to rent or resell. You can be successful if you research the market, know the laws associated with the type of property you are interested in pursuing, and move carefully to acquire it.

Chapter 4

Working with
Real-Estate Agents

There will be times when you use a real-estate agent to help you buy and sell investment properties. The trick is finding the best agent and understanding how the agent's loyalties affect your transactions. Learn your local laws and customs, then put that knowledge to work to help you find a real-estate agent who will give you a call every time a property that suits your needs comes on the market.

How Can an Agent Help?

Successful real-estate agents keep track of their local markets on a daily basis. That's critical, because other investors are on the lookout for properties and homebuyers are always searching for a deal. The most desirable properties just don't last. By establishing a relationship with one or more agents, you will be among the first to hear about new opportunities.

QUESTION?

Should real-estate investors become agents?
Real-estate agents are usually required to disclose that they are licensed agents—an immediate turn-off for some "for sale by owner" sellers, sometimes called FSBOs. Agents must also comply with specific advertising guidelines and other state and federal laws. Hold off until you're sure a license will help.

Working with a real-estate agent simplifies some of your research. Most agents have access to a local multiple listing service (MLS), a conglomerate of agencies that have decided to band together to show and sell each other's listings.

Agents can research properties sold through the MLS as easily as they can view current listings. Knowing the sales history of properties is a real plus because it allows you to find out exactly how much each property sold for without having to dig through local public records. Working with an agent who actually viewed those sold properties can help you make even better comparisons, since the agent will have personal knowledge of each property's condition at the time of sale.

FACT

An agent may refer to MLS printouts of sold properties as comps, or comparables. They look exactly like the MLS sheets for current listings, but they also include the listing and sale date, the sales amount, the name of the selling agent, and sometimes even the type of financing used. Comps help you make comparisons to determine a current listing's market value.

Buying Listed Properties

Using an agent is the only way to access properties listed with a real-estate agency, so it's best to prepare for that ahead of time by finding a good agent now. Don't let the agent forget about you—make occasional contact even if you work mostly with FSBO properties.

Selling and Leasing Properties

You may decide that you want to use an agency to sell and lease your own properties, especially if you own real estate that's located a long distance from home. Hiring an agency is a good choice when you don't have the time or expertise for effective marketing or if you own a unique property that could be handled better by a specialized professional.

Working with a Seller's Agent

A seller's agent is any agent working for the real-estate firm employed by the seller to sell a property. In an MLS arrangement, all offices work to sell each other's listings, so even if Firm XYZ holds the actual contract, all real-estate agents who can show the property are probably subagents for the seller. Because agents work for the seller, buyers should never disclose confidential information to them.

Important Agent Disclosures

Real-estate agents in the United States used to operate on a buyer-beware basis. Agents worked to get the best deals for the seller, but they did not disclose the agent-seller relationship to potential buyers, who often incorrectly assumed that the agent was working for them. Buyers often felt free to give the agents confidential information—such as how much they were prepared to pay for a property—unaware that it was the agent's duty to pass that information on to the seller.

Nondisclosure resulted in thousands of lawsuits and complaints to state real-estate licensing boards, so disclosure rules began to evolve. Nearly all real-estate agents in the United States are now required to disclose that they are agents for the seller, and in most cases the disclosure must be in writing.

This means a seller's agent may ask you to sign a document that verifies she discussed real-estate agency status with you. It is not a contract but simply a statement that verifies she explained her affiliation with the seller and the choices you have when you work with a real-estate agent. The document is usually accompanied by a handout that explains the different types of agency relationships available in your state.

Disclosing Material Facts

Seller's agents must disclose material facts about a property. That includes things like leaking roofs and foundations, plumbing and drainage problems, sewer and septic issues, broken appliances—anything that is wrong with the property.

Disclosure doesn't just focus on repair issues. A restaurant that's doing business in an area not zoned for that type of business is a problem that should be disclosed to potential buyers. If a structure on the property touches the property line of a neighbor, the details must be communicated.

Commonly disclosed material facts differ from area to area. In California, agents are asked to disclose whether or not the property is on a fault line. In areas prone to flooding, the property's relation to the flood plain is an important disclosure.

FACT

Foreclosure may or may not be considered a material fact. If no legal documents have been filed, foreclosure doesn't usually have to be disclosed. If legal filings have taken place, foreclosure is generally considered a material fact.

There's also information that is not subject to disclosure. A seller's agent needs the seller's permission to disclose personal information about the seller. For instance, the agent won't tell you that the sellers are getting a divorce, can't stand to be near each other, and will take any offer that comes along! Learn as much about disclosure customs in your area so that you'll recognize if a commonly disclosed item is absent and what kind of information you should not expect to get from the agent.

Working with a Buyer's Agent

Many agents will offer to work as a buyer's agent, someone who agrees to represent *your* interests. If you're in the market to buy property and prefer to work with a buyer's agent, the buyer agency contract you sign may require that you work exclusively with that person. Nonexclusive agreements are available, but most agents will not work in that capacity. Being a buyer's agent takes a great deal of effort, so agents aren't inclined to devote time and energy to your search if you are not committed to stick with the relationship.

If you sign a contract with an agent—as either a buyer or a seller—you are the agent's client. If you sign a disclosure for a seller's agent, you are a customer. The agent must act in an ethical manner and treat a customer's transaction with care, but he owes more loyalty to a client.

Some states allow buyer's agents to work temporarily with a verbal agreement, giving the agent and the client the opportunity to get to know each other before signing a formal contract. Usually, the verbal agreement must be put in writing before an offer is made on a property. Never sign a contract with an agent until you are sure the agent is the best choice for your needs.

The Agent's Duties and Responsibilities

Buyer's agents have additional duties and responsibilities to the buyer that seller's agents either aren't obligated to perform or cannot perform. First and foremost, a buyer's agent must be loyal, keeping the buyer's personal information confidential. The buyer's agent must also disclose all known facts about the properties that are up for sale and the sellers—anything that could influence the buyer's decision to make an offer.

Buyer's agents also provide help by researching past sales to help formulate an appropriate offer for the property; suggest contract contingencies to protect the buyer's interests; and are closely involved in the closing process. This includes helping the buyer to find a lender, tracking the progress of the loan, ordering inspections, working with the closing officer—every detail that will get the buyer's contract to the closing table.

Negotiating the Buyer Agency Agreement

The details of a buyer agency contract can be negotiated with the agent. Here are specific points you might consider including in the contract:

- **Search area:** You can limit the geographical area an agent works in, preventing agent overlap if you are searching for properties in multiple areas.
- **Time period:** Agreements can remain in force for any length of time you both agree to, even as little as one day or for the showing of one property.
- **Exceptions:** You can ask the agent to insert an exclusion that allows you to work with and purchase FSBO listings on your own, without paying the agent a fee.

ALERT!

A real-estate agency that calls itself an "exclusive buyer agency" deals only with buyers and does not accept listings from sellers. That type of agency always works to obtain the best contracts for their buyer clients.

Buyer's agents are usually paid a portion of the seller's commission at closing. Ask your agent if any scenario exists under which you would owe him a commission. Don't sign an agreement until you understand every term within it.

Working with a Dual Agent

Dual agency occurs when a buyer's agent shows the buyer a listing held by the agent's real-estate firm. Dual agency is a little tricky because the agent has responsibilities to both parties. The agent cannot disclose personal information to either client about the other, but must still be careful to make sure the needs of both clients are met.

Dual agency is usually easier to deal with if the buyer is not working with the agent who actually holds the listing for the property. Many real-estate offices are so accustomed to handling dual agency that they encourage their agents not to chatter about the personal business of their clients. Then, when dual representation occurs, only the listing agent is privy to personal information.

Dual agency is not allowed in all states. Where it is allowed, it must typically be disclosed to the buyer and seller in advance, and both must agree to it in writing.

Other Agency Arrangements

Your agent may explain other types of agency rules, and these seem to constantly change in order to meet the needs of buyers and sellers. Pay close attention as agents disclose working relationships, and ask as many questions as necessary to understand where their loyalties are.

Here are some additional terms you might hear:

- **Single agent:** A single agent can work for either the buyer or the seller.
- **Designated agent:** In some states, the broker in charge may assign a designated agent to a transaction, bypassing the dual-agency situation to allow more complete buyer and seller representation.
- **Transaction broker:** A transaction agent helps facilitate a closing but does not have a contract with either party. (This arrangement is legal in Florida.)

Finding the Right Agent

The best agent for you depends on how you plan to use that agent. Even if you're in the market to buy, a seller's agent might be the best choice if you don't need advice and like to handle the bulk of transactions by yourself. You simply need an agent to submit offers to sellers with listed properties. There's no reason not to use a seller's agent if you feel comfortable proceeding on your own, developing contract contingencies and time frames and determining the best price to offer for a property.

If you'd like a little more help, a buyer's agent can provide it. If you plan to buy and sell real estate, you should find an agent who excels in both areas.

Calling the agent on the "For Sale" sign puts you in touch with the seller's agent—not someone who's going to help you get the best price on a property. That's fine. You may not need any help—just make sure you don't tell the agent anything you wouldn't want the seller to hear.

Start Looking

If you know you'll use an agent periodically, you might want to start browsing the field to find one who clicks with your personality. It could take you awhile to find someone you trust, so start looking now. Here are a few tips to get you started:

- Ask your friends if they had a good experience working with particular agents on selling and buying properties.
- Pick up homes-for-sale publications and pay attention to the listings and marketing methods of individual agents and agencies.
- Surf the Internet to compare local real-estate agent Web sites or to find an agent in another area.
- Search for key phrases about your town on popular Internet search engines to find out which agencies in your area rank highest.
- Interview agents. Pay attention to each agent's enthusiasm and knowledge of the real-estate market.

- View properties with an agent without signing an agreement. Spending a few hours with an agent will reveal a great deal about her personality and motivations.
- Take note of each agent's interest and degree of involvement. Did the agent follow up with you after the appointment to suggest other properties?

FACT

A brand-new agent can be just as effective as a seasoned pro. They're enthusiastic, they need the business, and since they're working with fewer clients, they often provide excellent customer service for each one.

There's no best way to find a great agent—it can take time, or it can happen on your first try. Sometimes you just have to go with your gut instinct to decide if an agent is the "right" one for you.

Working with Multiple Agents

Sometimes buyers think they will find more properties by working with someone at every agency in town. Whether that is effective or not depends on your area, but the practice can backfire.

If you're looking in the city, where agents sometimes work a very specific area, it might be best to develop a relationship with more than one agent. Even if they belong to an MLS that covers a broader base, they may only tell you about properties listed in the neighborhoods they want to work in. It can be a logistical problem for them to move beyond those boundaries, and they might not feel knowledgeable about properties located in other areas. Ask each agent to define the areas where he works.

The same is true in rural areas, where properties can be spread out over a multicounty area. The agents probably know about listings outside their base, but they may not be anxious to drive you hundreds of miles to find them. Just ask, and they'll tell you where they can realistically work.

Calling all of the agencies in town can actually backfire in small towns, where every agent knows each other and everyone draws from the same group of listings. You might be surprised how fast word travels about customers who call every agent asking for details about the same properties. Contact as many agents as it takes to find a good one, but keep in mind that if you call everyone all the time, you won't be taken as seriously as you might like.

Getting the Most from Your Agents

In the real-estate world, we spend a lot of time talking about agent duties—what agents should and shouldn't do to comply with laws and ethics. We don't hear nearly as much about buyer and seller duties, and they are every bit as important. Simply put, your real-estate transactions will be more successful and less stressful if you treat your agent in the same way you want to be treated.

Get Your Finances in Order

Talk to a lender to find out exactly what types of financing are available to you. Don't waste everyone's time looking at listings that are out of your price range unless you feel a property can be bought for much less than its asking price. If you're preapproved for a loan, you'll feel much more confident about making an offer, and your lender will have given you a close estimate of how much you can expect to pay in closing costs—an important consideration when you make an offer.

Be Clear and Honest

The type of information you give a real-estate agent depends on your relationship with the agent, but no matter what the relationship is, be honest. If you're working with multiple seller's agents, let them know so that their efforts don't overlap. It's a waste of everyone's time and will ultimately create hard feelings. You plan to be in this game for a while, so let everyone know you are honest and sincere.

When you're buying or selling any unique property, do a bit of research to find an agent with the expertise to handle the transaction. For example, if you're buying or selling commercial properties, a commercial broker is probably your best choice.

It also helps if you're able to communicate what you need and want. The perfect property may not be out there. Do you want to wait for it, or do you want to compromise and find something that you can alter with a little work? Determine which qualities are most important to you, and share the list with your agent. An agent can't create something that doesn't exist, but most of them can do a pretty good job of finding properties with the majority of your must-haves.

Cooperate with Your Agent

Don't blindly follow an agent's directives, but do try to cooperate. If contracts must be signed, don't let them linger. Your offer may be discarded if you wait too long to deliver documents or promised deposit money. A better offer could be presented at any time—can you guess whose unsigned contract is void when that happens?

Don't refuse to enter a property just because you don't like its exterior. When you have an appointment, you should at least take a quick walk through the property. It's rude to drive away, and it creates hard feelings among agents. It's in your best interests if your agent is on good terms with the other agents in town.

Don't assume you can accurately judge a listing by looking at an MLS sheet. Your agent has probably been to the property and knows that the photo or description is terrible and not a true representation of the property. Choose some of the properties you want to see, but trust your agent to choose some, too. You'll be surprised by how many properties that you would have discarded are actually good finds.

Your agent will likely go to the home inspection, but you should attend too, if possible, so that the inspector can show you problem areas and talk with you personally about them. Being there to ask the inspector questions gives you a much better feel for which repair issues are important and which ones are minor. Some things sound much worse on paper than they truly are. Hearing about them secondhand through your agent simply isn't as informative and forces the agent to describe something that may be out of his field of expertise.

Stay on Top of Closing Issues

Handle all issues required for your loan. Choose your closing agent if that applies in your area. Work with your agent to make sure everything is ready for closing, such as switching utilities and obtaining insurance binders. Your agent will help, but those items are your responsibility.

Real-estate closings don't just happen. They happen because at least one person is following through, usually on a daily basis. You'll find that the road to closing is a lot smoother if everyone does his share of the work.

Don't expect your agent to do anything illegal or anything involving fraud or deception. Sellers shouldn't ask their agent to help cover up a structural problem. Buyers shouldn't expect their agent to write a fraudulent contract. Remember that agents must comply with fair housing issues; they cannot steer a buyer to or away from specific neighborhoods.

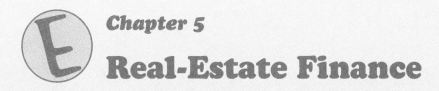

Chapter 5

Real-Estate Finance

A look at the world of real-estate invest-ment wouldn't be complete without a review of real-estate finance. Knowing how real-estate finance works will help you understand where you should look for a loan and what lenders require of bor-rowers. Not all loans are suitable for all properties, and not all borrowers are of-fered the same types of loans. To make good financing choices, you'll need to know how the industry works.

How Will You Pay for Your Purchase?

Most beginning real-estate investors need a loan to pay for their initial purchases, and sometimes even investors who can pay cash for properties choose to secure a mortgage instead of depleting their cash reserves. So where will you go to find a loan? You can start at the bank where you have checking or savings accounts. If the bank does not make real-estate loans, it can surely refer you to someone who does.

FACT

Ask friends if they have worked with a loan officer who helped them through the loan process. If that doesn't work, look for lenders who advertise in the "mortgage" category in the Yellow Pages of your local telephone book.

What Your Options Are

The type of loan you can secure will depend on many factors, including the property you intend to buy—a house, a multifamily dwelling, land, or commercial real estate. Different properties qualify for different types of financing, and your credit history will have an impact on all of the loans you are offered.

Savings associations and savings banks have always specialized in home mortgages. Commercial banks sometimes prefer to make short-term construction loans that are paid off with another loan when the job is complete. They also finance larger commercial projects and make many other kinds of short-term loans.

Credit unions have become a major source of mortgage loans in recent years. State and federal laws that control many banking activities do not apply to credit unions, so their loans are sometimes more flexible and can be tailored to meet your needs. You do not usually have to be a member of a credit union in order to use its services.

When you apply for a real-estate loan at a bank, credit union, savings-and-loan association, or other lending institution, you will work with a loan officer who evaluates your financial information in order to determine which types of loan products are suitable for the type of purchase you intend to make. That person can be an important contact as you move forward to acquire properties.

Important Lending Terms

There's a brand-new language awaiting you in the world of real-estate finance. Learn the meaning of important terms before you go shopping for a loan so that you'll understand the information well enough to ask questions on the spot, while the details are still fresh in your mind.

Amortization

An amortized loan is one where the regular payments include an amount for the current interest that is due on the loan and an amount that is applied to the principal balance of the loan. Negative amortization takes place when the amount of the monthly payment isn't enough to cover the interest, so the unpaid interest is tacked on to the principal balance each month, *increasing* what you owe.

The only good thing about negative amortization loans is that payments are lower and can help increase your cash flow (how much cash you have available to invest in other properties). Reserve this type of mortgage for properties you plan to sell or refinance right away and for properties purchased for a price below market value or located in an area of quickly escalating values.

Balloon Mortgage

Balloon loans are loans in which the full balance is due at some future date. You might make regular monthly payments that are calculated based on a longer time period, but at some point those payments stop, and the full balance becomes due.

For instance, you buy a property and the monthly payments are calculated the same way they are for a typical thirty-year loan. But instead of paying the loan for that length of time, the balance becomes due in five years.

Balloon mortgages are risky unless you are sure that on the due date you will have either the cash to make the full payment or another loan to take its place.

Real estate finance is an ever-changing field. New types of loans and guidelines for existing loans change constantly to meet the needs of borrowers. Find a loan officer whose opinions you value, and work with that person to gain an understanding of the loans that apply to the types of properties you wish to buy.

Mortgage and Deed of Trust

Remember, a mortgage isn't technically a loan. It is a security instrument, a document that says the property being purchased is collateral for the loan. When you take out a mortgage on a house, that house is the collateral for the money you borrowed to purchase it.

When combined with a promissory note—your promise to pay—the mortgage creates a lien (the legal right to keep or sell somebody else's property as security for a debt). If you do not fulfill your promises to repay the loan or adhere to other terms of the agreement, the lender can foreclose and take the property.

A deed of trust is a special kind of deed that gives someone temporary, limited title to a property. It serves the same purpose as a mortgage, but it is easier to foreclose.

Both types of documents give the lender the right to take back a property if you do not make payments on the loan or fulfill other obligations, such as paying your taxes or hazard insurance. Read more about both types of security instruments, and how they affect your deed, in Chapter 13.

Prepayment Penalty

Some loans have a prepayment penalty clause, charging you a fee if you pay off the loan before a stated date. Investors usually avoid loans of this type if they plan to resell a property, but you should evaluate the other terms of the loan to decide if the benefits override the negatives of paying a penalty.

Due-on-Sale Clause

The due-on-sale clause is a loan condition that kicks in when you transfer ownership of a property to another person. If the lender finds out you've sold the property, the lender can demand that you pay the remaining balance that's due on the loan. Not all real-estate loans have due-on-sale clauses.

Working with a Mortgage Broker

Mortgage brokers are business people who charge a fee to bring together borrowers and lenders. Mortgage brokers do not lend money, but they can help you find a loan. They usually network with dozens or even hundreds of lenders, so they can usually find loans for all types of borrowers and properties.

A mortgage broker analyzes your loan needs, then shops for a lender who will make the loan. Good mortgage brokers have a thorough understanding of the types of loans each lender makes and large networks of lenders to draw from, so they sometimes have the ability to secure loans that a single bank or other lending institution cannot make.

The lender gives final approval for any loan, but the mortgage broker prequalifies buyers and makes an assessment of their borrowing power. Brokers pull credit files for the lender and assemble all of the paperwork that the lender requires to approve the loan.

Conflicts of Interest

Mortgage brokers work with you in the same way that a bank-loan officer does, so they have access to your credit records and all of your personal information. Most brokers are honest and attempt to find you the best financing they can, but you must keep in mind that the lender pays them a fee for their services. A better deal for the lender results in a higher fee for the broker. Do not disclose the terms you will accept—let brokers tell you what loan terms they can secure for you. Shop around to make sure that the terms are reasonable, using your own copies of credit reports for the initial interview, so that your credit files are not accessed numerous times. (See Chapter 6 for more information on your credit report.) That can have a negative affect on your credit history.

Some borrowers prefer to work with mortgage brokers for all of their real-estate finance needs. You'll have a better feel for the type of lender you like to work with after you've completed a few real-estate transactions.

Primary Mortgage Market

The primary mortgage market is made up of the businesses that lend borrowers money to pay for real estate—such as the bank you visited to find a loan. They are also called *originators*, because they initiate—or originate—the loan paperwork and the cash that's transferred to buyers at a real-estate closing. In addition to banks, the primary mortgage market includes savings associations, credit unions, and individuals—any person or business that provides cash for someone seeking a mortgage.

QUESTION?

Are mortgage brokers part of the primary mortgage market?
Mortgage brokers are considered part of the primary mortgage market, even though they do not make loans, because they work to bring lenders and borrowers together.

Originators all make loans as an investment, but the way they earn an income from the loans varies. The majority of loans made by originators are sold in order to free up funds so that the originator can make more loans. Less frequently, originators hold on to their loans, receiving regular payments from borrowers and earning an income from the ongoing interest that borrowers pay.

How do originators sell the loans? They assemble many similar loans into groups and sell them to members of the secondary mortgage market, typically receiving cash or mortgage-backed securities for them.

The securities are a type of bond that the originator can then sell to other investors for cash. The end result is that the originating lender gets back the cash they gave the borrower, plus a fee for originating the loan.

The originator sometimes continues to service the sold loans, collecting payments from borrowers and handling their customer service issues. The originator charges the new loan owner a fee for the service, thus creating another way to make a profit for originating the loan.

Secondary Mortgage Market

Members of the secondary mortgage market are the businesses and organizations that buy loans from the originators. Think of them as kind of a clearinghouse for loans. They assemble the loans into even larger groups than the groups they bought from originators and then turn them into securities that can be sold on the stock market.

There's always been a secondary market, but before the 1950s it was less organized. Sometimes there were buyers that originators could sell loans to, but sometimes there weren't. Sometimes there were plenty of secondary market buyers in one area of the country but not in another. The result was a poor cash flow for originating lenders, which resulted in fewer loans to homebuyers.

The government stepped in to better organize the secondary market, creating agencies and the funding they required to keep the flow of money going back to originators so the originators could make more loans. Businesses and organizations purchasing the securities that have been assembled on the secondary market include life insurance companies, real-estate investment trusts, and others looking for long-term investments.

Major Players

The major secondary market organizations are Fannie Mae, Freddie Mac, and Ginnie Mae. Others include Farmer Mac, Munie Mae, and private Real Estate Mortgage Investment Conduits (REMICs). They all have slightly different purposes, as explained here.

Fannie Mae

Formerly a government agency called the Federal National Mortgage Association, Fannie Mae is now a corporation. Fannie Mae plays an important part in the development of the guidelines lenders use to determine if buyers qualify for a loan. Even though it is no longer a government agency, Fannie Mae is regulated by the U.S. Department of Housing and Urban Development (HUD). It can borrow funds from the U.S. Treasury, if necessary, to help keep funds flowing back to primary market lenders.

Ginnie Mae

The Government National Mortgage Association, commonly called Ginnie Mae, was created when Fannie Mae became a private corporation. Regulated by HUD, Ginnie Mae provides a secondary market for low-income and other special-assistance loans and guarantees that principal and interest payments will be made to investors who buy mortgage-backed securities.

Even though you'll never deal directly with the agencies and corporations involved in the secondary market, knowing they exist and understanding how they work makes you more familiar with the mortgage market in general and may give you a better appreciation of the tools that are in place to help buyers in every income category acquire a home.

Freddie Mac

This private corporation was formerly a government agency called the Federal Home Loan Mortgage Corporation. It was originally created to provide a secondary market for savings-and-loan associations, but Freddie Mac is now involved in buying and selling a variety of loans on the secondary market.

Other Major Secondary Players

Three other members of the secondary mortgage market are Real Estate Mortgage Investment Conduit, REMICs, which issue mortgage-backed securities; Farmer Mac, which is involved with the secondary-market sale of loans for farms and ranches; and Munie Mac, which handles tax-exempt multifamily developments.

Underwriting Guidelines

Underwriting is the lender's process of evaluating a borrower and the property the borrower wants to buy. The borrower must be creditworthy, and since the property will act as security for the debt, the documents gathered during the loan process must show that its value meets or exceeds the amount of money that will be lent. That's important, because if the borrower stops making payments and forces to lender to take the property back, the lender wants to make sure it can quickly sell the property and recover its investment.

The secondary market members, especially Fannie Mae and Freddie Mac, have worked with the Department of Housing and Urban Development, known as HUD, to develop underwriting guidelines that help lenders determine which borrowers are more likely to have problems making payments after a loan is granted. Originators who plan to sell their loans on the secondary market must follow the guidelines very carefully. If they don't, their loans won't be marketable.

FACT

Portfolio lenders keep all or a portion of their loans instead of selling them on the secondary market. Those lenders do not necessarily follow the secondary-market underwriting guidelines, so they will sometimes tailor a loan to suit your needs.

Applicants with a favorable credit history are granted loans that require a lower down payment than borrowers who have had prior credit problems. Good credit usually equals a lower interest rate, too. The loan package that you—or your buyers—will be offered is based on risk studies that secondary market lenders have done on past loans throughout the United States. So even though you don't deal with them firsthand, secondary market members play a big part in your ability to finance real estate.

Insured, Guaranteed, and Conventional Loans

If you qualify, your loans may be insured by the Federal Housing Administration (FHA); if you've served in the United States Armed Forces, you may be eligible for a Department of Veteran's Affairs (VA) loan. However, the majority of mortgage loans that are made are conventional loans, loans that are not insured or guaranteed by any government agency. Lenders who make conventional loans must follow guidelines established by Fannie Mae and Freddie Mac in order to sell them on the secondary market.

Insured by the FHA

The FHA does not make loans—it insures lenders from loss if FHA guidelines are used to determine loan approval. The most common FHA loan program, known as Section 203(b), requires a very small down payment and is reserved for single-family, owner-occupied residences. Other FHA-insured loans that can be used by investors include the following:

- Section 221(d)(4) insures up to 90 percent of loans to build rental housing for moderate-income families.
- Section 223(f) insures loans for existing apartment buildings that are at least three years old.
- Section 234 insures loans for the construction or rehabilitation of apartments that are being converted to condos.

A mortgage broker or loan officer is your best source of information about loans that can be issued for all types of properties.

FHA offers a loan program for owner-occupied duplex, triplex, and fourplex units. Live in one unit and let rent from the others make your payments. Many real-estate investors have started their careers using that method.

VA-Guaranteed Loans

The VA guarantees a portion of each mortgage made through its program for qualified current and former member of the United States Armed Forces. The VA does not make loans, but it does guarantee a portion of each borrower's loan. VA loans are attractive because they can be processed with no money down. Closing costs cannot be financed, but the seller is allowed to pay them. VA loans are for owner-occupied residences only. Your lender can give you complete details about the VA loan-guarantee program, including specific armed service requirements.

Conventional Mortgage Loans

Conventional loans are divided into two categories: conforming and nonconforming. Conforming loans have the most rigid underwriting guidelines. They are less risky to the lender, so they carry low interest rates. Lenders look for borrowers with little debt and excellent credit histories. The traditional down payment is 20 percent, but you can opt for private mortgage insurance, PMI, to reduce the amount. You might choose to take a second loan to add to the down payment and avoid PMI. It's a good idea to discuss your payment options with your lender.

Nonconforming loans are variable from one lender to another. They are sometimes referred to as "subprime" loans because the majority of them are geared to applicants with negative credit histories. Guidelines are not as strict as those for conforming loans, but borrowers can expect to pay higher interest rates. Your lender will explain your options if you qualify for a nonconforming loan.

Fixed-Rate Loans

When you take out a loan, your two options are a fixed-rate loan and an adjustable-rate mortgage. If you get a fixed-rate loan, you'll be paying it off at an interest rate that remains the same throughout the life of the loan. That means the amount you pay each month for principal and interest will never change. The specific rate you are offered is a result of the lender's assessment of your loan application—putting less money down is one action that usually results in a higher interest rate. Borrowers with better credit scores are offered lower rates than those with problems on their credit reports.

FACT

Loans are made by combining components. A fixed-rate loan can be conforming or nonconforming. It can be a conventional loan, an FHA loan, or another loan type. A loan can be made for different lengths of time and carry different interest rates. You'll find that lenders will juggle loan components to come up with a package that suits your needs.

The length of the loan period also affects rates. Loans for a period of ten or fifteen years have lower rates than loans for longer terms, such as a thirty-year mortgage. Payments for a shorter-term loan are naturally higher, because you have less time to repay the debt, but the combination of higher payment and lower interest rates allows borrowers to build equity much faster than they can with a longer-term loan.

If you have a fixed-rate mortgage, and interest rates go up, your payment does not increase, so it's easier to plan your long-term budget. If rates dip, you'll have to refinance the loan to decrease your payments and the amount of interest you pay on the loan.

Adjustable-Rate Mortgages (ARMs)

Another option you've got as a borrower is an ARM, a mortgage with a variable interest rate that is linked to a specific economic index, a guide that lenders use to measure interest rate changes. If the index goes up, so does your interest—and your payments. One, three, and five-year Treasury security indexes are often used as the basis for ARMs, but lenders can choose from many others.

ARMs are described using figures such as 1-1, 3-1, and 5-1. The first figure in each set refers to the initial period of the loan, during which your interest rate will be the same as it was on the day of closing. The second number is the adjustment period, which tells you how often adjustments can be made to the rate after the initial period has ended. Here are two examples:

- A 1-1 ARM has an initial period of one year, with rates that can change annually.
- A 3-1 ARM has an initial period of three years, with rates that can change annually.

Ask your lender to explain the different types of ARMs it offers.

Terms to Know Before ARM-Shopping

There are several terms that apply to adjustable-rate mortgages. It's a good idea to become familiar with them before you start shopping for a loan:

- **Margin:** This is the lender's markup, an interest rate that represents the cost of doing business plus the profit on the loan. The lender adds the margin to the index rate to determine your interest rate. The margin usually stays the same during the life of the loan.
- **Buy-down:** This is the fee that real-estate sellers sometimes pay to temporarily reduce the initial interest rate. Homebuilders often use buy-downs to offer their new homes at attractive interest rates. It's a good marketing method that you might want to use someday.
- **Adjustment period:** This is the time between possible rate adjustments.
- **Interest-rate caps:** Rate caps limit how much the lender can increase your interest rate. Periodic caps limit how much it can increase the rate from one adjustment period to the next, and overall caps limit how much the rate can increase over the life of the loan. Overall caps are required by law.
- **Payment caps:** Payment caps limit the amount your monthly payment can increase at each adjustment. If an ARM has a payment cap, it probably won't have a periodic rate cap. The lender can carry over increases that would take a payment past the limit, implementing them at the next adjustment.

ALERT!

You can't choose which index a lender uses, but you can choose a lender based on which index will apply to your loan. Find a loan tied to an index that has remained fairly stable during various economic conditions. When you compare lenders, consider both the index and the margin rate that's being offered.

Financing Ideas for Investment Properties

Many loan products that are designed for investment properties require a minimum of 20 percent down and carry a higher interest rate than mortgages for owner-occupied homes. Those terms can be difficult for new investors to handle, especially when they don't have excess funds or haven't yet generated a cash flow from their investments. There are methods you can use to work around the problem.

For a home, you can take advantage of owner-occupied loan programs if you are open to living in a residence that you are refurbishing. Lenders usually ask you to sign a form that states it is your intent to live in the house yourself for at least one year. Many loans, some for rehabilitation purposes and some with little to nothing down, are available to buyers who can answer "yes" to that question.

After the period you've agreed to, you can sell the house and start over with another. If you use that method a few times, you'll hopefully have enough funds to obtain more conventional investor funding for future purchases. It's a good way for beginners to enhance their cash flow since it means they only make payments on one real-estate loan at a time.

Home Equity Loans

If you have no desire to live in your investment property, your funding could come by taking a home-equity loan on your permanent residence. This method works well for those who have good equity in their homes, but equity loans can be a dangerous solution. If you do not repay the loan, the lender can foreclose, and you will lose your home. Use them only in an emergency for properties you know you can turn around quickly for a profit.

Credit Cards

Credit cards with cash access are another way to raise funds in a hurry. You'll probably pay high interest rates for the use of the money, so reserve this method as a short-term solution.

Private Investors

Mortgage brokers sometimes work with private investors who make real-estate loans. Using someone you know and trust is a better solution than contacting an unknown private investor who advertises in your local paper.

Seller Financing Options

Seller financing is an important and popular tool that can be used to get buyers into properties they could not otherwise purchase. Sellers are sometimes willing to be the bank for a buyer, taking payments just as the bank would until the loan is paid in full. The deed is transferred into your name as it is with any purchase, and you simply make your payments to the seller instead of a bank.

If the seller finances the entire purchase price, a bank won't be involved at all, so you won't have an underwriting department to critique the property—deciding if it's a good buy is entirely up to you. Order an appraisal, and perform all inspections required to help you determine the condition of the structure.

Sellers might check your credit reports, but qualification for a seller-financed loan is usually easier than getting a bank to finance you, especially if you already own many investment properties. You can usually buy a seller-financed property with better terms than a bank can offer for investment properties—at lower interest rates and less money down.

It's not unusual for a seller to ask for a balloon note, but you can usually negotiate to allow a healthy period of time before the note is due. If you plan to refurbish and sell the property, make sure there's enough time to get both tasks handled before the deadline. If you're keeping the property for a rental, make sure you can access payoff funds by the time the due date comes around.

You can usually go to closing very quickly with a seller finance package, but slow down long enough to consult with a real-estate attorney about your offer to purchase and the seller financing agreement.

Contract for Deed

"Contract for deed" is a special type of seller financing. For this type of purchase, the deed remains in the seller's name as security for the debt. The buyer takes possession of the property and maintains it as any owner would, paying taxes, insurance, and maintenance costs. When the debt is paid, the deed is turned over to the buyer.

Contract for deed is sometimes used in order to get around the due-on-sale clause contained in the seller's existing mortgage. That clause states that if the deed changes hands, the mortgage must be immediately paid in full.

Financing issues apply to many aspects of a real-estate transaction. You'll find more information about the various aspects of real-estate finance throughout this book, discussed in the chapter that's most related to each topic.

Since the contract for deed is an agreement between individuals, it requires little or no entry in public records. Before you choose this option, your real-estate attorney should study the seller's existing loan documents to find out if a due-on-sale clause exists.

Before You Sign the Agreement

There are risks that you should evaluate before you accept a contract-for-deed agreement. If the seller has a mortgage, you must make provisions to ensure that he continues to make the loan payments. If he doesn't, the original bank can foreclose and take the property back—even if you've been making timely payments to the seller. You must also be able to prevent the seller from placing future liens on the property, such as acquiring a home-equity loan.

The contract must clearly outline your rights if for some reason you cannot continue to pay the loan. How will foreclosure be handled? Will you be given time to sell the property? Always consult a real-estate attorney before signing a contract-for-deed agreement.

Chapter 6

Your Credit Reports and Credit Scores

For the best interest rates and other attractive loan terms, you must be able to show lenders that you're a good credit risk. Developing and maintaining a positive credit history is essential, and it involves more than paying your bills on time. Use the techniques in this chapter to get your credit reports in tip-top shape before lenders review them.

Credit-Reporting Agencies

There are three major credit-reporting agencies in the United States, Equifax, Experian, and TransUnion, and each one keeps a detailed record of your credit history. They are all storehouses of information, places where your creditors send details about your payment histories, current balances, credit limits, and personal information.

Credit-reporting agencies also receive reports about you from collection agencies, the court system, and other sources of public records. If there's a negative report floating around about your credit history, always assume it will make its way to at least one of the reporting agencies.

Each agency operates independently of the others, so records sometimes differ. Maybe a creditor didn't submit details about an account to all three, or perhaps a mistake occurred during the transfer of data. Each of the agencies handles hundreds of thousands of entries a day, so mistakes are common. It isn't unusual for the records of the three agencies to reflect a different set of "facts" about you and your credit history.

What's on Your Credit Reports?

Your credit reports include your personal information as well as your detailed credit history.

Personal Information

This section of your credit report includes the following data:

- Full name, including any previous names, such as a maiden name
- Social security number
- Birth date
- Current and previous addresses
- Current and past places of employment
- Driver's license number and the state that issued it

Most personal information is not used to evaluate your credit history, but a lender might notice if you've changed jobs frequently and question you about the reasons for the changes. You'll also be questioned if your credit application lists an address or other information that doesn't match the information on the reports.

Although the records contained in your report can go back many years, each report that is generated is very specific for the day and time it is pulled from the records. Information is constantly flowing into the report from your creditors, so it can change at any time.

Detailed Credit History

The core of each report is a detailed history of the credit granted to you for the past several years, with facts about the way you have handled your accounts. Reports offer information about each credit account, including the following:

- Dates accounts were opened and closed
- Current account balances and credit limits
- Payment history for each account, including notations of late payments
- Types of accounts (revolving, such as credit cards; installment, such as auto loans; and real-estate loans)
- Details about who closed the account—whether the request came from you or the credit grantor

Your credit reports include details about liens and judgments against you, bankruptcies, foreclosures, wage attachments, accounts in collection for nonpayment, unpaid child support, and overdrawn checking accounts.

Reporting agencies also keep track of inquiries that are made when you apply for new credit. Too many new inquiries in a short time may be viewed negatively. If the lender feels you've been seeking too much new credit, it might decide you are either already overextended or on the verge of living beyond your means—making you a credit risk.

Credit inquiries made for promotional mailings, requests from your current creditors as they update files, and by you for informational purposes are tracked, but they do not have a negative impact on your reports.

When you buy real estate, the lender will analyze all three reports. Even if you are certain that you've never made a late payment, you should order reports from all three agencies before you decide to buy. You might be surprised by the information that's recorded in your files.

Your Credit Scores

Credit scores were developed to help lenders estimate the risk of lending money—the higher your score, the less likely you are to default on a loan. The techniques used to calculate scores have been developed over time by comparing millions of borrowers with specific types of credit histories. Credit scores are generated by plugging the elements of your credit report into a mathematical formula.

FACT

A loan application isn't the only thing that triggers a credit check. Your reports might be accessed when you apply for a job, purchase an insurance policy, or sign a lease.

The exact formulas used to calculate scores are not public information, but this pie chart offers a basic look at the elements of a credit report, and shows how each one contributes to the calculation.

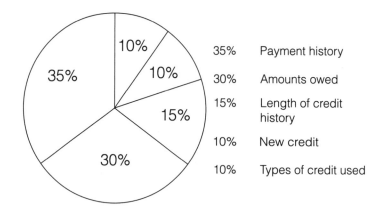

35%	Payment history
30%	Amounts owed
15%	Length of credit history
10%	New credit
10%	Types of credit used

▲ Elements of a Credit Score

The Elements of Your Score

So how do the elements of your credit history come together to create a credit score? We don't know exactly how it happens, but we do have a basic idea, enough to help you see which areas of your credit files have the biggest effect on your scores.

Credit scores are sometimes called FICO scores, because the software used to generate a vast number of score reports was created by Fair Isaac Corporation (FICO), a company that specializes in analyzing data. However, lenders and credit-reporting agencies don't always use the same method to generate scores, so it isn't unusual for scores from each agency to differ.

Your Payment History

Your payment history accounts for approximately 35 percent of your credit score. One part of the calculation looks at the number of accounts you pay as agreed. Another aspect of the formula considers prior and current delinquent accounts, looking at the total number of past-due items, the length of time you stayed in past-due status, and how long it's been since you made a past-due payment.

Older past-due items that were brought current do not usually lower your scores as much as new problems, but they do continue to affect your scores in some way for the entire time they remain on your credit report. Negative public records and accounts turned over to collection agencies are another part of your payment history that can bring your scores down.

Amounts You Owe

The second most important category for scoring is the total amount you owe, accounting for 30 percent of your credit score. Lenders want to see that you are using credit responsibly. Keeping your balances low in relation to the amount of credit available is one way you can demonstrate that you can manage your credit. Maxed-out accounts are a signal that you may be paying a majority of your living expenses with credit, rather than with regular income, making you more of a risk.

Installment loans, such as auto loans, are reviewed with a look at the current amount due versus the original balance—have you brought them down significantly? A well-managed installment or home loan can help raise your scores, because it sends the message that you are settled in, building equity, and handling your finances.

Length of Credit History

The total length of time tracked in your credit report accounts for 15 percent of your score. A history of at least three years is viewed more favorably than accounts and activity that reflect a shorter reporting time.

Types of Credit Used

Credit-scoring software looks at the types of credit you use, such as installment loans, revolving accounts, and mortgages. No single combination of account types will help or hinder this 10-percent portion of your credit score. Every individual's credit history is different, so the impact of this category varies for each of us.

FACT

Equifax calls its score a BEACON score, while Experian uses the term Experian/Fair Isaac Risk Model. TransUnion's scoring process is called EMPIRICA. Each company uses a slightly different formula to calculate scores.

New Credit

Information about new credit extended to you makes up 10 percent of your score calculation. The formula analyzes the number of accounts you've opened recently and then compares how many new accounts you have to the number of seasoned accounts. If the new accounts greatly outweigh the old accounts, your score can go down.

Recent credit inquiries enter this part of the formula, telling lenders if you are seeking credit from many different sources. Numerous inquiries, combined with the opening of new accounts, raise a red flag that you might be overextending your obligations. Allowing time to pass between inquiries and the opening of new accounts lessens their impact on your scores.

New credit can have a positive impact on your credit scores if you've opened new accounts and re-established a good credit history after bankruptcy or past payment problems.

Scoring software recognizes that multiple inquiries from mortgage or auto lenders within a short time usually indicate that you are shopping for a single loan. Groups of similar inquiries are counted as one during calculations.

What's a Good Credit Score?

Credit scores range from 340 to 820—and a few types of scoring reports go as high as 850. The higher your score, the less risk a lender believes you will be. As your score climbs, the interest rates you are offered will most likely decline. In general, borrowers with a score over 700 will be offered more financing options and better interest rates than individuals with lower scores.

Fair Isaac Corporation reports that scores in the United States are distributed as follows:

Up to 499: 1 percent
500 to 549: 5 percent
550 to 599: 7 percent
600 to 649: 11 percent
650 to 699: 16 percent
700 to 749: 20 percent
750 to 799: 29 percent
Over 800: 11 percent

Credit-scoring software only considers items in your credit report, but lenders typically look at other factors that aren't included in the report, such as your income and detailed employment history. For most real-estate loans, you will be asked to provide additional information, such as bank statements and tax returns.

Checking Your Credit Reports

It's a good idea to order your credit reports and study the information presented there, even if you have no immediate plans to seek a mortgage or other loan. Unless you've kept track of all three of your credit histories, it's likely they contain errors. Corrections aren't difficult to make, but it sometimes takes thirty days or more for records to be changed. Check your reports regularly (annual or more frequent checks are a good idea), and notify the agency immediately if you find an error.

Credit-reporting agencies offer options to help you check your credit history online. You can choose from several different types of reports.

- A credit report with or without your current credit score
- A three-in-one credit report that lets you view a side-by-side comparison of records from all three major reporting agencies, with or without scores
- Report services that notify you every time your credit history is requested
- Reports that include daily and weekly notifications of changes to your file
- Subscriptions that allow you to access your current credit report any time you like

When you purchase a three-in-one report, the information displayed from each agency is usually the same as the data found in its files. However, the credit scores shown for the agencies that did not sell the report to you are not always accurate. For best accuracy, order a score report directly from each agency.

You are entitled to a free credit report if you have been turned down for credit or employment (due to your credit report) during the past sixty days. You can also receive a free report if you believe it contains fraudulent information, if you are on public assistance, or if you are unemployed and plan to apply for unemployment benefits within the next sixty days. Ask agency staff if you are eligible for a free or reduced-rate report.

Contact Information

Here's the complete contact information for the three credit agencies:

Experian
NCAC
P.O. Box 9595
Allen, TX 75013
1-888-397-3742
✍ *www.experian.com*

Equifax Information Services, LLC
P.O. Box 740256
Atlanta, GA 30374-0256
1-800-685-1111
✍ *www.equifax.com*

TransUnion
P.O. Box 34012
Fullerton, CA 92834
1-800-916-8800
✍ *www.transunion.com*

Getting Your Credit Reports Online

The first time you order an online report, the agency will ask you to establish a user name and password. You'll be asked to verify your social security number. You'll also be asked a series of multiple-choice questions about your credit history—all designed to ensure you are truly who you say you are.

Some online credit reports can be viewed for thirty days, while others disappear as soon as you close your screen. Be sure to read the instructions carefully and print out your report so that you have a permanent record of it.

Getting Your Credit Reports by Mail

Credit reports can also be ordered by telephone or by mail for home delivery. The typical cost for a mailed report is $8 to $10, but many states give consumers the right to receive a report at a reduced rate.

When you order a credit report by mail, be sure to include your payment, your full name and address, your social security number, and your most recent former address. You might also be asked to send a copy of your driver's license or a utility bill in your name that verifies your identity and home address.

You probably get offers for free credit reports in the mail. Some of those offers require that you subscribe to a service or buy products in order to receive the free report. Read the fine print before you respond to an advertisement offering a free credit report.

Cleaning up Errors and Negative Items

You might discover errors in one or more of your credit reports—or even worse, accurate references to late payments, liens, and collections. Don't panic because the errors can be fixed, and it's possible that some of the negative items can be removed—without help from so-called credit-repair companies.

Once an entry is added to your report, it doesn't drop off for some time unless you prove that it's an error. Positive records are always a plus, but negative entries by your creditors can affect your buying power for many years. Most negative records can stay on your report for seven years. Bankruptcies can remain there for ten.

Disputing Errors on Your Credit Report

Follow these steps to dispute errors that you find on your credit report:

1. Make a copy of your credit report and circle every item you believe is incorrect.
2. Write a letter to the reporting agency (the address will be printed on your credit report).

3. Explain why you are disputing the item, and request an investigation to resolve the issue.
4. Include copies of supporting paperwork, coding the pages in some way to match dispute paragraphs. Do not send your originals.
5. Send all materials by certified mail, return receipt requested, so that you can prove the packet was received.
6. Send a letter of dispute to the creditor whose reports you disagree with. Most billing statements include a special mailing address for disputes.

If your dispute involves your current employment, include a copy of a pay stub or your current W-2 form. If the error involves your current address, include a copy of your driver's license or a utility bill in your name that shows the correct address. Ask the agency for recommendations if you aren't sure what type of proof is required to correct the error.

The reporting agency will initiate an investigation, contacting your creditors or others to verify the accuracy of the disputed entries. If the creditor cannot verify that the information is correct, it must be removed. When the investigation is complete, the reporting agency must send you a free copy of your credit report if changes were made to it.

If the investigation reveals an error, you have the right to ask that a corrected version of your report be sent to everyone who requested it during the past six months.

FACT

You can also initiate an investigation from an online credit report. It's an intuitive process, so follow the links and check the disputed items as directed. There sometimes isn't a place for remarks—you must select a multiple-choice reason for each dispute. If you feel that you must be more specific, submit your dispute by mail instead.

If Requested Changes Aren't Made

If the reporting agency verifies that the information is accurate, it must provide you with a written notice that includes the name, address, and phone number of the provider. If you still disagree with the findings, you can initiate another investigation.

If your attempts to correct an entry are unsuccessful, you can ask the reporting agency to insert a 100-character explanation in your credit files that gives your side of the story.

Removing Accurate, but Negative Items

You can dispute a negative item even if you believe it is accurate. You'll have to follow your conscience on that, but some people have been able to have negative entries removed by repeatedly disputing them with their creditors and the reporting agencies.

If an account that was previously past due has been brought current and has been either paid off or kept current for at least a year, the creditor might agree to delete references to past-due payments. Write a letter requesting that action. Chances are good that they will remove the late notation.

Improving Your Credit Scores

The only quick fix for low credit scores is paying down debt and successfully disputing negative information in your credit files, but there are many things you can do to start improving your credit scores from this day forward. The thought of waiting another year to see an improvement might be daunting, but what if you don't have a solid plan of action? You'll be another year down the road with unimproved scores. Don't put it off. Start working toward a better credit history today.

Always pay your bills on time, because late payments play a major role in driving down your scores. Your goal should be to accumulate a long history of on-time payments.

Contact your creditors as soon as you know you cannot pay accounts on time. Most creditors will work with you to bring an account up to date, and you might even avoid being flagged as a late payer. If you have late payments now, get them current and keep them that way. If your debt situation is serious, see a legitimate *nonprofit* credit counselor for help (see Appendix C). Avoid the scam artists who promise a quick reversal of your credit problems—it just isn't realistic.

Other credit-related actions are just as important as paying your bills on time. Every piece of the credit pie you saw earlier in this chapter must come together in a positive way in order for you to have a positive credit history.

> Managing your credit files should become a part of your regular routine. Once they are in good shape, monitor them often to make sure that new errors do not pop up.

Don't open several new accounts in a brief period, especially if your credit history is shorter than three years. Opening many accounts makes lenders feel you aren't handling your credit responsibly.

Try to keep your credit card balances low, because high debt-to-credit limit ratios bring your scores down—and maxing out even a few accounts can create a significant drop. Don't rush to close unused credit cards, because untapped credit can raise your scores. On the other hand, don't open new cards that you don't need just to show that you don't use all of your available credit. That can backfire and lower your scores, since it generates additional credit requests and makes it appear you are loading up on available credit. The bottom line is that you should pay off your debt instead of moving it around. Ⓔ

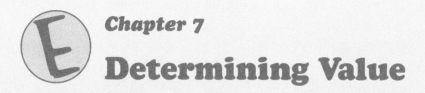

Chapter 7

Determining Value

Once you find a property you're interested in and the financing that will make the purchase possible, you'll have to consider what the property is worth. You want to buy for a low price and with excellent terms, but how do you know when the price is right? Sometimes gut instinct tells you—but that instinct must be acquired. Plan to spend time researching the market and learning about the different types of valuations assigned to properties by appraisers and others within the world of real estate.

Fair Market Value

Have you ever assembled a jigsaw puzzle? You gather the pieces in front of you so that all are visible, and you sort them into groups to help you determine which piece fits in where. Putting a value on real estate is a little more complex, but the process is very similar. You gather facts and opinions from several different sources, sort them into groups, and then determine how each piece fits into the overall picture of the property's value.

FACT

You'll hear the term *fair market value*, or simply *market value*, when you begin to shop for real estate. The term refers to the highest price a property would sell for in a reasonable length of time, provided both buyer and seller are knowledgeable about the market and not under pressure to buy or sell instead.

Can Tax Values Help Determine Value?

A tax value is the value of the property as assessed by your local taxing authorities for the purpose of determining property tax. Tax values do not usually offer a good estimation of a property's market value, but they do provide some insight into individual properties and the local real-estate market. Details about building elements and heated square footage are often stated within documents that accompany public tax records. The records contain details about the dates improvements were added to land. Thus, tax values offer a snapshot of the differences in property values from neighborhood to neighborhood.

Become a regular at your county courthouse or equivalent location where public records are housed. The staff will teach you to look up tax records and find copies of the deeds that contain details about the properties you are researching. Ask the staff if there are general guidelines to help determine tax value versus approximate market value. For instance, in some areas tax value equals approximately 80 percent of market value. Using that type of formula won't give you true market value, but it does provide a starting point for your research.

Real-Estate Appraisals

Appraisals are important to buyers, sellers, and real-estate lenders. Buyers want to know that the value of the property they are purchasing meets or exceeds the amount they are paying for it. Sellers use appraisals to make sure they don't price a property too low. Lenders depend on the results of a formal real-estate appraisal to help determine if they should lend money on a property. It tells them whether or not they are likely to sell the property in a reasonable length of time for at least the amount they are investing in it if you default on the loan and force them to take the property back.

The property being appraised is called the *subject property*. Recently sold properties an appraiser chooses to compare to the subject in order to help determine value are called *comparables*. You may hear both of those terms during your real-estate transaction.

Three types of appraisals are common in real-estate transactions—sales comparison, cost, and income capitalization. Often only one approach is used, but for some properties, it makes sense to look at value from different angles. Another option is to calculate the gross rent multiplier.

Most appraisers belong to real-estate multiple listing services, so they are able to quickly find sold properties to use as comparables. Since they don't show properties when they are for sale, appraisers often call listing agents for feedback about the condition of the comps they choose.

Sales Comparison Approach

The sales comparison approach develops an estimate of the subject property's market value by comparing it to similar properties that have recently sold in the area. The sold properties are called *comparables,* or *comps*. Sales comparisons are commonly used for residential properties, including single-family homes, condos, townhouses, and duplexes. The method is sometimes used to appraise fourplexes and larger, multiunit properties.

The appraiser typically selects three sold properties to compare to the subject property, adjusting the components of the comps to make their features closely match the subject. For instance, a subject with an open deck could be compared to a comp with a screened deck. The appraiser would adjust the comp, taking away the value of the screening. After adjusting the sales price of all three comps, the appraiser has a good idea of the subject property's market value.

Cost Approach Appraisals

A cost approach appraisal is an opinion of the subject property's value that is determined by calculating how much it would cost to replace it. The appraiser estimates the value of the structures and other improvements to the property, then deducts an amount for depreciation—a lessening of value that occurs over time from general wear and tear or because elements of the structure are obsolete. The value of land is determined by using recent sales of similar sites. Depreciation does not apply to the land.

FACT

Cost approach appraisals are most suitable for newer properties because it's easier to estimate replacement costs for the materials and methods used in the structure. This approach is also useful for appraising unique properties, where comparables cannot be found.

Appraisers consider different types of depreciation:

- Physical depreciation is caused by normal deterioration of the property. An aging roof and peeling paint are both considered physical depreciation.
- Functional obsolescence refers to aspects of the improvements that make the structure less desirable or less marketable. Outdated designs, such as homes with four bedrooms and only one bath, fall under this category.
- External obsolescence is caused by elements that make a property less desirable but are out of the control of the owner. A neighborhood that

has changed from residential to industrial is one example of external obsolescence.

Income Capitalization Approach

The income capitalization approach is used to place a value on property based on its income-producing capabilities. It is most commonly used to estimate the value of office and apartment buildings, retail stores, strip malls, shopping centers, and other similar rental real estate.

The appraiser uses the sales comparison approach to find similar properties in order to determine if the subject property's rental fees are higher, lower, or similar to typical market rents.

The appraiser calculates the subject property's annual gross income and then deducts a figure for the normal operating expenses, such as taxes, routine maintenance, management fees, pest inspection and control, vacancy allowances, insurance costs, and other expenses associated with operating the property. The appraiser might also include an amount that represents a reserve for major repairs.

Net income is determined next by subtracting the operating expenses from the total amount collected from tenants, called gross income. The appraiser inserts the investor's desired rate of return into a mathematical formula with the other elements to calculate value: value = net income / capitalization rate.

Gross annual income	$100,000
Less expenses	($33,000)
Net annual income	$67,000
Capitalization rate	0.10
Estimated value	$670,000

Gross Rent Multiplier

The value of single-family homes destined to be rentals is sometimes estimated by using a gross rent multiplier (GRM). The appraiser locates comparable properties and then divides their sales prices by a typical monthly rental fee.

For instance, let's say you have a property with a sales price of $100,000 that could be rented for $800 per month: $100,000 / $800 = 125 GRM.

The appraiser locates a series of comparables to develop an average GRM, then the formula is approached from a different angle. If he finds that the average GRM in the area is 120, and the subject property could be rented for $875 per month, the estimated value of the property is $105,000. Here's how it works: $875 per month × 120 GRM = $105,000 estimated value.

Hiring an Appraiser

Real-estate appraisers are individuals who are trained to help determine the market value of real estate. They are typically licensed by state agencies after completing coursework and an internship with an experienced appraiser. Coursework teaches appraisers the mechanics of performing an appraisal, but it's real-life experience that makes them good at their job.

An appraiser should be an objective third party, someone who has no connection to any person involved in the real-estate transaction. The bank won't be too likely to accept an appraisal if they know it was done by the buyer's brother! Likewise, an appraiser who works for the real-estate agency that holds a listing shouldn't be used to appraise property for a buyer.

Buyers are normally asked to pay for an appraisal when they apply for a home loan. The lender might use an appraiser on its staff or hire an independent appraiser to work on the transaction. If you are allowed to choose the appraiser, it's possible that the lender will ask a third party to review the results, just to make sure you didn't select someone who is biased in your favor.

Dealing with a Low Appraisal

Your lender wants to be sure its investment is covered in case you default on the loan. If the property under contract appraises lower than the sales price, the loan may be declined. Don't panic if that happens, because there are steps you can take to make the deal work if you still want the property.

ALERT!

Cash buyers should always insert a clause in their purchase contracts stating that they can back out of a contract with no penalties if the property does not appraise at or above the sales price. Buyers seeking financing are usually protected by a financing contingency—poor appraisal, no loan.

You can dispute an appraisal if you feel it is incorrect. Be prepared to tell the lender—in writing—why you do not agree with the report. Perhaps you know that one or more of the comparables the appraiser used was in terrible condition, and not a good comparison to the property in your transaction. Do you have proof? An old multiple listing service description showing the property was sold "as is" would help your position. Similar statements from the former listing agent would offer more reinforcement that the property needed repairs.

Appraisers rely on written documentation to select comps. They will usually adjust their reports if you can show them that a property doesn't truly match the one under contract.

If that doesn't work, the seller might be willing to save the sale by reducing the sales price. The realization that future appraisals might not be much better is a powerful motivation for the seller to get the transaction over with and move on.

If the seller won't reduce the price, and you still want the property, you could talk with the bank and offer to make a larger down payment, but more down does not guarantee they will approve the loan. Banks often don't like to lend money if the borrower ends up with negative equity in a property. That occurs when the value of a property is less than the amount it sold for.

Appraisal Limitations

Appraised value does not necessarily indicate market value. When a lender orders an appraisal, it wants to verify that its investment is covered, so a large number of appraisals come back showing a value that closely matches the sales price. Appraisers focus on the needs of the lender, and they don't spend a lot of time analyzing a property beyond what's necessary to establish minimum value.

Appraisals don't tell you how much or how quickly a property might increase in value, either over time or with the addition of key improvements. Those are important topics that you must analyze to determine if you have an interest in a property.

Always remember that an appraisal is an opinion. If you order three appraisals from three different appraisers, you're very likely to get three different results. They're usually similar, but sometimes the differences are surprising. Variations are most common when an owner orders multiple appraisals for her own purposes, since the appraiser is starting from scratch—there's no target figure associated with a sales contract.

Appraisers do not verify property boundaries. Unless an encroachment, where a neighboring property owner has built on or too close to your property line, is obvious, it won't be on the appraiser's report, even though it might have a large impact on market value.

The same is true about title issues. An appraisal wouldn't show that a former owner has never relinquished rights to the property, or that two generations ago the owner granted someone a permanent right-of-way across the property. Those issues are usually discovered by an attorney or other title researcher when a sale takes place.

An appraisal does not take the place of an inspection to verify that all components and systems of a structure are in good operating condition. A house or other building that looks great on the surface could turn into a fix-up nightmare for its new owner. Appraisals are a useful tool, but they are just one piece of the puzzle you must assemble in order to determine a property's market value.

Comparative Market Analysis

Real-estate agents use a process called *comparative market analysis*, or *CMA,* to help home-sellers determine a realistic asking price, and although their less formal evaluations are not accepted by banks, an experienced agent can come very close to a property's true market value.

Most real-estate agents have access to the records of a multiple listing service, which provides a history of recently sold properties that can be compared to the subject property. Agents who work with many buyers have an even greater advantage—they have shown those properties and have a personal knowledge of their conditions, making comparisons easier and more accurate.

You may not always want to work with a real-estate agent, but since a larger percentage of properties are listed with agencies than sold by owners, it makes sense for you to find at least one real-estate agent you trust to help you evaluate properties. Develop a business relationship with that agent so that you can call on him when you need to research comparable properties for an anticipated sale or purchase.

ALERT!

An agent will be more responsive to your ongoing research needs if you reward that agent with the business of handling at least a portion of your sales and purchases. Who do you think an agent will call first when the perfect property is listed—someone who helps the agent make a living, or someone who only calls when they need advice?

Hands-On Evaluation of Comparables

A real-estate agent won't be inclined to show you properties if you're not truly interested in purchasing something, but if you are planning a purchase, working with an agent to view properties is definitely a good way to get an overview of the market. Another option is to attend as many open houses as possible. Viewing FSBO properties is a third way for you to evaluate properties that are for sale in your area.

Keep accurate records of all the properties you visit. If an agent gives you multiple listing sheets, make notes on them to help you remember the specifics of each property. Most sellers prepare handouts for potential buyers—keep them. Keep open-house flyers, too, jotting down your recollections of each property. A FSBO seller might feel uncomfortable if you take interior photos, but if they'll allow it, do it.

Pick up real-estate for-sale publications that are distributed in your area. They're free and usually distributed at real-estate agencies, grocery stores, gas stations, and other similar locations. Don't miss reading your local classifieds. Search the Internet for listings in your area. If you spend enough time researching properties, it won't take long to become accustomed to typical real-estate prices in your area.

Once you know that a property has been sold, research your local public records to find its sales price. If you're not sure how to do that, ask the staff who work in the records department to show you how to find the information.

If you're serious about real estate, public records will be one of the first items you look at to find details about a property. While you're researching, keep in mind that the amount the owner paid for a property has nothing to do with its current value. The prior sales amount doesn't show you improvements that have been made and it isn't a reflection of the property's appreciation or current condition. You expect your own property values to appreciate over the time—so do sellers.

Knowing how much the current owner paid for a property can help you negotiate a contract when you know that the seller needs to sell quickly. A divorce, a forced move, a possible foreclosure—all three are events that can motivate a seller to accept a lower offer.

The best way to alienate a seller is to remind them what they paid for the property and use that figure to justify a low offer. Sellers know what they paid for the property, and they very likely know what it's worth now. If you expect future negotiations to be amicable, don't come across as an arrogant buyer who has no regard for the true value of someone else's property. That tactic usually backfires.

There are many factors to consider before you make an offer to purchase any piece of residential real estate. Facts about restrictions, easements, rights-of-way, and property boundaries are important details that help you determine the limitations and best use for a property. When you know its best use, you're closer to making a determination of its value.

You'll feel more confident about your buying and selling decisions when you become an active participant in property research and stay informed about the real-estate market where you are participating. Acquiring that knowledge takes time and dedication on your part. It won't happen overnight, but when it does, you'll be able to make speedy judgments about current and potential market values. (E)

Chapter 8

Disclosures and Inspections

Property disclosures and home inspections are two important issues that affect real-estate transactions. Buyers want sellers to disclose facts about a property. Buyers and sellers want inspection feedback that verifies that the property is in excellent condition, with no hidden problems. Inspection issues can create stress if problems are found, but try to relax, because you can usually work through it.

Residential Property Disclosures

Property owners in most U.S. states are required to give buyers a written disclosure that describes facts about the structure they are selling. Each state that requires disclosure provides its own forms, so the specific questions sellers must answer differ in every area. Most disclosures do cover many of the same topics, giving the seller the opportunity to answer "yes," "no," or "no representation" to questions about all components of the property.

Sellers sometimes answer questions with "unknown" or "no representation" when they are unsure if a problem exists. The property might be part of an estate settlement, and the person handling the sale simply doesn't know the answers. The property might be a vacation home that hasn't been used for some time. It's also possible that the seller is being evasive. Sellers should not declare "no representation" about an item they know is defective, but it does happen.

Some FSBO sellers don't realize that they are required by law to give potential buyers a residential property disclosure. Not following through on that duty in states where it's required can create liability for the seller if a pre-existing problem is discovered after closing.

Even if sellers are not required to give potential buyers a specific disclosure form, local real-estate laws probably do require them to disclose information about any known problems associated with the property.

ALERT!

Ask for a disclosure for all properties you want to look at, then refer to it during showings to remind you of the age of components and known problems associated with them. You might even find that there are properties you don't want to see because disclosed problems are excessive.

One way to learn more about the disclosures required in your area, along with many other facts about real estate, is to take a real-estate agent licensing class. You don't have to become an agent—just taking the class will give you a head start on learning about real-estate laws in your area.

Common Items on Disclosure Forms

A property disclosure contains details about the condition of the property, the age of its components, and any defects that may exist. That type of information is called a *material fact*. Here are a few topics you might see on a property disclosure:

- Age of shingles and other roof components
- Facts about known leaks in the roof or foundation
- Details about past or present mold or mildew within the structure
- Information about prior or current infestations of wood-destroying insects
- Problems with sewer lines or septic systems
- Paid or unpaid fees for upcoming assessments, such as sidewalks
- Information related to planned roadways or other events that will affect the property
- The existence and location of a buried fuel storage tank

In some states or localities, certain facts might be disclosed on a special form. Your state or city might require specific disclosure if a property is in an airline flight path, within a flood plain, located on a fault line, or affected by other conditions of a local nature.

Chapter 9 includes more information about disclosures and inspections that are related to environmental hazards, such as lead paint, radon, molds and mildew, and asbestos.

What's *Not* a Material Fact?

Some things you might like to know more about are *not* material facts. That includes personal information about the sellers, especially things that would convey the impression they are eager to sell. Sellers don't have to disclose that they've been transferred and must report to a new job in a different city in three weeks. A possible foreclosure isn't considered a material fact until the information is part of the public records. An impending divorce never needs to be disclosed.

Buyers always want to know the seller's reasons for moving. Most sellers are moving for the same reasons that buyers are buying—they want a change. They've grown out of the house. Their kids are gone and they don't need the space. They want to move to a warmer climate. For some reason, buyers think that a seller will disclose negative details when they ask why they are moving, or give them a clue as to their motivation to sell. It doesn't usually happen.

Items that *Might* Be Material Facts

Some items are regarded as borderline material facts, differing from state to state. Information that someone died in the house may not be considered a material fact in some areas, even if it was a homicide, but if a buyer asks a question about it, the question should be answered truthfully. The same is true for structures that some people consider to be haunted. If a buyer asks, the seller should be truthful about a property's ghostly reputation.

FACT

People who have AIDS or are HIV-positive are considered legally handicapped by fair housing laws. A real-estate agent cannot legally answer you if your questions are about that illness, even if the agent is working for you as a buyer's agent. The correct response to your questions is that the subject cannot be discussed.

Commercial Property Disclosure

Disclosures for apartment buildings and other commercial properties usually include details that help a buyer evaluate the structure and the property's support systems. Disclosures are also required for vacant commercial land in some states. Information about zoning, disability issues, garbage pickup, environmental hazards, encroachments and numerous other topics might be included in a commercial property disclosure.

It's critical to understand all local, state, and federal laws before you purchase commercial or industrial properties. There are many pitfalls for the novice investor, so commercial transactions aren't usually the best place for a beginner to start investing in real estate. Gaining experience in dealing with residential properties is a less risky way of beginning your real-estate investment career.

If you feel commercial real estate is the only way to go, find a mentor to whom you can turn for advice about disclosures and inspections. Use an experienced commercial real-estate agent for your transactions. Employ a real-estate attorney who can lead you through the process. Study governmental Web sites to learn about laws that control the type of property you are buying. Read as many books as you can about commercial purchases. When you're ready to proceed, do it with caution.

The Purpose of the Inspection

Home inspections are usually optional—but always a good idea. Qualified inspectors can tell you if systems within the house are adequate and working correctly. How would you feel if you bought a property during cold weather, then found out the next summer that its air-conditioning system isn't capable of cooling the house? A good inspector can provide those details and will give you feedback on nearly every aspect of the structure.

A home inspector evaluates the structure of the house and gives details about components such as the roof, plumbing, electrical system, heating and air-conditioning units, appliances, insulation, doors, and windows. Inspectors may have seen hundreds, or even thousands, of homes and know exactly what to look for. They usually know all the little quick-fix tricks that sellers try and will alert you if they find cover-up attempts.

ALERT!

Some buyers decide an inspection isn't necessary for a brand-new structure. That's a bad decision, because new constructions are rarely problem-free. Builders offer warranties, but it's a lot easier to get a builder to resolve problems before the sale than afterward, when the money has already changed hands.

If you want a property so much that you're ignoring severe problems, an inspection can help bring you back to reality. The inspector will take a clinical look at the house, then give you only the facts—and that's what you need to make decisions about going forward with the purchase. If you do decide to proceed, at least you'll have a better understanding of the time, energy, and money you must devote to a property that needs many repairs.

The property might be such a wreck that, even if you know you want it, you don't know where to start. A thorough inspection can be valuable because it will uncover areas in critical need of repair and point out safety issues that can help you prioritize your repair schedule.

Finding a Qualified Home Inspector

Most U.S. states offer little or no regulations for the home inspection industry, so finding a good inspector sometimes takes a little legwork. One of the best methods you can use is to get referrals from friends who've been happy with an inspector's services. Your real-estate agent can also provide you with the names and phone numbers of multiple inspection companies.

Questions to Ask the Inspector

Ask each inspector for references—but keep in mind they won't give you the names of unhappy clients! Ask which systems are included in their inspection. Find out if the inspector charges an extra fee to inspect septic systems, private wells and related water testing, radon, and mold.

Ask to see a sample of the report you will be given after the inspection. Does it include plenty of specific details, with photos of problem areas? It should include a checklist that shows results for all systems evaluated. It should also include detailed reports in paragraph form.

Find out how long the inspection will take, and be prepared to set aside three to five hours or more for a thorough inspection. Compare fees and services among the inspectors you interview. Other questions you should ask include the following:

- Where were you trained, and how long have you been a professional inspector?
- Are you an engineer or general contractor? (Both of those designations take extensive study.)
- Do you attend continuing education classes for home inspectors?
- Do you belong to a professional organization for inspectors?
- What are the requirements for organization membership? (Entry should require more than just an application fee.)
- Do you carry errors and omissions insurance? (This is a type of malpractice insurance that covers mistakes made by inspectors.)

A septic report and a water test are required if you're obtaining FHA or VA financing for a home that's not on public utilities. You can usually save money if you ask the inspector to perform the tests at the same time other systems are inspected.

Other Options

Some buyers ask a friend or relative to step in to do an inspection. That's okay—it's your choice, and some people truly do have a friend or family member who can do a thorough job. Be sure you understand the differences between someone with building experience and someone who inspects real estate for a living. A person with construction experience may not have the equipment or expertise that's required to conduct a thorough evaluation of a home or other structure.

Conduct Inspections on Time

Inspections must typically be completed by a specific date specified in your contract. Other dates that should be listed in your contract are the date a buyer must have repair requests to a seller and the date by which a seller must respond. If your contract says that *time is of the essence*, the dates stated within it are not flexible unless all parties agree to the change.

You'll find that there are different methods for handling inspections throughout the United States. In some areas, inspections are done after the parties have signed a contract. In other areas, inspections are completed before the actual contract is signed. Talk to real-estate professionals where you live to find out how inspections are handled.

If you can, attend the inspection along with the inspector. Inspectors report all defects they find, no matter how minor. It is not unusual for buyers to get excited about minor problems simply because they weren't there for a firsthand explanation of each one. Witnessing the problems gives you a better grasp of what is and is not an issue.

Your Inspection Contingencies

An offer to purchase should include a detailed statement regarding the buyer's rights to an inspection and the seller's rights related to the inspection. It should spell out the options both parties have if an inspection uncovers serious problems.

Real-estate agents use standard forms that include provisions for home inspections. Real-estate attorneys draft more specific contracts for buyers and sellers in some areas. It's common for the buyer to be given the right to back out of a contract with no penalties if an inspection uncovers more problems than the buyer feels she can deal with. In most cases, the seller can be asked to complete repairs, but he isn't obligated to do so. Closing on a property in need of repairs is very often a give-and-take situation, with each party compromising to make the transaction work.

Lender Requirements

Your lender might require a separate inspection to verify that there are no active infestations of wood destroying insects in the structure. Environmental inspections might also be on your list of important tasks to complete before you close on the property.

Lenders sometimes ask for a structural inspection if the appraiser's report comes back with comments about foundation cracks, standing water in basements or crawl spaces, or negative remarks about other areas related to the building's structure. If that happens, and your inspector holds the type of license the lender wants to see on a structural report, you're ahead of the game. Lenders will usually accept a letter of structural integrity from a licensed general contractor or a structural engineer.

Lenders that require wood-destroying insect inspections want to see a report that's dated within thirty days of closing. Monitor your estimated closing date, moving pest inspections forward if necessary to remain in the accepted timeframe.

Additional inspections might be a routine occurrence in your specific area, especially for commercial properties. Research your market, and talk to experienced real-estate agents and to others who can tell you if certain inspections are required or recommended.

Facts about Home Warranties

Home warranties insure against repair and replacement costs for appliances and other components of a home that quit working. They can be purchased for any home, no matter what its age. Home warranties are a plus for any property, but sellers sometimes offer them for residences with older components, especially if a home inspector has red-flagged an item as past its prime. A warranty helps assure the buyer that he won't have to buy new appliances or other covered items if they fail a month after closing. Warranties are often purchased at closing, but can be acquired any time.

Standard home warranty coverage differs quite a bit by provider, so you should study each policy carefully before selecting the one that's best for your needs. Many standard policies cover plumbing and appliances. If heating and cooling units are not covered by the basic policy, you can include them by paying an additional fee. Some home-warranty policies cover the roof. Coverage for private wells and septic systems must usually be tacked on to the basic policy.

Home warranties that are ordered while a house is for sale can be used to make repairs for the current owner, but coverage for the owner and future buyers might differ. A standard policy might not pay a seller's repair bill if the furnace quits working before the house is sold, but it will cover the buyer if that happens after the property changes hands. Read the fine print to determine how each party is covered. Many policies cover the seller, without payment, for up to 180 days while the property is listed. Payment is due at closing.

QUESTION?

What's the difference between a home warranty and hazard insurance?
A home warranty replaces items that fail on their own, while hazard insurance replaces items damaged or destroyed in fires, by wind, or during other covered events.

When you call to report a problem, the home-warranty provider sends out a local repairperson who is licensed to represent them. The warranty company pays the repairperson a fee, and you pay the person a copayment for your portion of the repair. Copayments vary but often range from $35 to $55 per visit.

One complaint that real-estate agents hear is that warranty providers sometimes send out a repairperson more times than necessary, attempting to have the person repair an item that should have probably been replaced on the first visit. Talk to each warranty company about their policies to verify how they determine when replacement should be made.

Evaluating Coverage and Companies

The cost of a home-warranty policy varies. A basic policy is similar among the major providers, even though the items covered sometimes differ. Evaluate coverage by jotting down covered items in a column on the left side of a blank sheet of paper. To the right, make a separate column for each policy, and check off the items that are covered by each provider's basic policy. If you must purchase coverage for some systems separately, jot down the price. Doing this side-by-side comparison will help you determine which policy covers the most components for the best price. Other items you should consider are how long the company has been in business and how easy it is to reach their customer service department.

Most home warranty policies are effective for one year, with an option to renew coverage when they expire. Be aware that the renewal cost is often higher than the fee paid for the initial policy.

Warranties Help Sellers Sell

A home warranty is a good marketing tool, and it also offers sellers a little more peace of mind that buyers won't come knocking on their door if a system fails after closing. Offering a home warranty for a home with older components helps put potential buyers at ease about possible break-downs. The price of a home warranty is minimal, and since the policy can be paid for at closing, you're not out any cash until the home sells. Home warranties are a relatively inexpensive way for a seller to add value to a property.

Benefits to Buyers

Buyers are often short of cash after coming up with the funds required for closing. Replacing an appliance or making repairs to major systems a short time later can be devastating. Ask your seller to pay for a home warranty at closing, or negotiate a deal where both of you kick in funds to pay for the policy.

Chapter 9

Getting a Grip on Environmental Hazards

Environmental hazards are an important consideration for anyone who plans to buy and sell real estate. Federal laws regulate disclosure about paints made with lead. Buyers are concerned about moving into homes with high levels of radon, a potential carcinogen. Molds are a potential health risk and can cause structural damage if left unchecked. Investors must consider those topics and others before they move forward with a purchase.

Federal Lead-Based Paint Laws

U.S. federal regulations require that sellers and landlords disclose any known information about lead-based paint that exists in residential structures built prior to 1978, when its use was banned in residential dwellings. Buyers and tenants must be given a pamphlet developed by the U.S. Environmental Protection Agency (EPA) in association with other governmental agencies, titled *Protect Your Family from Lead in Your Home*. In addition, home-buyers must be given at least ten days to conduct lead tests and risk assessments.

Regulations do not require you to test for lead-based paints; they simply state that if you have conducted tests to detect their presence, the test results must be shared with buyers and tenants. Most sellers and landlords do not conduct tests for the presence of lead in paint.

These laws were implemented because lead paint is a potential health risk. Depending on the level of exposure, lead can cause damage to the brain and nervous system, behavior problems, slowed growth, headaches, difficulties during pregnancy, high blood pressure, digestive problems, and muscle and joint pain.

Lead can affect everyone in the family, but children are often at highest risk, especially small children who are more likely to chew on painted objects or pop a paint chip into their mouths.

Landlords who renovate structures built prior to 1978 are required to notify tenants of the risks of lead exposure that could take place during those renovations. The EPA's Web site includes a self-test to help you determine if disclosure is required for your project. You'll find EPA contact information in Appendix C.

A permanent solution to the presence of lead-based paint requires work by a certified lead abatement contractor, someone who will remove the paint or seal and enclose it with special materials. Landlords who choose lead abatement may be required to disclose information about the process to their tenants.

Radon and Its Effects on Health

You can't see or smell radon. This colorless, odorless, tasteless radioactive gas is formed during the natural breakdown of uranium in the environment. It can enter buildings in well water or seep into the air through cracks and holes in the foundation.

Health officials have labeled radon a carcinogen, stating that it is responsible for some cases of lung cancer. Studies have shown that while radon exposure is most likely to trigger cancer in smokers, nonsmokers who breathe the gas have a slightly elevated risk of developing the disease, too.

Because more buyers are now educated about radon, testing is becoming routine. Your real-estate purchase contracts should be contingent on test results that show an acceptable level of radon gas as recommended by the EPA. If levels are found to be high, you should have the option of backing out of the contract with no penalties. You may not be concerned about the health risks of radon for yourself, but if you're buying for resale, it's a good idea to make sure you have a structure with low radon levels.

FACT

Written proof that the air inside of a structure contains low levels of radon can be a good marketing tool when it's time to sell the property. Results from a professional inspector are more convincing to potential buyers than tests you conduct yourself.

The EPA recommends you install a system to reduce radon if the amount of gas detected in a residential structure is 4 picocuries of radon per liter (pCi/L) or higher. Some states have issued their own standards for acceptable radon levels.

Radon Testing Methods

Even if the house next door is radon-free, your property might have elevated levels of the gas. You may have heard that structures without basements don't have problems with radon, but that isn't true. The only way to know if radon is present in a structure is to test the air quality.

There are two basic types of radon testing devices, passive and active. Passive devices do not need power to function. These devices include charcoal canisters and similar units made from materials that absorb the gas. They are placed in the structure for a specific amount of time and then sent to a laboratory for analysis.

Active testing devices require power to function. They are meters that continuously measure and record radon in the air, making it easy to see when gas spikes and dips occur. Active devices are considered more reliable than passive testers, but since the equipment is expensive, they are used primarily by home inspectors and air-quality professionals and are not readily available to a homeowner.

Active devices sometimes have an anti-interference feature, which records when the device is moved. That can be an important factor when testing structures where you're not sure the seller will allow the device to remain in place during the testing period.

The most commonly used radon testing devices are passive units left in place for forty-eight to ninety-six hours. Long-term testing, done over a ninety-day period (or more), is usually more accurate, because time helps level out the spikes and dips in radon concentration. Investors and home-buyers don't usually have the luxury of taking ninety days to complete a test, so it's more common to see long-term tests used after a real-estate closing by an owner who wants to verify radon levels.

Tester Placement

The EPA recommends that you place the testing unit in the lowest level that can currently be used for living space. Choose a room that's used regularly but not a kitchen, bathroom, laundry room, or hallway.

Follow the EPA's recommendations for testing:

- Close the room's windows and outside doors for at least twelve hours prior to beginning.
- Keep windows and doors in the tested room shut, except for normal entry and exit.

- Do not perform short-term tests during times of high humidity or high winds.
- Place the testing unit at least twenty inches above the floor so that it is out of drafts. Do not disturb it during the testing period.
- Follow the manufacturer's instructions to record the starting and ending times.
- Reseal the package and return it to the lab for analysis.

Labs typically have test results ready in forty-eight hours or less.

FACT

Buyers usually want to do their own radon tests, but knowing the levels beforehand helps you price a property that might eventually require installation of a radon reduction system—something you will probably be asked to pay for.

Lowering Radon Gas Levels

Radon levels are lowered using a process called mitigation. Some mitigation methods keep radon from entering a structure, and others are designed to remove the gas after it enters. There is no single "best" method. The mitigation expert will determine where the radon is coming from and explain how levels can be reduced.

The soil suction method draws radon from beneath the house and moves it away from the house through pipes. The house pressurization method uses a fan to create pressure differences that helps keep radon from ever entering the structure. Sealing cracks usually doesn't lower radon levels significantly, but it can slow down its entry. It also helps reduce the amount of radon that must be removed by other systems, making those systems more effective.

Filters are used to remove radon from well water. Charcoal filters or aeration devices used at the water's point of entry are the most effective. Point-of-use devices are an option for removing radon at the tap so that you won't ingest it. Those devices do not reduce radon in unfiltered taps, such as showers and laundry areas, so they are not a solution for structures with high levels of radon. If radon-tainted water is used throughout the house, the radon will continue to escape and increase gas levels.

A mitigation contractor performs tests to determine how the radon is entering the structure and then offers suggestions about suitable radon reduction systems. Mitigation can usually be done as a two-stage process. A simple system is installed first, after which the air is tested again. If radon levels are still too high, supplemental items are added to the system. The second round usually eliminates even high radon levels.

If you're building a home, it's a good idea to go ahead and install a radon reduction system now. The cost is far less than the cost of fitting a system after the residence is built, and future buyers will love it.

Mold and Mildew

Molds and mildews are fungi that reproduce by releasing tiny spores into the air. If the spores land on moist objects, they will likely begin to grow and eventually release more spores. We encounter mold and mildew every day, inside and outside, but we certainly don't want to find them growing in our homes.

Some molds, like *Stachybotrys chartarum* (also known as toxic black mold) are dangerous to our health. Toxic molds produce hazardous by-products, called mycotoxins. Individuals with asthma or other respiratory problems can have reactions to any type of mold, but researchers believe that mycotoxins can trigger health problems in healthy individuals. Some medical professionals feel that mycotoxins are related to memory loss and severe lung problems, especially in infants and the elderly.

Stachybotrys chartarum is a greenish-black mold that grows on damp cellulose like wood, paper, drywall, and other similar products; it does not grow on tile or cement. Greenish-blue mildew isn't as picky—it will flourish on just about any damp spot where it gets a foothold.

There have been cases in which homeowners have burned down their homes, and everything in them, because they felt that it was the only way to get rid of the mold. The real-estate community has had a surge of liability issues involving toxic black mold. Juries have awarded large sums of money to homeowners whose insurance agencies did not pay for moisture-related repairs in time for mold to be eradicated. The problem was so severe for a while that some insurance companies put a moratorium on issuing coverage for mold-related problems.

Mold is a hot topic with buyers and tenants, so it's critical to take care of it immediately if your home or other property is affected. Even if the mold in your investment property is not toxic mold, it can still be a problem because mold growing on organic materials will destroy them if left unchecked. Too much mold or mildew of any type smells bad and degrades air quality—and odors are one of the biggest buyer turnoffs you'll encounter.

Mold and Mildew Prevention Tips

The best way to control mold and mildew is to prevent it from occurring. Use these tips to protect your property:

- Install an exhaust fan.
- Repair leaky water pipes.
- Fix roof leaks.
- Clean up flood waters as quickly as possible.
- Vent clothes dryers and exhaust fans to the outside, never under the house or back into a room.
- Don't use carpeting in damp areas.
- Install storm windows to eliminate condensation on glass; insulate pipes and other cold surfaces for the same reason.
- Ventilate the structure's crawlspace and cover crawlspace dirt with plastic.

Keep your eyes open for mold and mildew growth. If you find it, try to determine why it is growing and make changes to eliminate the cause.

Cleaning off Mold and Mildew

Ventilate the room and clean visible mold and mildew with detergent and water. Allow it to dry, using fans to speed up the process. Finish by applying a solution of ½ cup bleach per gallon of water to help kill the remaining spores. Remember that mold and mildew will return unless you eliminate the problems that allowed it to thrive.

FACT

The EPA publishes a book for owners of larger buildings, called *Building Air Quality: A Guide for Building Owners and Facility Managers* (BAQ Guide). Landlords will find answers to many of their questions about indoor air management.

Asbestos in Residential Structures

Breathing high levels of asbestos fibers increases the risk of developing lung cancer. There are only a few products that contain asbestos on today's market, but up until the 1970s it was a component of many products found in homes.

Some items, such as vintage asbestos siding with its textured surface, are immediately recognizable, but you can't tell if most materials contain asbestos just by looking at them. A professional testing laboratory can analyze samples for the presence of asbestos if you are in doubt.

Here are some items that may be made with asbestos fibers:

- Insulating blankets that cover steam pipes, boilers, and furnace ductwork
- Vinyl flooring and the adhesives used to install them
- Cement sheet, millboard, and paper insulation around furnaces and stoves
- Soundproofing and decorative materials sprayed on walls and ceilings
- Textured paints and patching compounds
- Shingles and siding

Asbestos is not dangerous if it is intact—it's the loose asbestos fibers that cause problems. If you are selling a property with asbestos-containing products that are in good condition, you don't really have to worry about it. But if you're purchasing a rental property and you know there's a possibility your tenants might disturb the asbestos-containing materials, causing some fibers to permeate the air, it might be best to seal or remove them.

A common form of control is to do a repair, which is accomplished by sealing or covering the asbestos. Sealing binds the asbestos fibers together or coats the material in such a way that the fibers cannot be easily released. Repair by covering is accomplished by placing another material over the asbestos.

Removing asbestos is more expensive, and it is not usually the best option unless state or local regulations require it. The EPA is your best source for any questions you might have about asbestos repair and removal.

ALERT!

Fear of asbestos is enough to make many home-buyers go straight to the next property without even looking inside the house. Keep that in mind when you buy a resale property that has asbestos siding or shingles.

Underground Storage Tanks

Most of the underground tanks associated with private residences and farms are used as storage for furnace oil or gasoline. When you are looking at investment properties, you'll find some buried tanks that are in service and others that have not been used for some time.

Residential storage tanks holding less than 1,100 gallons are not controlled by the federal underground storage tank program, but they can still be a problem—particularly if they are no longer used. Buyers worry that a tank will leak its contents into the soil or rust away and cause a cave-in of the surrounding earth. They often want storage tanks removed prior to closing, which means the seller has to pay for it. If the tank has already leaked fuel into the ground, buyers certainly don't want to pay to clean up the spill.

If buyers do agree to leave a tank in place, they usually ask for a reduction of the property's sales price to compensate for removing the tank later. The reduction they ask for is typically quite a bit more than the actual cost of removing the tank. Solve that problem by getting rid of the storage tank before you put the property on the market.

QUESTION?

Is the seller required to disclose the presence of an underground storage tank on the property?
It depends on local or state laws, but in many areas the seller is in fact required to disclose the presence of an underground storage tank.

Removal is the best solution, but empty tanks can sometimes be filled with a special concrete-like mixture and left in place. The EPA Web site offers information to help you determine if filling a tank makes sense for your situation.

The hazards mentioned in this chapter are common, but they are not the only hazards you will encounter. Some areas have problems with pesticide residue that's entered private wells; other are plagued with high levels of arsenic in the soil.

Chapter 10

From Contract to Closing

Many real-estate offers never result in a contract, and some that do never make it to closing. Contingencies can't be met, title problems are found, the buyer might not get financing—there are many reasons that contracts die. Your transactions have a better shot of making it when you understand how interest proceeds to an offer, an offer proceeds to a contract, and a contract proceeds to a closing.

Making an Offer to Purchase

You've researched the property. You know the fundamentals about its benefits and limitations—enough to make you think that it's a good buy. Now it's time to put it on paper. Grab a legal pad, a computer, or use any other organizational method you prefer. It's time to consider all of the pros and cons associated with the property in order to formulate an offer.

FACT

A real-estate closing, or settlement, is the event where the actual transfer of property takes place. The escrow period is the time that elapses between your contract date and the closing.

The basics are behind you, but there are no doubt some additional facts that you want to know before you're certain this is the right property for you. These facts are most often items that you don't want to spend money pursuing until you're sure you can come to an agreement with the seller to purchase the property. After all, why spend time and money on research and inspections if you and the seller are far apart on the sales price or other important issues?

Make an Offer on Paper

Most real-estate agents can provide you with some blank sample residential and commercial offer-to-purchase contracts. Take some time to study the wording before it's time to make the offer. Be sure the agent includes commonly used addenda, pages that cover topics that aren't in the main body of the contract. An experienced real-estate attorney can draft a contract for you if standard forms are not used in your area or if you need a more specific contract to cover the purchase of a unique property.

Don't rely on a handshake to conduct business. Oral real-estate contracts can and do go to closing, but if something goes wrong, they are not enforceable. A valid contract must be in writing and must be an agreement made between competent parties who are not being pressured to sign. It must not contain an agreement that is illegal, and some type of consideration must pass between the buyer and seller. Consideration can be in the form of money to the seller, or it can be another benefit, such as a traded property or service.

Counteroffers

If an offer is changed in any way by either party, it becomes a counteroffer, a new offer that is presented back to the other party. The offer is not a contract until all parties agree to all provisions, initialing changes and inserting signatures as required on the form.

Contract Contingencies

Your questions about a property can be inserted into the contract as contingencies, facts or events that you must verify before you complete the purchase transaction. Contingencies dictate whether or not a sale will actually take place, and they can be written for any topic that needs further exploration. The seller does not have to accept all of your contingencies; they're often negotiated so that both parties are happy with the outcome.

For example, your offer to purchase is dated April 1, with a date of July 30 to close, or finalize, the purchase. The seller doesn't want to wait that long to sell the property, so responds by changing the closing date to June 1. You can agree to the new date or go back to the seller with another time that works better for you.

Sellers can also insert contingencies. What if you wanted to close on June 1, but the seller cannot sell until later? The seller would change the closing date, and negotiations would begin.

Contingencies aren't just questions you want answered. Instead, they are questions that must be answered *to your satisfaction*. Standard forms usually contain carefully worded contingencies for several issues, such as inspections and resulting repairs. You might need to consult with a real-estate attorney for contingencies that aren't part of a standard contract.

In some areas, attorneys draft the majority of real-estate contracts. In other areas, real-estate agents use "fill in the blank" contracts that have been prepared by attorneys and approved by Realtor associations and the state agencies that enforce real-estate laws. Most of the contracts used by agents include wording for contingencies that are most commonly used in the area, plus blanks to fill in the date by which the outcome of a contingency must be complete and reported to the seller.

Your Title Should Be Guaranteed

Contingencies that should be part of any contract include the guarantee that, at closing, the seller will deliver to the buyer a clear deed, one with no problems, and a legal right-of-way if the property is not accessible by public roads. Most standard forms have a clause that states the seller will give existing title information to the buyer or buyer's closing agent so that it can be shared with the person performing the new title search.

The Financing Contingency

A financing contingency should always be included if you depend on a lender to complete the transaction. This contingency is a statement that tells the seller what kind of loan you are seeking. It states the type of loan you will accept, but it does not dictate that you must accept those terms if better terms are offered to you. If you cannot get the loan and terms you disclose on the offer, you should have the option of backing out of the contract with no penalties.

Buyers sometimes attempt to insert an unrealistic financing contingency, planning to use it as a possible way out of the contract if necessary. For instance, you could insert a very low interest rate in the slot where you state the rate you will accept—one you know is not possible. When it isn't offered, you have the option of backing out of the contract. That tactic can throw up a red flag to the seller that your offer is questionable, so be realistic if you really want the property.

Your Rights to Inspect the Property

If your offer is for a structure, you should insert inspection contingencies. That might include a structural inspection, testing for the presence of radon, mold, lead paint, or other hazardous items, and inspecting for wood-destroying or other insect infestations. Contracts for commercial buildings will likely trigger specific inspections that vary depending on the type of structure involved. You'll find advice about inspections in Chapters 8 and 9.

FACT

A real-estate contract must be in writing to be valid, but it does not have to be in a specific format. You can draft your own contracts if you wish, but for your own protection, seek advice from a real-estate attorney before you present them to a seller.

Other Common Contingencies

Here's a list of contingencies that are commonly seen on an offer to purchase real estate.

- Buyer's approval of the property lines and tract size after a survey is complete
- Buyer's approval of topography mapping
- Requirements that the property appraise for at least the contract price
- Requirements that land with no sewer connections be approved for a septic system
- Time to review and approve deed restrictions or restrictive covenants
- Time to review and approve leases executed between the current owner and tenants
- Verification that radon gas levels are below minimum standards
- A contingency that states the buyer must sell another property in order to complete the purchase

Remember that every offer to purchase real estate is unique, so no single list can cover all of the possible contingencies you might require. Brainstorm to come up with all the what-ifs of your purchase to determine contingencies that might be important to you.

Contingency Roadblocks

Buyer contingencies sometimes result in further negotiations if the information that's discovered isn't agreeable to the buyer. Let's say a new boundary survey indicates that property lines are not where the seller thought they were, resulting in less acreage than the seller promised. The buyer will surely want a reduction in price. If radon levels come back above minimum standards, the buyer might ask the seller to install a radon reduction system. Sellers don't have to bow to buyer demands, but compromises are usually possible if everyone keeps a cool head during negotiations.

The statement "contingent on a survey," doesn't mean a thing because it doesn't say what you expect to see on the survey. The statement "contingent on buyer's approval of property lines indicated by a new boundary survey," is more specific. State what's important about the contingency. Get advice from an attorney if necessary.

Contingencies are for your protection. Use them as a tool, but try not to overdo it. Too many unreasonable contingencies send a message to the seller that you may be looking for a loophole, something that will let you back out of the contract if you wish. No seller wants to take a property off the market for an offer that's full of nitpicky contingencies. Get the answers to as many issues as you can *before* you make an offer. The cleaner the contract, the more likely the seller will negotiate the fine points with you.

Purchases Contingent on Another Sale

You might find a property that you'd like to buy, but you can't move forward with the sale until you free up funds by selling another piece of real estate. When that happens, you can make an offer that's contingent on the sale of your property. Most sellers will accept contingency offers if they can continue to have their property on the market.

A contingency contract locks you into the deal and gives you some time to explore your financing options. Here's how it works. You prepare an offer as you normally would, bumping the closing date forward a bit. The length of time you bump it up depends on the estimated time you think it will take you to sell and close on your other property.

Your real-estate agent or attorney probably has a special form that can be used with the offer. It states that you must sell your existing property before you can close on the new one. It will contain a space to insert a time associated with a *kick-out clause*, which says that if another acceptable offer comes in, the seller can come to you and ask you to back out of the contract or decide that you will move forward with the new purchase immediately, even if your sale has not occurred.

ALERT!

Most sellers won't be inclined to accept a contingency offer if the property you are selling is not on the market yet or if you haven't at least made plans to get it there. Enhance your offer to purchase by telling the seller when you plan to list the property or begin marketing it yourself.

The time you have to make that decision varies dramatically by area. In towns where competition for properties is high, twelve to twenty-four hours might be a commonly accepted timeframe for the kick-out. In other areas, you'll see more time given, usually forty-eight to seventy-two hours.

The contingency form will also include a space for you to state how quickly you will close on the property if you move forward after being notified that the seller has another acceptable offer.

It Comes with the Property

Buyers and sellers often have very different ideas about what should transfer with the property. Sellers might have a sentimental attachment to an object that you regard as permanent, and you might encounter renters who have installed fans or light fixtures that they plan to take with them when they leave. Fixtures that will not remain should all be noted on the property disclosure, but sellers sometimes forget to list them.

Fixtures are items that are permanently attached to a structure. It's common for commercial fixtures to be removed before a property is transferred, but residential fixtures nearly always remain. Built-in appliances, furnaces, light fixtures and ceiling fans, weathervanes, built-in spas, and gas logs are all regarded as fixtures.

Take a look around the structure and write down any object you want to be sure is in the structure at closing. Chandeliers, decorative weathervanes and statues, birdbaths, built-in fireplace screens, generators, hot tubs—all these are items that should be addressed in the contract. If an item you want is not covered in the standard contract, insert text stating that you wish for it to remain. Always clarify exactly what you expect to see in the structure when you take possession.

The same is true for items you want the seller to remove, such as old satellite dishes, cars, or trash of any kind. Make sure the contract contains wording that the seller agrees to remove those items before you close on the property.

How Long Does It Take to Close?

An offer to purchase should include target dates by which each step of the process should be complete. It should list dates for completion of each inspection and associated dates by which you must report the results to sellers if you ask for repairs. There should be a deadline to meet the loan commitment, the bank's formal approval of your loan. One of the most critical dates is the projected date of closing.

If your contract states, *time is of the essence*, it means that dates are rigid unless each party agrees to change them. In some states, stated dates are more flexible, and the contract remains valid if an event goes past the deadline, but takes place within a reasonable length of time (often thirty days).

Your bank will probably *preapprove* you for a loan, but *loan commitment* doesn't take place until much later, after the appraisal is back and both you and the property are approved and on the way to closing. Don't confuse the two terms when inserting dates in an offer to purchase.

The typical length of time it takes to close a property varies from region to region and by the type of property you are purchasing. An attorney or experienced real-estate agent can give you a good idea of realistic timeframes that should be used for the events associated with your contract.

The final closing date is often dependent on your contingencies. For instance, if you require a survey, but all of the surveyors are booked for the next six weeks, you won't be able to close in thirty days.

The same is true of inspections for septic permits. In some areas, it might take as much as three to four weeks for that type of inspection to be performed. Since you probably don't want to tie up too much time and money on other issues before you are sure the land will be suitable for a septic system, you'll want to move your closing date forward and perform other tests after you know a septic system is doable.

When you're estimating a closing date, you should always determine the order in which contingencies should be handled so that you invest as little as possible into the transaction until you become confident it will close. For instance, don't pay for an expensive survey until you have the results of the home inspection. Don't perform special home inspections until you know the outcome of the first. If you think the property might not appraise at or above the sales price, don't do any extra work until a positive appraisal comes back.

It's Important to Negotiate

The seller might accept your very first offer, but a more common scenario has the contract going back and forth between buyer and seller until everyone agrees on every term within it. Some people are born negotiators, but for most of us it's a learned skill. If you're buying or selling through a real-estate agent, the agent will handle most (if not all) of the negotiations for you, but you'll have to learn to express your wants and needs to the agent to make sure you end up with a favorable contract.

If you're dealing directly with a buyer or seller, hold off on discussing price, because that topic sends everyone into a defensive mode. Starting out with a period of friendly conversation is usually a better way to get

ALERT!

Decide which issues are most important to you before you begin negotiations. That way, you'll already have a clear idea about those issues where you might be willing to be a little more flexible.

No matter who you are dealing with, ask as many questions as it takes to get the answers you need. Learn to ask open-ended questions—questions that cannot be answered with a simple *yes* or *no*. Listen carefully, and pay attention to answers and body language. You don't have to be an expert in body language—most of us can tell when another person is turned off by the conversation. It's essential to be empathetic, showing the other party you understand and care about his problems.

If you are a buyer, ask the seller to respond to questions in writing, because those records could be important later if problems are found. Sellers are usually honest when asked questions about their properties, but it doesn't hurt to be cautious.

Negotiations typically go back and forth until each party is satisfied with the contract, but there will be times when you won't be able to reach an agreement. Even those negotiations are worthwhile because they are an important learning experience. They will help you with the next contract you attempt to resolve.

Your Good-Faith Deposit

The deposit you submit with an offer is referred to as earnest money, or a good-faith deposit. It is credited back to you at the closing and should always be refunded to you if your contract contingencies are not met. You are not required to submit earnest money with an offer, but sellers regard the funds as a sign of your seriousness and your ability to close on the property.

Your attorney or real-estate agent can tell what percentage of the sales price is considered an average good-faith deposit in your area. If you go with a lower amount, consider showing the seller documents that prove you can close on the property, such as a preapproval letter from your lender.

A hefty earnest money deposit can sometimes offset a low offer, especially when combined with a quick closing date. Always try to put some type of a positive spin on a low offer.

Very low good-faith deposits usually trigger a request from the seller for more funds. When that happens, the amount the seller requests is often considerably more than she would have accepted if the buyer had been more realistic with the initial offering. Try not to wave a red flag at the seller that you don't have the funds to complete the transaction.

Who Pays for What

If you buy or sell property across the United States, you'll find that there are wide variations in the typical expenses paid by buyers and sellers. There are no rules about who pays for what, but there are basic guidelines to help you estimate costs before you make an offer.

Buyers typically pay for expenses related to obtaining a loan. That includes the down payment, fees to buy-down the interest rate, loan origination fees and other similar costs. Appraisal and inspection fees are normally a buyer expense. Buyers pay for hazard insurance policies. The title examination and title policy fees are usually paid for by the buyer. In some areas, a buyer is expected to pay for a survey, but in other areas, it's regarded as a seller expense.

Sellers usually pay the real-estate agency commissions. Many sellers must pay off one or more existing mortgages at closing in order to deliver a property with no liens attached to it. Sellers must usually pay for tax stamps, an excise tax assessed on the sale of the property. In some areas, sellers pay for all or part of the title examination and policies.

Some costs are shared by buyers and sellers. Property taxes, homeowner's association fees, and other fees paid on a yearly basis are prorated, with each person paying his share based on the number of days he owned the property during the billing period. If the seller has already paid fees for the year, the buyer must reimburse the seller for his share. Unpaid accounts are usually paid by the closing agent when the property transfers, with each party billed for his share of the costs.

You can read more about closing costs in Chapter 11.

It's common for buyers to ask sellers to pay for items that are typically regarded as a buyer expense. A motivated seller is often willing to pay additional expenses in order to get the property sold.

Making It to Closing

Monitoring the progression of contingencies is an important ingredient that takes you closer to closing on the property, but there are other equally important events that must take place. Getting a transaction to the closing table takes the cooperation of every person involved—the real-estate agents, the buyer and seller, the lender, attorneys, and title search companies— everyone who has a part to play.

Sometimes one closing is dependent on others. If you're buying residential property, the sellers might be closing on a new purchase the same day they sell to you. Someone needs to make sure that transaction is progressing smoothly, too. The seller or seller's agent should notify you immediately if there are delays.

There are plenty of things to do after the appraisal is in and all other contingencies have been satisfied. If you're buying a structure, you'll need to secure hazard insurance and make sure it goes into effect the minute the property is transferred to you. You'll also have to arrange for all utilities to be switched into your name as of the day of closing.

Work with the Lender

The lender might have last-minute questions for you. It helps to touch base with the lender every few days to make sure they have everything they need and that the contract's timeline is still doable. If you're working with a real-estate agent, she should help you with this task. Answer the lender's questions as quickly as possible, submitting any supporting documents that are required.

Important Don'ts!

If you're getting a loan, don't apply for new credit until after you close, because lenders sometimes check your credit history again as you near closing—sometimes even the day of closing. That new car payment could kill your mortgage loan if the lender isn't sure you can handle both payments.

Don't spend large amounts of cash. The bank might want to verify your account balances before closing, to make sure the funds that were there when the loan was approved are still in your possession.

Don't change jobs if you can help it. The switch might not make a lender refuse the loan, but it could create a delay while your new situation is analyzed.

The Final Walk-Through

If you're buying a house or other structure, you should plan to do a final walk-through prior to closing on it. This is your way of making sure the place is in the same (or better) condition it was in when you made your offer to purchase, or in the condition agreed to by the seller. Hold off on the final walk-through until the sellers have moved, just to make sure that you have an opportunity to inspect for damage that could have occurred during their departure.

ALERT!

Early walk-throughs are important whenever the seller agrees to make repairs, because you don't want to find out on the day of closing that the repairs have not been made. Plan to re-check the property as soon as you are notified that the repairs are complete. Take along your inspector to help verify that repairs were done correctly. Return on the day of closing for your final walk-through.

What to Look For

Have items been damaged during the seller's move? Check flooring for rips and gouges. Look at the walls to make sure there's no damage, especially to walls and areas around doorframes.

Your contract probably stated that all major systems in the building must work at the time of closing. You might want to do a quick check of appliances, gas logs, furnaces, air conditioners, and other fixtures to make sure they haven't failed since the building inspection.

All items that the sellers agreed to leave should be in place. All items they agreed to remove should be gone. You probably don't want to be stuck with the expense of hauling away Uncle Harry's 1975 truck that's been sitting in the garden for ten years.

Resolving Problems

Problems found immediately before closing can sometimes be resolved quickly. The seller wants their proceeds from the sale, and the buyer has the power to hold it up until a resolution is found. Funds can be placed in a neutral party's trust fund to pay for repairs, removal of trash, or whatever is needed to bring the seller in compliance with the contract. Or you might prefer to fix the problems yourself after negotiating a flat amount to be paid to you at closing.

Make sure all issues are addressed before the deed changes hands. If you cannot come to an agreement with the seller, it might be best to postpone closing until they have performed the necessary tasks. Ⓔ

Chapter 11

Settlement and Transfer of Title

A real-estate settlement is the event that occurs at the end of a successful real-estate transaction, when a property officially changes hands. Buyers and sellers both have settlement expenses, and many are the result of decisions made in the days and weeks leading up to the event. This look at settlement costs and ownership options helps you make plans for a smooth closing day.

Federal Settlement Disclosures and Requirements

The costs of obtaining a loan are a significant expense for buyers, but in the past, lenders often didn't disclose all of their fees until after a buyer had committed to using their services. Nondisclosure created problems at settlement and beyond, because buyers didn't understand how fees would impact their settlement expenses and long-term loan costs. The federal government stepped in with the Real Estate Settlement Procedures Act (RESPA), which requires lenders to make certain disclosures about the costs of loans so that buyers are better equipped to compare lenders.

FACT

The terms *closing* and *settlement* are both used to describe the end-point of a real-estate transaction. The time leading up to settlement is called the *escrow period,* or simply *escrow,* a word used to describe a situation in which money or another item is held in trust.

Within three days of applying for a loan, your lender or mortgage broker must give you a good-faith estimate (GFE) of anticipated settlement costs, listing in part the loan-related charges you are likely to pay at your real-estate closing. If the lender requires that you use a specific settlement agent to handle the closing procedure, it must be disclosed on the GFE.

The mortgage servicing disclosure statement is another RESPA requirement. It includes information that explains what steps you should take to resolve current or future complaints you may have against the lender. It also tells you if the lender intends to service the loan itself or transfer it to another company after settlement. Servicing lenders are the ones you deal with on a regular basis for payments and customer service issues, and it isn't unusual for the originating lender to transfer that job to someone else after you close on the property.

The lender should also give you a special information booklet that contains details regarding real-estate settlement services in general. Note, however, that the lender is not required to give you any booklets or other documents related to settlement if it turns down your loan application within three days.

Uniform Settlement Statement (HUD-1)

The HUD-1 is a form on which the settlement agent itemizes all charges and expenses incurred by the buyer and the seller in a real-estate transaction. RESPA requires that settlement agents use the HUD-1 for all transactions that involve federally related mortgages. That category includes loans made by banks and other lenders whose deposits are insured by the federal government—such as loans insured by the FHA or guaranteed by the VA, and loans that will be sold to Fannie Mae, Freddie Mac, or Ginnie Mae. In short, it includes the majority of real-estate loans made in the United States. Settlement agents are accustomed to using the HUD-1, so you'll probably see it used to complete many cash transactions, too.

RESPA bans kickbacks and referral fees that increase settlement costs. For instance, an appraiser, real-estate agent, or other related professional should not receive a fee for referring a borrower to a lender.

RESPA rules require that buyers and sellers be given a copy of the HUD-1 at least one day prior to settlement, but that sometimes doesn't happen. The bank packets, which outline the details a settlement agent needs to fill out in the HUD-1, sometimes arrive shortly before closing, leaving little time to prepare the statement. Sometimes repairs or other actions that create expense are still in progress and cannot be added to the statement until the last minute.

Even if you do receive the settlement statement early, entries can change as all parties review it for accuracy. Never assume that the statement is correct because mistakes are common. Your real-estate agent and your settlement agent should both review the HUD-1 with you. The more eyes looking at the statement, the more likely errors will be found.

Closing Costs Charged by Lenders

You probably know how much down payment is required to buy the property, but that's not the only portion of your closing expenses that will go to the lender on the day you sign the loan documents. Other lender-related closing costs will be estimated on your GFE.

Some lenders charge borrowers a loan origination fee. It's usually referred to as costing one or more *points*, an amount that's equal to 1 percent of a loan amount. For instance, one point for a $100,000 loan equals $1,000. Not all lenders charge an origination fee.

Your lender will probably charge an application fee. This fee covers their costs of processing your application from beginning to end, and this might be called a processing fee or an underwriting fee. It might include prepayment for the appraisal the lender requires to evaluate the property you are buying.

A document preparation fee is another closing expense that lenders charge. As its name suggests, it covers the costs of preparing your loan documents.

Discount points are optional fees paid to the lender at closing in order to lower your interest rate. Each discount point you buy on a thirty-year loan typically lowers the interest rate by 0.125 percent. That means a 6.5-percent rate would be lowered to 6.375 if you purchase one discount point.

Like the origination fee, each discount point costs one percent of the loan amount—or a point. Buying points can be a good choice for properties you plan to keep for awhile, but they aren't helpful for properties you intend to sell quickly. Do the math to find out if points make sense for your transaction:

1. Calculate the amount of your monthly payment at the interest rate you will be charged if you *do not* pay points.
2. Calculate the amount of your monthly payment to reflect the payment you'll make if you *do* purchase points.
3. Deduct the lower payment from the higher payment to find the amount saved each month.
4. Divide the amount you would pay for points, $1,000 in our example,

by the monthly amount saved. The result is the number of months you must keep the loan to break even on paying points.

Here's an example:

$100,000 Loan on a 30-Year Term
7.5% Interest, no points = $699.21 monthly payment
Buying 1 point for $1,000 = monthly payment $690.68
Monthly Savings = $8.53
$1000 ÷ $8.53 = 117 Months to Break Even

That's nine years. Do you plan to keep the property that long? If not, save your cash and forget the points.

Can the Seller Pay Points?

Talk with your lender, because the seller might be allowed to pay for your points. The seller might want a higher sales price if she agrees to give back closing funds, so you'll have to analyze your total costs to decide if a seller contribution makes sense.

FACT

Points paid for residential real estate are tax deductible in the year they are paid. Buyers may deduct the amount paid for points even if those costs were paid by the seller at closing. Ask a tax professional how the cost of points affects your tax return.

Prepaid Expenses and Escrow Account Funding

Some fees are paid to the lender at closing in order to prepay interest and to begin building your escrow accounts, the accounts the lender uses to pay your property taxes and hazard insurance when the first bills come due after closing.

Interest is paid on mortgages in arrears. That means the interest included in each monthly mortgage payment covers the month prior to the payment. Your June payment pays the May interest. The May payment covers the interest due for April. If you are closing on a property October 18, your first payment will be due on December 1, and will include interest for the month of November, but not the days you owned the home in October. To make up for those days, your lender collects interest for October 18 through 31 at closing. The expense will be called *prepaid interest* on your settlement statement.

Each monthly loan payment you make will include approximately one-twelfth of the amount due annually for hazard insurance and property taxes. The lender accumulates the payments in a special account, called an escrow account, where the funds are held in trust until they are needed to pay your tax or insurance bill.

Lenders begin funding your escrow accounts at closing, usually charging you the equivalent of two to four months' payment for each expense. That way, your escrow account will be fully funded when the first payments come due the following year, and the account should contain excess funds to cover any increase in costs.

You've probably heard references to the term PITI during discussions about mortgages. The letters stand for "principal, interest, taxes, and insurance"—the components that make up your total monthly payment.

Don't confuse escrow funding with insurance and property taxes that are paid at closing. Those payments satisfy bills for the current year. Your escrow account accumulates funds for future payments, which your lender will mail for you to ensure they have been made, protecting their interests in the property.

If your taxes and insurance go up, so will your monthly escrow payments. The lender's goal is to collect enough money throughout the year so that payments can be made when bills become due without creating a negative balance in the escrow account.

Other Common Closing Costs

Nearly any expense that's associated with transferring a property can be classified as a closing cost. Most buyer closing costs are associated with requirements to obtain a loan, to verify the value of a property, and to assess the property's components. The seller's most significant closing cost is often the real-estate commission, unless the seller has agreed to pay all or a portion of the buyer's expenses.

The lender will require a title examination to make sure there are no problems associated with the property's deed. Depending on where you live, a title examination might be done by an attorney or by a company that specializes in title work. The examiner looks back at the history of the deed to make sure that it has passed from one owner to another in the correct way, examining old liens on the property to determine that they were paid and that the deed reflects the payment. Buyers usually pay for the title examination fee.

If you are using a loan to buy real estate, your lender will expect you to purchase title insurance, a special type of insurance that covers losses that can occur when the title examiner fails to find problems with the deed. Buyers usually purchase two title insurance policies, one for the lender and one for themselves. Title searches and insurance are covered in more depth later in this chapter.

Closing Agent Fees

The closing agent might be an attorney, the lender, an escrow company, or even a real-estate brokerage. The closing agent prepares the HUD-1 settlement statement, analyzes and explains the buyer's loan documents, makes sure all documents required for closing are signed by the buyer and seller, makes all required payments from closing funds, and takes care of any document that must be recorded in public records. The buyer should plan to pay a fee for these services.

The agent usually charges a separate fee for recording of documents, sending overnight mail packages, making wire transfers to pay off existing mortgages, and other similar costs.

Preparing the Deed for Transfer

The seller is usually responsible for preparing the new deed that transfers the property to the buyer. The seller typically signs the deed in front of a notary public, someone who verifies that the person signing the document is the person whose name appears on it. The buyer's name is shown on the new deed, but the buyer's signature is not required.

Boundary Surveys

A survey involves permanently marking the boundary lines of a property with concrete posts, iron stakes, or other markers. Natural landmarks, such as trees and rocks, are sometimes used to identify points along a line. A licensed surveyor completes the survey and converts the findings into a paper document. Structures and topographical elements of the property are usually drawn to scale inside the image of the tract.

In some areas, lenders require a boundary survey before making a loan. In other states, a survey is optional and only done at the request of the buyer. The convention of who pays for a survey varies around the United States, but even if it's regarded as a buyer expense, the buyer can ask a seller to pay for all or part of the process. Surveys are often paid for at or shortly before closing.

Propane and Other Fuels in Storage Tanks

Every offer to purchase contract should have a provision that states what happens to unused fuels. Sellers are usually reimbursed at closing for propane and other fuels that remain in storage tanks when the property changes hands.

ALERT!

Don't forget to arrange for utility service if you're buying a house or other property where utilities already exist. Readings for electrical service, water consumption, natural gas, and other utilities should be scheduled to take place on the day of closing.

The buyer should find out if the seller owns or rents the tank. If it's a rental, the buyer must likely buy future fuel from the company that owns it. If the buyer does not wish to keep a rented tank, seller and buyer should coordinate a removal and replacement date just prior to closing.

Excise Taxes

The seller might be required to pay an excise tax based on the sales price of the property—a charge that is sometimes called tax stamps. In some cases, buyers are asked to pay the fee for the sellers. The amounts due for this type of expense vary quite a bit from state to state.

Hazard Insurance

Buyers who are using a loan to buy real estate with a house or other buildings on it are required to pay for a hazard insurance policy at or prior to closing. No insurance, no loan—the lender wants to make sure its interests are protected if the structure is damaged two minutes after closing. Flood insurance or other types of special policies might be required for properties in your specific area.

Fees Paid Outside of Closing

Appraisal fees, charges for credit reports, loan application fees, and other similar expenses are part of your closing costs, even though they might have been paid prior to closing. They should be recorded on your settlement statement as "POC," paid outside of closing. The same is true for payments you made directly to service providers, such as home inspectors, pest inspection companies, and water-testing services.

The settlement statement is your permanent record of the transaction, and you will likely need it for future income tax returns, so it's handy if every expense associated with purchasing the property is listed in one spot. Be sure to tell your closing agent about all fees paid outside of closing.

Prorated Closing Costs

Some costs of property ownership must be shared at closing to make sure each person who owns the property during the current billing period pays his share of the expense. Property taxes, homeowner association fees, and rent for a fuel storage tank that a buyer leaves in place at closing are three examples of expenses that are split, or prorated. Ownership share is calculated by determining the length of time each party owns the property during the billing cycle.

Suppose a bill is paid annually, and is due on January 1 of each year. If closing takes place on April 1, the seller is the owner of the property for three months of the year, or one-fourth of the billing period, so the seller owes one-fourth of the annual bill. The buyer's ownership runs from April 1 through December 31, making her responsible for three-fourths of the expense.

If the seller has already paid an expense at the time of closing, the buyer's share is paid back to the seller. If the seller has not paid the bill by the time closing takes place, but the bill has been issued, both buyer and seller must pay their share and the closing agent pays the bill. If the bill has not been issued, the seller's share can be paid to the buyer at closing, and the buyer is responsible for paying the bill when it arrives.

The closing agent calculates how much each party owes for this type of bill and enters it on the settlement statement, but it's always a good idea to check the figures.

What Can the Seller Pay?

Buyers can often work out a deal in which sellers agree to pay for at least a portion of the buyer's closing costs. Just how much a buyer can obtain depends on the seller's motivation and how much the buyer offers for the property. Sellers might ask for a higher offer to offset the paid expenses, but that can be a win-win solution for both parties. The seller gets the property sold, and the buyer has long-term financing for some of the costs of closing.

The lender expects the property to appraise at or above the amount of the sales price, not the amount of the loan, so this technique might not work for properties that are borderline when it comes to meeting appraisal requirements. If you inflate the price too much, and the property doesn't appraise for an amount the lender feels is suitable, the loan might be denied.

Talk to your lender to find out exactly how much the seller is allowed to pay at closing. The maximum amount the seller can pay differs depending on the type of loan used.

Title Examinations and Title Insurance

A title examination is a search of all public records that involve documents that have been recorded in association with a property. The examiner looks at past deeds, wills, and trusts to ensure that title passed correctly to each new owner and that prior owners all released their claims on the property. The examiner attempts to verify that all prior mortgages, judgments, and other liens have been paid in full and officially released. Examinations usually cover the past thirty years of a property's history. Title examinations also review additional facts about the property, such as easements, details about mineral rights, and pending legal actions.

Title insurance protects against many types of losses that could occur if someone else claims a right of ownership of the property. Title insurance is required by lenders, and two policies are normally issued, one for the lender and one for the new owner. The lender's coverage is usually for the loan amount, while the owner's policy is for the sales amount.

Title insurance covers the following:

- Problems that were not apparent during the title search or were missed by the title examiner
- Problems that occur when a deed or other document in public records is found to be a forgery
- Liens that result from unpaid taxes or liens by a former owner
- Easements that aren't shown in public records
- Several other types of mistakes in public records

FACT

Title problems are called *clouds on the title,* or *title defects*. A real-estate attorney can advise you about the severity of title issues and how they might affect your rights to the property.

A title policy will pay your legal fees if you must go to court to defend the deed. If you lose the property, the insurance pays you for your loss up to the amount of the policy. However, title insurance companies are not usually quick to pay, and they often pay the least amount possible to settle a claim, so there's no true guarantee that you'll recover all of the losses associated with a problem property.

Title policies do not cover title defects that occur while you own the property. Policies often exclude problems related to easements, liens, and mineral and air rights. Ask your closing agent to explain your title insurance coverage, including its exceptions—items that are *not* covered.

Title policies are paid with a one-time fee that you submit at closing. Ask your closing agent about future purchases of inflation riders to increase your coverage as the property increases in value.

ALERT!

Buyers can sometimes save money on the title search if the current owner's policy can be updated and reissued. Ask your closing agent if that is possible for your purchase.

Transferring the Property

Transfer of property is often made using a general warranty deed because it offers the most protection for the buyer. By offering a general warranty deed, the seller guarantees good title, not only during the time the seller owned the property but going back throughout its history.

That doesn't mean that problems won't surface, but if a title examination was done, it means that the settlement agent who prepares the deed feels comfortable that it is free of problems.

A seller, called the grantor, who conveys property with a general warranty deed guarantees that the following are true:

- He or she is the property owner and has the right to sell the property.
- The property is free and clear of liens and encumbrances, except those in the public records.
- No one else has a right to claim ownership of the property.
- He or she will pay the buyer for loss if future problems arise.

That last guarantee isn't always valuable since the seller might not be in a position to pay the buyer if problems surface. For that reason, title insurance is always a must, even when problems seem remote.

Transferring Property with a Special Deed

Property is sometimes transferred on special types of deeds if one or more of the provisions of a general warranty deed cannot be guaranteed. Special deeds are also used to allow an individual to relinquish all claims they have on a property.

A *quitclaim* deed is used to transfer real estate with only one guarantee, that the person signing the deed relinquishes all claims he has in the property. Quitclaim deeds are most commonly used to clear up title defects or allow an individual to relinquish rights to a property. For example, an ex-spouse can relinquish a claim on property by signing a quitclaim deed. An easement can be recorded or released by having the relinquishing party sign a quitclaim deed. A former owner whose signature was not acquired when a property was sold can use a quitclaim to relinquish rights to the property.

A *special warranty* deed is often used to guarantee that the property was free and clear of encumbrances during the time it was owned by the current seller, also called the grantor. The grantor offers no guarantees for dates prior to his ownership.

You might encounter *special purpose* deeds when you buy real estate. A *correction deed* does just what its name says—it corrects an error on a previous deed. A *deed of release* is used to release a property when a loan using it as security has been paid in full. Other types of deeds are used to transfer foreclosures to a lender. Ask your closing agent to explain the facts about your new deed to help you understand the property guarantees you are acquiring.

Types of Ownership

There are two broad categories of rights to real estate: freehold estates and leasehold estates. A freehold estate involves ownership, while a leasehold estate involves tenancy, more commonly called rental. Each category breaks down into many subcategories that can affect your rights to use a property.

A free simple estate gives an owner all rights to a property for an unlimited time. A free simple defeasible estate puts limits on a property, stating ways that it can and cannot be used. For instance, an owner might stipulate on the deed that the property can only be used for a church or that it cannot be used as a restaurant. In some cases, if the agreement is broken, the land reverts back to the grantor.

FACT

In a real-estate transaction, a seller is called a grantor and a buyer is called a grantee. In a similar manner, in a rental transaction, a landlord is called a lessor and a tenant is called a lessee.

Shared Ownership

If you purchase property with others, your deed might state that your share of the ownership transfers to the other owners upon your death. Or it might state that your heirs receive your ownership interests. There are also specific types of wording designed specifically for married couples.

Life Estates

A life estate gives an individual the rights to use the land based on the life of specific person. Those rights end with the death of that person, and they revert to whomever the documents specify. Here's an example. You have inherited a house, but you have no need to live in it. Your father needs a place to live, but you don't want to sell the property to him or give him full ownership. You can grant your father a life estate. Upon his death, the property can revert back to you or to anyone else you specify.

A life estate can be based on the life of an individual other than the owner of the life estate. You might grant someone a life estate that terminates upon your own death, with the property going directly to your heirs.

QUESTION?

Can life estates be sold?
Yes, they can, but since they are based on the life of an individual, which is always uncertain, they are not very marketable.

The owner of a life estate is expected to maintain the property in a reasonable manner. For instance, the property cannot be stripped of natural resources such as trees.

Chapter 12

Investing in Distressed Properties

Now that you've got down the basics of purchasing a property, let's move on to strategies. One obvious option is to invest in a distressed property—a fixer-upper that won't sell or rent until moderate (or even major) repairs or updates are completed. There are plenty of those on the market, but there are also properties where a little imagination is just as important as repairs. A successful investor recognizes both categories of distressed properties and knows how to profit from them.

Browse the Real-Estate Market

For some reason, when a property is advertised as a fixer-upper, or as-is, we immediately think, "It's a deal," because we've been programmed to expect that the price tag is a reflection of the condition of the property. Look closely, and you'll find that many so-called fixer-uppers are actually not priced too far below market value. It takes some research to determine which properties have the most potential—and can be bought at a discounted price.

Real-estate agents can tell you which locations and types of houses are in most demand in your area. Agents also have an excellent feel for the features buyers are looking for. They know if one type of buyer outweighs the others who are looking in that market, and whether it's mostly families, professionals, senior citizens, or a mixture of buyer types.

If any one type of buyer greatly outweighs the others, it might be a good idea to focus on the types of houses they are looking for. Here are the kinds of things you should consider:

- Seniors like one-level homes with few—if any—steps.
- Families might want a house on a street where there are other children.
- Families might be looking in specific school districts.
- Professionals want a house with creature comforts—one that's close to shopping and entertainment.

Don't spend all of your time looking for distressed houses—you can't recognize a good value unless you know the typical selling prices of all types of properties in your real-estate market. You'll find you also get plenty of decorating ideas from faster-moving real estate.

Read classified ads and all of the real-estate magazines that are published in your area to find out which features are mentioned most often. When multiple real-estate agents repeatedly talk up a feature, you know it's something in high demand locally. Features that are popular in nearly every area include these:

- A split bedroom plan, where the master suite is on the opposite site of the house from other bedrooms.
- A nice view of mountains, a forest, city line, or the ocean—it varies greatly by market.
- Basements are an important feature in some areas.
- Privacy is a must for many buyers.

Every market has its own set of popular features. Study local advertising materials and network with agents and buyers to find yours.

Cosmetic Updates Versus Major Repairs

Do you recognize the differences between cosmetic updates and true repairs? If not, find a contractor or homebuilder whose opinion you trust to help you learn. Can you accurately estimate the expense of necessary repairs and updates? The person who will do the repairs should inspect the structure before you make an offer on the property, and multiple estimates will help you come closer to the true cost.

ALERT!

Potential buyers may ask you to disclose proof of building permits and inspections, especially when they see repairs and updates that are obviously fresh. Not having proof that work was done correctly can kill a deal or drive the price down.

Become savvy about components used to build properties in different eras. If you pull down wallpaper, what do you expect to find behind it—drywall or paneling or plaster? How will that find affect your remodeling plans?

If you plan to tackle repairs and updates yourself, make sure they are within your level of expertise. Cosmetic updates can be a breeze, even for novices, but problems that involve plumbing, electrical systems, and structural issues will require help from an expert. Many of those repairs should not be attempted without building permits issued by your local city or county government, followed by inspections when the repairs are complete. Doing it correctly the first time will ultimately save you money.

It's a fact of life—repairs are nearly always more expensive than estimated. Unless you can buy it for an absolute rock-bottom price, don't take on a project that involves massive structural repairs until you're confident you can handle them *and* sell the property for a nice profit. Sometimes it's better to forget about a problem property and move on to the next one.

Changing Your Perspective

Distressed properties aren't always true fixer-uppers. They can be properties that simply haven't sold for some reason. Go visit your favorite real-estate agent and ask her to search for properties by the number of days they've been on the market. Start with properties in your price range that have been for sale for 180 days or more, because those sellers are the most likely to be anxious to sell.

The agent should give you printed sheets that describe each property. Take the sheets home, and study them to see if you can determine why the properties haven't sold. You'll find that the majority of them are overpriced. Some might have been described poorly by the listing agent. Others might include an unflattering photograph.

FACT

Now that most multiple listing services are on the Internet, agents can e-mail you links that allow you to view information about listed properties. Many listing services also have public Web sites that allow you to browse all listings in a specific MLS.

Many buyers make decisions about which properties to look at based solely on the printouts. A good real-estate agent won't allow that type of selection process, but many agents either don't know how to handle a buyer's refusal to keep an open mind or don't bother to show them the properties because it's more work. As a result, listings that are poorly described and photographed often go unnoticed.

The informational sheets should include drive-by directions for each house. Go for a ride and view the exterior of each property. How's the curb appeal? Is it so bad that a typical buyer wouldn't even look inside? Yes? Then it's a property *you* should know more about.

Most Buyers Have No Imagination

It's true—most home-buyers have no imagination at all when it comes to envisioning changes that will turn a ho-hum property into something special. It might not be that they aren't creative. Perhaps it's simply because most of them want to buy a house that's already finished to their liking.

Sometimes the current owners can't see the negatives, either. They typically don't even consider that there might be ways to improve room layouts and designs because the old ones have worked for them for years. Or maybe they don't have the funds to make changes. They just want to sell the house, and it's been on the market longer than they expected. That's where you step in.

Assess the Exterior

Sometimes the negative aspects of a property are obvious. If the problem is curb appeal, what would you do to change the situation? Is the porch sad and sagging? Is the landscaping full of weeds and so overgrown that it touches all of the windows and the roof? Is the paint peeling off the siding? Envision what the house would look like if those items were repaired.

ALERT!

If the neighborhood is the problem issue, it might be better to pass, unless you know that the area is in an upward swing due to community action. You should only consider properties with negative features that you can correct.

Take a Look Inside

Schedule a showing for houses that look like they have the most potential. View the interiors in the same way you did the outside components.

- Is the color scheme dated? Sometimes that's an easy fix.
- Are the rooms dark, with little natural lighting? Skylights and sun tunnels would brighten it up.
- How about the flooring—should it be replaced or cleaned?
- Does the house show poorly because the current owner's furniture is a wreck?
- Are there walls that could be opened up to make living areas feel more spacious?
- Is it a one-bath house? Sometimes adding a second full bath does the trick.

Inspect the house with an open mind, trying to determine why it hasn't sold and if there are ways you can turn it into a more attractive offering.

Some houses don't sell because they are dirty. Unkempt houses make buyers fearful that important components have been neglected, too. A thorough cleaning and fresh paint are sometimes all it takes to turn a profit.

If the Numbers Make Sense

The price you pay for a property and the amount of work you put in it don't always tell you if it's a good investment. Properties you plan to fix up and sell are evaluated differently than properties you plan to fix up and rent. No matter how you plan to use the real estate, crunch the numbers to find out if the purchase makes sense.

What's the anticipated market value of a property you intend to resell? You have to know that figure before you can decide if you want to purchase it. Start by estimating what the property's fair market value will be after all of your work is complete, then deduct your expenses:

1. Write down the amount you would agree to pay for the property.
2. Add up the costs to acquire the property, such as loan-related fees, title work, and inspections.

3. Estimate the total amount it will cost to fix up the property.
4. Figure the amount of interest you'll pay during the time you expect to own the property.
5. Add in property association dues, property taxes, and other similar fees for the period you expect to own it.
6. Calculate the amount of commission you will pay if you use a real-estate agency to sell the refurbished property.
7. Estimate your closing costs for the second sale.

Total your expenses and initial investment, and deduct that figure from the property's anticipated fair market value. What's left over is your potential profit before tax deductions are considered. Is it enough of a profit for the time and effort you plan to invest in the property? Is there a large enough gap between the amount spent and the market value to buffer expenses that exceed your estimates, because expenses have a habit of doing that?

You can juggle the numbers around, looking at them from different perspectives. Take away the fix-up expenses and look at your profit. Can you cut those costs to yield a better return? Can you negotiate a better price for the property? Evaluate the variables to come up with the best scenario.

Income Producing Properties

You can use the gross rent multiplier (GRM) method, described in Chapter 7, to help determine property values based on their sales price and the amount of rents you can charge for them. The GRM is helpful, but it is only one part of the picture you must look at to determine if a property is a worthwhile investment.

Income capitalization is another way to look at the deal, using this formula:

VALUE = NET OPERATING INCOME (NOI) ÷ RATE OF RETURN

1. Estimate value by using the GRM formula.
2. Calculate the NOI by adding up all potential rents for a year, then deducting the total of all projected yearly expenses.

Estimate the rate of return by doing a comparative market analysis of similar, but not rehab, properties that have sold recently. A commercial real-estate agent can help you find the comps. If you know the sales price of those properties and their NOIs, you can plug the numbers into the formula to calculate the rate of return.

Calculate the average rates of return for the comparables, and divide your own projected NOI by that percentage to estimate the property's value.

FACT

The rate of return, or capitalization rate, helps you determine how much future rents are worth by today's standards, which helps you determine current market value.

Flipping Properties

Some investors use a technique called flipping to profit in real estate. Instead of contracting and closing on a property, the investor puts it under contract and then finds another buyer to assign, or transfer, the contract to. The first investor never closes on the property but receives his profit when the buyer he found does.

Successful flippers have a list of buyers who they know are interested in distressed properties. It takes a while to develop a network like that, but once you do, it's definitely worth the effort.

Another Flipping Scenario

It's possible to flip properties that have not yet been built. The investor signs a contract with a developer for a property that's under construction, speculating that when the property is actually built it will be more valuable than it is prior to construction. The important term here is *speculation*—an educated guess that values will climb. It's just as possible that values will stay the same or decline.

The Risks Involved

There are some obvious risks to flipping. If you can't find a buyer in time to close, you might lose your deposit money, or you could be forced to buy the property unless additional contingencies provide a way out of the contract. You must have a thorough understanding of property values and rehab costs in order to ensure there will be enough mark-up potential when you sell the contract to the new buyer.

Flipping is a fast-moving game that some real-estate investors like to play. If you are good at it, and can take the pace, flipping can pay off in nice profits. But if you're not sure, it might be one type of real-estate investing you'd do best to avoid.

ALERT!

If you plan to flip a property, make sure your offer to purchase includes a clause that states you are allowed to assign (or transfer) it to another party. If that clause isn't added, you might be forced to purchase the property yourself before selling it to someone else.

Chapter 13

Foreclosures and Foreclosure Auctions

Foreclosure is the process of taking possession of a real-estate property from a debtor who can no longer make mortgage payments. Foreclosure can also result from failure to pay property taxes or property owner association fees, or selling the property to another person without the original lender's approval. Foreclosed properties can often be purchased for less than market value, and that's where foreclosure auctions come in.

Property Is Security

When someone obtains a loan to buy real estate, the property he purchases becomes security for the loan. That means the property guarantees the debt. Before money changes hands, the borrower must sign security instruments, documents that give the lender the right to take the property back if the loan conditions are not met.

Over half of the states in the United States use mortgages as security instruments. The other states use a deed of trust, which serves the same purpose, but with a few important differences. Why should you care? One type of security allows a lender to move through the foreclosure process at a faster pace and with less cost. When you're dealing with an owner who's nearing foreclosure, it helps to know how it will be accomplished and how much time they have to negotiate a contract and sale.

Mortgages

Many people don't see a difference between real-estate loans and mortgages, but a mortgage is not a loan, and it is not something that a lender gives a borrower. A mortgage is a security instrument that creates a lien on the property being purchased, and the lien is the lender's security for the debt.

QUESTION?

What is a lien?
A lien is a legal claim against a property that usually must be paid when the property is sold. Liens are recorded in public records so that anyone researching a property's deed is aware the debt exists.

There are two parties to a mortgage. The borrower is the mortgagor; the lender is the mortgagee. Even though a loan is secured by a mortgage, the borrower owns full title to the property—no one else has any rights of ownership. In order to foreclose, the lender must usually progress through the court system to prove it has a right to take the property.

The Deed of Trust

A deed of trust is a special kind of deed that gives someone a limited interest in a borrower's property. Like a mortgage, the deed of trust is recorded in public records, where it notifies everyone that there is a lien on the property. The deed of trust involves three parties: the borrower, who is the trustor; the lender, who is the beneficiary; and the third party, who holds a partial interest, is the trustee.

The trustee is someone who holds temporary, limited title to a property by way of the deed of trust and is responsible for releasing the deed of trust when the lien is paid. The release shows up in public records to notify anyone who is looking for information that the debt no longer exists. Documents are in place to ensure that a trustee cannot take the borrower's property for no reason.

FACT

The trustee must be a neutral third party, someone who will not favor either the borrower or the lender if problems develop with the loan. In some areas attorneys act as trustees, while in other areas title insurance companies provide the service.

The deed of trust gives the trustee the power to sell the property at auction if the lender gives the trustee proof that the borrower has not complied with the terms of the loan. The trustee progresses as allowed by law and as dictated by the terms in the deed of trust. But the process bypasses the court system, making it a much faster and cheaper way for the lender to foreclose when compared to a mortgage foreclosure. A property owner with a deed of trust might not have as much time to negotiate with you as an owner with a mortgage.

Avoiding Foreclosure

Banks and other lenders don't benefit from foreclosure, and they prefer not to be involved in it, but if the borrower can't pay the mortgage, lenders are forced to take back the property and sell it to recover their funds. This is why lenders are very careful about screening borrowers and appraising the properties—they want to be sure that they can recover their money if foreclosure becomes necessary.

Foreclosure is an expense for lenders, so they nearly always try to resolve past-due payments before they set the process into motion. Here are some of the options a delinquent borrower has:

Reinstatement: A borrower can ask to have an account reinstated when he is behind in payments but can promise a lump sum to bring the account current by a specific date.

Forbearance: A borrower is allowed to delay payments for a short period, with the understanding that another payment option will be used at the end of that period to bring the account current. A lender might combine forbearance with reinstatement when the borrower knows that funds will be available by a certain date.

Most real-estate loans contain a *due-on-sale clause* that makes the outstanding balance due immediately if a borrower transfers ownership of a property without the lender's approval. Seek the advice of a real-estate attorney before you decide to buy from an at-risk owner without refinancing the property.

Repayment plans: If an account is past due but the borrower can now make payments, the lender might agree to add a portion of the past-due amount to a specified number of monthly payments until the account is current.

Mortgage modification: The lender may agree to modify a mortgage for someone who can now make payments but would have a difficult time catching up on late payments. The past due amount might be added into the existing loan so that it could be financed over a long period of time. The lender might even agree to extend the length of the loan if the borrower cannot make payments at his former level.

Selling the property: If a catch-up is not possible, the lender might agree to put foreclosure on hold to give the borrower time to sell the property.

Deed in lieu of foreclosure: This occurs when the borrower gives the property back to the lender, and the lender forgives the debt. The lender might require the borrower to attempt to sell the property before offering this option, and it might not be possible if there are other liens against the property.

FHA and VA Loan Solutions

Borrowers who have an FHA loan can sometimes receive a one-time payment from the FHA Insurance Fund to bring them up to date. For a borrower to qualify, the loan must be at least four months but no more than twelve months past due, and the borrower must be able to begin making full mortgage payments immediately.

The loan must eventually be repaid. The borrower signs an interest-free promissory note, and HUD places a lien on the property. The lien becomes due when the first loan is paid or the property is sold, whichever occurs first.

The Veterans Administration (VA) offers financial counseling for borrowers at their regional offices. Staff at those offices have been trained to help borrowers find solutions to avoid foreclosure.

Moving on to Foreclosure

Once a lender decides that an owner can't or won't work to resolve past-due payments or other problems, it moves forward to acquire the property. The lender files all required legal documents at the courthouse in the county where the property is located—or its equivalent. The documents state when the property will be sold to satisfy the lien. Notices are printed in local newspapers, and some localities put them on the Internet.

Others who have liens against the property have a stated amount of time to come forward, at least thirty days but often longer. The lender might even choose to add other lienholders to the lawsuit.

During the time prior to the sale, the property owners can file documents to try to stop or postpone it. They might file bankruptcy, since that action puts at least a temporary halt on the foreclosure process.

Some states have initiated investigations into the practice of filing for bankruptcy solely to stop or stall a foreclosure, without ever intending to move forward with the process or enter into a bankruptcy repayment plan. Companies or individuals who help borrowers initiate fraudulent bankruptcies might be subject to fines.

Investing in Foreclosed Properties

Some investors specialize in pre-foreclosures, real estate that is on the verge of being foreclosed but where the owner still has some time to sell the property or recover from the problems. Network with friends and family to help you find these individuals.

Another option is to acquire foreclosed properties. Investors who are interested in foreclosures should have a good understanding of the steps that property owners are going through to avoid or deal with foreclosure. That knowledge helps you be more empathetic to owner problems, and it gives you clues as to owner motivation and contract timing.

Pay attention to the foreclosure notices; the first sale date you see advertised in the paper is rarely the date a foreclosure sale will actually take place. You can keep up with current sale schedules by following their progress at the courthouse.

ALERT!

Some states have a redemption period, where owners have up to a year *after* foreclosure to recover their property. To avoid surprises, you should always become familiar with your local laws before you attempt to buy foreclosed properties.

When the sale does occur, cash bidders meet to place their bids. Sometimes an individual walks away with the property, but the winner is often one of the lienholders, protecting its interests by entering a bid just over the total amount that's owed plus any expenses it has incurred.

The lender might keep the property and sell it "as is," by itself or through a real-estate agency. It's more likely that the lender will turn the property over to the secondary market agency associated with the original loan, such as Freddie Mac. That agency then sells the property.

If You Decide to Bid

There are many pitfalls to buying a foreclosure at an auction sale. However, if you're willing to spend some money and do a fair share of legwork before the auction, there's plenty of opportunity to profit from a transaction. Auctions aren't something you should jump into unprepared, so get ready to research the properties that sound most appealing to you.

Auction bids must be paid for in cash, usually within twenty-four hours or so of winning. If you don't have excess cash, consider obtaining a home equity loan or a line of credit prior to the auction—or maybe a cash advance from a credit card would be enough to pay for the property. You can seek a conventional loan afterward to replenish your funds or pay off high-interest debts.

FACT

Foreclosed properties acquired by the lender at auction are referred to as real-estate owned properties, or REOs for short. Many investors like to purchase REOs, since the foreclosure has already been completed and there's no waiting time before they can resell the property.

Properties sold at auction are transferred by means of a sheriff's deed or another type of special deed that does not guarantee clear title. If you want details about the condition of the property's deed, conduct a title search yourself prior to the auction, or hire someone to do it for you.

You might or might not have a chance to inspect the property prior to the sale. If utilities are turned off, you definitely won't be able to run appliances. You will *not* receive a property disclosure. The less you know about the property, the more risks you take if you purchase it. You can attempt to talk to the current owner, but don't be too surprised if you are not warmly welcomed. That person is losing his home, so he might not be in the frame of mind to offer you help unless you can offer some sort of help in return.

Even worse, the owners might not have moved out of the property yet when the sale takes place. You can eventually get them out, but if they want to be difficult, there are many ways to stall a formal eviction, all costing you time and money. A distraught owner might even leave the property in disrepair.

Debts Associated with the Property

A property owner might owe money to more than one lender, with each lender having a recorded lien on the property. The initial lender's lien is usually called the senior lien, senior mortgage, or first mortgage. It takes precedence over most liens that come after it. Liens that are recorded later, such as home equity loans and other lines of credit that ask for property as security are called junior liens, junior mortgages, or second mortgages.

Liens for unpaid taxes, homeowner association fees, and assessments generally take precedence over all other liens. They are paid first from sales funds, then the remaining money is used to pay other liens, usually in the order they were recorded.

Mechanics liens are liens that become attached to real estate if an owner fails to pay for work done at the property, such as a new furnace installation, a new roof, a new appliance, and other repair and update work. Judgments, which are court rulings that state a person owes a debt, can become liens on property.

All liens take their place in line for payment when the owner sells the property, typically in this order:

1. Taxes, assessments, property-owner association fees
2. First mortgages
3. Other liens in the order in which they occurred

Are All Liens Paid at Foreclosure?

A foreclosure sale usually wipes out most of the liens that are attached to a property, even if the property does not sell at a price sufficient to pay them all off. The outcome depends, in part, on who is forcing the foreclosure, a senior lienholder or a junior lienholder.

The senior lienholder is often the holder of the first mortgage, but remember that some people do not have a mortgage. In that case, the senior lienholder would probably be the person who has the oldest recorded lien against the property.

When the senior lienholder forces foreclosure, it usually protects its interests by bidding an amount slightly over the amount of the debt plus all expenses it has incurred. If a junior lienholder believes the property will sell for an amount above the first lien and its own lien, it might place a bid just over the sum of those two amounts. An investor or home-buyer might outbid them both.

FACT

It's in the senior lienholder's best interests to include junior lienholders in the suit. If they are not included, junior lienholders could possibly re-emerge after the sale as the senior lienholder. The new lien would then have to be paid when the original senior lienholder sells the property.

A junior lienholder usually prefers not to bring the senior into the foreclosure suit. Instead, it sells the property at auction subject to the senior lien, which means it does not have to pay the senior lien. The senior lien stays in place for the new purchaser to deal with.

This type of foreclosure can go several different directions if the senior lienholder enters the picture. The junior might pay off the senior mortgage, or the senior might ask the courts to step in and make sure its lien is paid no matter who buys the property. One result is usually certain—a foreclosure by a junior lienholder voids other liens that are junior to it.

If the sales price is not enough to pay off all secured debts, and the debts will survive the foreclosure, you won't be able to acquire a bank loan for the property, because lenders will not allow the old liens to stay attached to the title. Someone must pay the debts or negotiate a reduction in them in order to clear the title when the property changes hands.

Carefully evaluate your risks before you bid on any property at auction. Talk to an attorney who can offer advice about liens that could survive the foreclosure. Make sure you are aware of every lien attached to the property. Be realistic, and don't get carried away with your bidding. If you think smart, you can come out a winner.

Buying Real Estate at Tax Sales

Real estate can be sold for nonpayment of property taxes. Properties with first mortgages are not usually sold at tax sales because mortgage companies pay taxes if they must to protect their interests. When a tax sale does occur, the high bidder wins a tax certificate, not an immediate deed. The certificate is subject to a redemption period, which gives the owner time to pay the taxes before the property is lost. The time of redemption varies from state to state.

An owner who redeems the property must pay the holder of the certificate the amount paid at auction, plus a percentage that is in part dependent on the amount of time it took the owner to pay. If the owner chooses not to redeem the property during the redemption period, the holder of the certificate receives a deed to the property.

A tax sale generally wipes out all other liens, so the title is delivered free of liens. However, the sale does not wipe away other problems with the title—things such as possible encroachments and easement issues. Only a full title search and in-depth look at the property will tell you if there are additional problems that must be considered.

A former owner who does not redeem the property could initiate a lawsuit at a later date, stating that the tax sale was not handled properly. That action can affect your ownership and create legal fees.

Laws regulating tax sales differ, so it's critical for you to study the practices at your location. Talk to staff at your county or city tax collector's office to find out when sales are scheduled and what happens before and after the sale. Talk to other people who have bought property at tax sales to see if they are willing to help you. Talk to a local real-estate attorney about the pros and cons of buying real estate at tax auctions.

The staff at your county courthouse will help you learn to research properties. Ask as many questions as you can think of regarding issues that affect titles. Find out how to look back at public records to discover possible problems. You may not ever become an expert title researcher, but you'll learn enough along the way to know when professional help is needed.

Sometimes you have to take a gamble, but don't be afraid to proceed with caution until you recognize which gambles are the ones with the best chances of paying off.

Other Types of Auctions

Foreclosures aren't the only kinds of auctions where you might find bargain properties. Private sales and probate auctions should both be on your list of events to watch. Both types of auctions are regularly advertised in local newspapers.

Some estates move through the courts through a process called probate and are usually sold by using a sealed bidding process. Talk to an experienced bidder or a real-estate attorney to learn the specifics of bidding in your area.

Private estate sales can be handled through sealed bids, but they are usually accomplished by holding a live auction. When a home is involved, the sale often includes both real estate and private property.

Land tracts are sometimes auctioned by developers. Land in a development that didn't do well can be a risky investment because desirability may never change. The up side is that this type of property usually sells at a very low price, so if you're willing to take a risk, sometimes you are rewarded with a property that has good resale value.

Sometimes vacant land is difficult to sell, but the same land will turn over rapidly with a house on it. Explore the option of joining forces with a builder to put a home on the property, then put it up for sale. Ⓔ

Chapter 14

Buying REOs and Pre-Foreclosures

The majority of investors are more interested in acquiring real-estate owned properties (REOs) and pre-foreclosures than they are in buying properties at auction. With REO foreclosures, the ownership of the real estate has already been legally switched to the lender, and in many cases the lender provides the buyer with a title search and title policy at closing. Pre-foreclosures are another possible source of bargain properties, and they're a good choice for investors who are prepared to treat at-risk sellers with great care.

Buying an HUD Foreclosure

Department of Housing and Urban Development (HUD) REO properties are foreclosures that are available in every state in the United States. If a foreclosed home was purchased with a loan insured by the FHA, the lender involved can file an insurance claim for the balance due on the mortgage. FHA pays the lender's claim and transfers ownership of the property to HUD, which then sells the house.

> You probably won't hear bank-acquired properties referred to as "REOs." They'll simply be called "foreclosures" by lenders, real-estate agents, and others in the real-estate community.

HUD begins by ordering an appraisal for the house, which helps them price it at fair market value for its location. HUD homes are sold as-is, so if the property needs repairs, the agency lowers the price to reflect the expense of projected repairs. HUD homes are sold with a guarantee of title that allows the buyer and new lender, if there is one, to purchase title insurance policies.

The Bidding Process

HUD foreclosures include many types of properties, such as single-family homes, duplexes and fourplexes, condominiums, and townhouses. They are sold through a sealed bidding process, and bids must be submitted on special HUD forms. Bids must be submitted through a real-estate agent.

HUD has a short initial offer period during which the first bids are accepted. Bids are collected, but they remain sealed until the offer period ends, then all are opened at the same time. If HUD accepts one of these bids, it's the one that best covers HUD's investment in the property. If no bid is selected during this first round, all future bids are opened as they are received.

The winning bidder is usually notified within a day or two after bids are opened, and settlement is scheduled to take place thirty to forty-five days from the date of acceptance. A buyer can sometimes buy additional time by paying extra fees to HUD. If the buyer fails to close, HUD can keep the buyer's earnest money deposit, so don't bid on a HUD home unless you're sure you can get the funds to purchase it.

FACT

When awarding bids, HUD looks at the bottom line—its net proceeds. Bidders asking for fewer monetary concessions have an advantage. One way to help the bottom line is to negotiate lowered commissions with the real-estate agent who is submitting the bid.

Can Investors Bid on HUD Properties?

Investors are not allowed to bid during the first offer period because HUD prefers to sell its homes to owner-occupants. If an owner-occupant is not found during the first round of bids, investors are allowed to enter the process.

HUD is concerned about fraud regarding owner occupancy. This is so true that they ask bidders who purchase a property during the initial offering to sign a statement that they have not purchased another HUD home in the previous twenty-four months and that they will occupy this home for at least twelve months. The real-estate agent must also sign a statement verifying that he has no knowledge that the buyer is an investor.

Won't Home-Buyers Snap Up All the Deals?

Maybe not. The price range that HUD homes typically fall in is attractive to first-time home-buyers, but the properties are sold as-is, which often alarms inexperienced buyers. Inspections must be done before the bid is placed, with no guarantee that a bidder will win. Spending several hundred dollars for inspections without being sure the house can be bought is more than many people are willing to do, especially when funds are tight.

That means fixer-upper foreclosures are often left for investors who are accustomed to dealing with repairs. But don't assume there won't be competition for the properties—there are plenty of investors out there who are looking for the same thing you are.

FACT

As required by federal law, HUD allows a contingency for buyers who want to perform lead-based paint tests on structures built prior to 1978. Read more about lead paint hazards in Chapter 8.

Finding HUD Homes

Talk to local real-estate agents to find someone with plenty of experience dealing with HUD foreclosures. If you can't find someone with existing experience, try to find someone who you think can learn the procedures quickly, keeping in mind that agencies must be registered with HUD before they can submit bids. If a property is hot, you might only have one shot at buying it, because incorrectly submitted bidding packets are discarded.

HUD provides links to current properties on its Web site. Links lead to homes categorized by state, and from there you can narrow your choices down to specific cities and towns. You'll find HUD's Web site address, along with many other helpful resources, in Appendix C.

VA Foreclosures

U.S. Department of Veterans Affairs (VA) foreclosures are marketed in much the same way as HUD homes. After the VA acquires the homes through foreclosure, they are sold through a bidding process, in which bids are submitted by real-estate agents. However, there is one important difference from the HUD process. The VA does not give preference to owner-occupants. Investors are allowed to bid from the very first day.

The VA also offers financing to investors who buy foreclosed homes, even if they are not veterans of the armed services. An investor might be able to buy a VA home with little down payment. The VA is somewhat more lenient about buyer credit requirements, and it does not use credit scores to determine a buyer's eligibility.

The number of VA-insured properties in most towns is far less than the number of properties purchased with an FHA loan, so you'll find that VA foreclosures are usually less common, too. The exception might be in towns located near a military base, where affordable housing for families is available nearby. A military town in your region could be a good source of potential properties. Search the VA's online listings to find out if there are clusters of foreclosures located in areas near you.

Fannie Mae and Freddie Mac

Two more sources for foreclosed properties are the Federal National Mortgage Association (Fannie Mae) and the Federal Home Loan Mortgage Corporation (Freddie Mac), both major players in the secondary housing market in the United States. Fannie Mae and Freddie Mac do not make loans, but they purchase loans from lenders. Both agencies always have foreclosures to sell.

Fannie Mae and Freddie Mac may work with the same real-estate agencies every time they list a property in a specific town. Find out which agencies in your area are chosen most often, and let agents know you are always looking for foreclosures.

Fannie Mae and Freddie Mac list their foreclosed properties with real-estate agents, who then place them in the multiple listing service (MLS) just like any other listing. Bids are not used—anyone can make an offer on a property at any time. The homes are sold as-is, but they are not typically bargains. They are usually priced at or above market value, sometimes even when repairs are necessary.

The offer to purchase must include special forms issued by the seller, usually dealing with the as-is condition of the property, the closing date, and often they include clauses that require a buyer use a specific closing agent. It's a good idea to have a real-estate attorney review all of the special forms before you sign them.

Even though the homes are sold as-is, Fannie Mae and Freddie Mac will accept contracts with inspection contingencies. They won't make any repairs, but the contingency gives a buyer the right to back out of the contract with no penalties if problems are discovered that are more than they want to take on.

It's important to do a thorough evaluation of any property's market value before you decide it's a good investment. Fannie Mae and Freddie Mac properties are no exception to that rule.

Pre-Foreclosures, Owners at Risk

Pre-foreclosure is a term used to describe owners who are on the verge of losing their property but aren't quite there yet. Maybe their payments aren't late enough for foreclosure proceedings to kick in, or maybe they've worked out a temporary agreement with the bank to stall the foreclosure process. Some of them will recover, but for many others it's just a matter of time before the property is lost. That's where investors step in, working a deal to help an owner salvage at least a part of his good credit and at the same time buying a property that can be sold or rented for a profit.

One problem with many owners who are facing possible foreclosure is that they are in denial—they don't believe it will really happen. They are too embarrassed to talk to anyone about their problems, even their lender. Those are the owners who find themselves in foreclosure quickly—unless their finances turn around—because they aren't asking for help.

You can't pluck these people out of thin air. Finding them is usually best accomplished by word of mouth. If you're new to the game, it will take awhile to get the word out that you are looking for properties. Make yourself known in neighborhoods where you are interested in buying. Think of the networking that a real-estate agent does and mimic it. Tell everyone from grocery clerks to auto technicians to bank tellers that you are searching for real estate. Eventually, someone's brother, sister, aunt, or uncle will tell a potential seller about you. It takes time, but you have to start somewhere, and it might as well be now.

After Foreclosure Is in Motion

Foreclosures that have been filed in public records are easier to locate, but at that point, other investors have found them, too. The earlier you discover the filings, the more time you have to research the properties and negotiate with the owners without competition from other investors.

The clerk of court at your county courthouse can give you a list of upcoming foreclosure sales. Another source of foreclosure information is the legal filings section of the classified ads in local newspapers.

Approaching At-Risk Owners

Every situation you encounter will be different. Some people have trouble paying their mortgage as a result of a job loss. For others, problems occur after a death or divorce. Each owner presents you with a unique situation, and you will find that your strategy must be flexible in order to negotiate a solution that benefits both you and the home-owner.

Knock on doors to talk to at-risk sellers—if collection agencies are calling them, they might not answer the phone. It's a lot more difficult to turn away someone who shows up on the doorstep.

Even if you don't truly care what happens to the homeowner, it's in your best interests if the outcome benefits all parties. By this time, the property owners may have been hassled by plenty of insensitive investors and collection agencies. Remember the importance of word of mouth. If you develop a reputation as someone who gets homeowners out of a bad situation, it will help your business grow in the long term.

The approach you use will vary. Are you responding to a FSBO ad in the newspaper? Don't immediately jump into pricing issues. Take some time to talk to the seller, asking questions that will help you determine why they are selling. If you ask that question directly, you won't get a straight answer, especially if finances are a problem. Sellers don't want you to know that they are under pressure to sell. If you take some time to explore the situation, you'll have a better feeling of the seller's true motivation.

Make a trip to your local courthouse. Find out what types of liens exist on the property and check the foreclosure filings. Find out if the property taxes have been paid. Unpaid taxes and a series of liens offer clues to the owner's financial situation.

If you're serious about the property, talk to the seller again after you've done your research. If you know there are problems, introduce the subject as tactfully as you can. Mention that, since you are very interested in the house, you did a pre-title search at the courthouse and found liens that must be paid at closing. *How can you help?* Those are powerful words. Once you know the facts and offer help, the sellers might be more likely to discuss their problems with you.

FACT

Just because a property isn't a foreclosure doesn't mean it isn't a good buy. The owners might have other reasons for moving on that are just as motivational. You must initiate conversations that uncover details about an owner's reasons for selling.

Establishing the Right Price

You'll encounter at-risk sellers who have honestly tried to price the property at market value, but a more common encounter will be with owners who have overpriced the property because the total amount they owe on the property *exceeds* the property's market value. You will have to show them a market analysis to convince them that selling an overpriced property is extremely difficult, especially when time is a factor.

Remember the information about liens, and what happens to them after a foreclosure auction? Most liens are wiped clean. Holders of second mortgages and other junior liens know this, and are usually willing to negotiate a reduction of the debt. If the property is headed for foreclosure, they know they won't get anything at closing, and they must pursue the seller later if they expect to collect funds. Most will agree to take less rather than risk getting nothing.

That's where you step in. The sellers might be ready to disclose details to you once they feel you are serious about helping them solve their financial problems. Make a list of every lien on the property, and find out how much is owed. A title search will uncover recorded liens if you'd like to make sure the sellers have disclosed all necessary information. Here's an example:

Owner's property taxes	$350
Owner's first mortgage	$40,000
Owner's second mortgage	$15,000
Owner's judgments	$8,000
Owner's mechanics liens	$4,000
Total	$67,350

Now, let's say you're willing to pay $65,000, including closing expenses. This would mean that the amount owed by the seller exceeds the sales price by $2,350 dollars, and that figure doesn't include the seller's closing costs. You can see why the seller feels he's in a real bind.

The holder of the first mortgage is less likely to negotiate a reduction in debt, since it is in a better position to protect its interests during foreclosure. The junior liens are the ones you'll usually want to focus on.

Get It in Writing

Sign a purchase contract before you begin negotiating for lien reduction. You don't want to spend time and money negotiating with lienholders and then lose the property to another buyer who enters the picture while you are doing the work. Make sure to insert a contingency that the sale will not take place unless all liens are paid at closing. That statement is probably covered by the standard contingency that deals with delivery of clear title, but making it a separate contingency reinforces your position with the seller.

Ask the seller to call all lienholders and give them permission to talk with you about the debts. Explain to junior lienholders that a foreclosure is imminent, and you wish to negotiate a debt reduction for the seller. Real-estate agents do this all the time. It isn't unusual for a lienholder to reduce the amounts owed to juniors by fifty percent or more. Get all reduction agreements in writing.

The owner might want a contingency too, one that states he is not obligated to sell if payoff reductions cannot be negotiated. If you plan to work in the area for the long term, think of your reputation and protect the seller, too.

In some cases, even the first mortgage holder will agree to reduce the debt required to release a lien. When you step in, they are assured of a quick sale. If that's more attractive to them than the time and expense required to force a foreclosure, they may negotiate with you.

You must remember that a reduction in the amounts that are required to release a lien does not usually erase the debt. The creditors can still pursue the sellers for the amounts owed unless they agree to accept the payment to satisfy the entire debt. You should make the sellers aware that their credit reports will contain negative remarks due to the reductions, but that the impact of those remarks will not be as negative as it would be after a foreclosure.

Developing Your Reputation

Most people don't know that lienholders will negotiate a debt. You do, and if you work it right the sellers will not only be able to sell their property, they will walk away from the sale with some cash. That's extremely important in order to help them make a fresh start, and *you* are the person who made it possible.

Where will the sellers go? It's likely they must rent for a while. Do you have a rental property you can put them into? By this time, you know the sellers pretty well, and you have a good feel for the reasons why foreclosure took place. You'll encounter some people whom you wouldn't want in one of your rentals, but most sellers with credit problems can turn their lives around if given the opportunity. Put them in a rental, and offer them information that helps them get their credit history back in good shape. It might not be too long before you can sell them a house.

The more people you can help in this way, the more your reputation will grow. You'll become known as the investor who helps people out of a bind, not as a scam artist who preys on their misfortunes. Even if you don't care about the human aspects of that reputation, your profits will increase, so it's definitely a win-win solution for every investor.

FACT

The property owner could request that if accounts are paid as agreed by the work-out, the creditor will not submit statements to credit reporting agencies that it had to write off a debt. Creditors might not agree to that, but it's worth a try.

Chapter 15

Vacation Homes and Time-Shares

The baby boomer generation owns more second homes than any generation in America's history. Some use vacation homes for regular getaways; others use them as income-producing properties. Either way, owners of vacation homes are building equity in real estate. Time-shares are another vacation property option, but one that should be bought only after you make a significant number of comparisons and consider the pros and cons of ownership.

Consider Purchasing a Vacation Home

The National Association of Realtors estimates that there are over 7 million vacation homes in the United States, and the number is growing rapidly. That makes another of their findings logical—values of vacation home are escalating more quickly than the values of most full-time residences. If you choose wisely, a vacation home offers a solid investment opportunity for your current and future finances.

How do you plan to use a vacation home? If you plan frequent trips to the location yourself, you might want to purchase a second residence within a reasonable distance of your home base. Grab an atlas and sketch in an area that's within a three-hour drive of home. Does any destination in that area appeal to you? If not, move out a bit farther, but keep the distance within a range that won't be a burden to get to regularly.

Distance isn't as much of a factor if you don't plan frequent trips, or if you want to rent the home and use a property management company to secure rentals. Branch out and consider any area that appeals to you—maybe even the spot where you hope to eventually retire.

A Suitable Location

Start exploring the most appealing destinations on weekends or during other time off. Subscribe to local newspapers and keep a close watch on anything that affects the real-estate market. For instance, loss of industry and other types of jobs can create a downturn in the local economy.

A temporary downturn could be a great time to buy if the real-estate market becomes overloaded with houses for people who can no longer afford them. However, a long-term downturn isn't attractive if you have plans to resell the property quickly.

What's Popular at the Destination?

Browse the Internet to learn about the destinations you've chosen. Contact the local chamber of commerce or visitors' center and ask staff to mail you information about the area. Learn what type of destination it is—is it attractive to seniors, a young crowd, families, or all three? Are buyers and renters looking for single-family homes, or are condos more popular? Is it a year-round tourist destination, or is this a town where vacation homes are in most demand during a single season of the year? Preferences change over time, but knowing which properties are in demand now helps you buy something with good resale potential.

FACT

The chamber of commerce or visitor's center will pass your name and address on to member businesses. Ask them not to do that if you aren't quite ready to receive a great deal of mail about the area.

Read real-estate ads in the area, in both online and print publications. An experienced real-estate agent is your best source of information about market trends. Agents are usually happy to mail out printed materials about listed properties or send you e-mail links to information online. Find an agent you feel comfortable working with, and ask her to keep you updated on new listings that meet your criteria.

Financing Your Purchase

Interest rates for a vacation home you plan to use yourself are generally the same as for your full-time home. Interest rates for second homes purchased as investment properties are higher. Some banks require a larger down payment for a vacation home purchase, but that requirement seems to be loosening up as more people buy second homes.

The Internal Revenue Service has many rules that apply to vacation home ownership. Here are a few that are important:

- The IRS allows you to deduct mortgage interest for a second home, but not a third home.
- Capital gains taxes are due on the sale of vacation homes.
- You must list income and expenses for homes rented more than fifteen days in a year.
- You cannot deduct rental expenses if the home is rented for less than fifteen days during the year, but the rent need not be included in your taxable income.

Always talk with a tax professional about the full implications of buying or selling a vacation home.

The Time-Share Option

In Europe of the 1960s, rising property values made it difficult for most people to afford a full-time vacation home. Developers found a solution—create properties with a shared ownership, where each person who owns the property has access to it at a specific time each year—usually for one week. The time-share industry was born, and it didn't take long for it to spread worldwide.

The cost of each time-share is split among the people who own it, making units affordable to a wider segment of the population. Costs to maintain the units and the common areas of the property are shared by all owners. Time-shares have been sold for cruises, recreational vehicles, campgrounds, and other types of properties, but the most popular sales are for condominium units at time-share resorts.

Time-Share Ownership Variations

There are two basic types of time-share ownership:

1. **Deeded ownership.** You receive a deed to the property that describes your specific rights.
2. **Right-to-use agreement.** A lease agreement that expires at a specified date, after which you no longer have any rights to the property.

From there, rights branch off to become more specific:

- A fixed-unit deed give you rights to use a specific unit.
- Fixed time deeds give you rights to use the property during a specific week or season each year.
- Floating time deeds offer usage dates that are more flexible, with reservations on a first-come basis.
- Vacation clubs or points-based programs allow owners to choose from the developer's entire inventory of destinations.

Time-shares might be a good option for real-estate investors who plan to search for other types of real estate in popular tourist destinations, because they help you avoid staying in a hotel while you search for properties.

Vacation clubs are popular with time-share buyers. That type of plan gives owners the option of choosing their destination from among multiple resorts in the same chain without paying a fee to an outside exchange facilitator. The downside is that many clubs have failed. Research the stability of the developer to help determine if their inventory of resorts will likely remain intact for future use.

Are Time-Shares a Good Investment?

Buy a time-share because you want to use it, not because you are looking for a real-estate investment. Time-share units generally have poor resale value. There are always thousands and thousands of people who are trying to sell their time-shares. Many of them have discovered that they never use their time, and others become tired of paying the required annual maintenance fees. However, there's one exception to this rule. Time-share resales are a good investment if you manage to find bargain properties.

FACT

A resale is a time-share unit that has already been purchased from the original developer and is now offered for sale by the current owner. Resale prices are often 30 to 50 percent of the original price or even less, unless the resort is rated "five star" or is in an extremely popular destination.

Costs Associated with a Time-Share

Developers of new time-share resorts secure financing for their units, but conventional financing is not usually an option for time-share resales.

Resale units are usually sold for cash although owners are sometimes willing to finance the buyer. It might also be possible to assume the current owner's loan.

If you do finance a time-share through a conventional lender, be prepared to pay significantly higher interest rates than you would for a house or other real estate.

Annual Maintenance Fees

In addition to the cost of the time-share, you'll have to pay the maintenance fees. This money is used to pay for repairs to the building and grounds, insurance, utilities, legal and other professional fees, management company expenses, and all of the other costs associated with running a large resort complex. You'll see fees that are as low as $200 and as high as $1,000 per year. They are increased as necessary to cover expenses and upgrades.

It's a good idea to look at each resort's fee history to see if there's a trend of rising costs. There's no guarantee that fees that have gone up slowly or remained stable for a time will continue to do so, but if you see that fees have climbed rapidly each year, it's a good indication the trend will continue.

Dealing with a Developer

If you purchase a new time-share from a developer, research the company as thoroughly as possible before you buy. There have been many time-share failures around the world, leaving owners with nothing for the money they paid. If the company cannot provide you with verifiable details about other successful time-share resorts they have developed, consider passing on the offer to purchase.

Developers sometimes offer free trips and lodging to potential time-share buyers in exchange for their attendance at a sales presentation. These vacation certificates are typically for a three-day, two-night stay at the time-share resort or a nearby hotel.

Sometimes the offers truly are free. Developers know that people are more likely to buy when a large crowd is there, giving buyers the perception that it's a hot property—one they shouldn't pass on. That makes it worth-while to the developer to have as many warm bodies as possible browsing the grounds.

Other offers are more questionable, and some are nothing but scams. You might be promised free airfare, but when you arrive, you find that your lodging bill is higher than it should be. Or you might be given free lodging but charged higher airfares.

If you are actually interested in buying one of the developer's new units, the free lodging might not be a bad deal. If you're going because it's free, reconsider—especially if you discover hidden costs. You'll have a better time at a destination of your choice, even if it does end up costing a little more.

If you are solicited by phone, ask the caller to mail you full details in writing. Reputable companies with valid offers don't hesitate to send written information. When it arrives, you'll have a better opportunity to study the facts and check the identity and references of the sender. As with any other solicitation, never give personal or financial information to an unknown caller.

Read the Fine Print

Nearly all vacation offers are subject to certain requirements:

- You must be twenty-one years old, and your annual income must be over a stated amount.
- If married, both you and your spouse must attend the required presentation.
- You may be asked for a deposit to guarantee your trip. The deposit might not be refundable.
- Your identity will be verified when you arrive at the resort.

A fee that's called a processing fee is probably nonrefundable. If the fee is called a deposit, it might be eligible for refund if you cancel the reservation. Ask the company to verify the facts, including deadlines for cancellation of your trip.

If you buy a new time-share and change your mind the next day, check the real-estate laws for the state the property is located in. There's often a "cooling off" period that allows buyers a specific time to back out of the sale with no penalties. Cooling-off laws do not cover time-share resales.

Buying a Resale Property

If you're planning to buy a resale time-share as an investment, you'll need to do lots of research to find the bargains. The Internet is the perfect place to do some exploration. For a small fee, you can join one of several groups that offer support for owners. Most of these groups provide ads and forums where members can arrange exchanges, rentals, or sell their time-shares. Studying the ads helps you get a very good feel for typical resale asking prices. You'll find time-share owner groups listed in Appendix C.

ALERT!

Time-shares with right-to-use agreements plummet in value as they near the expiration date. Use that knowledge to help you negotiate when you're searching for a deal.

A review area is an important feature offered by most online groups. That's where members give their opinions of time-share resorts worldwide. There's nothing like fifty good (or poor) reviews to help you decide if a specific resort should be investigated further.

Dealing with the Management

The original developer of a time-share resort manages the complex until a certain percentage of units have been sold. After that, it turns management duties over to a property owners' association, also called a homeowners' association. The association then usually hires a management company to take care of resort operations. The quality of service offered by the management company has a large affect on the resort's desirability.

Here are some tips to help you evaluate a resort's management team:

1. How long has the same management company been employed by the association?
2. Has their contract been renewed during that time, or was the initial contract a lengthy one?
3. Does the management company help owners find renters? What are the charges? What is the success rate?
4. Does the company offer real-estate sales services to help owners market their units?
5. Is there a program to help owners find and swap time-shares with other owners in the same resort or group?
6. Is the resort affiliated with Interval International (II) or Resort Condominiums International (RCI), two large exchange networks?

Exchanges and Rentals

Time-share owners who get tired of visiting the same resort every year can use an exchange company to arrange a one-time swap with another time-share owner. Exchanges open up a new opportunity for travel without requiring owners to purchase additional time-shares. If you don't want to exchange, renting your time-share might be a better option.

There are currently two major players in the time-share exchange business, Resort Condominiums International (RCI) and Interval International (II). Each company charges an initiation fee, but sometimes it's waived when you join. Owners deposit their time-share week into an exchange pool, and when an exchange takes place, they pay the company a fee.

The exchange companies each have their own systems for ranking resorts and describing the desirability of units that are available. You might be restricted to exchanging your time-share for one of equal or lesser value in their ranking system.

The management company at your resort might help you obtain a renter if you don't plan to use your time. User groups offer classified ads that might bring you a renter. Some owners try to recover at least the amount of their maintenance fee from the rent. One way you can make the rental more attractive is to price it below area hotel costs.

Selling a Time-Share

Selling a time-share is often a difficult task, but you're more likely to achieve success when you understand the market and know how to avoid questionable sales tactics. Gather your deed or agreement, mortgage information, tax records, and maintenance details to make sure you understand exactly what you own before you begin to market the unit.

Studios are not in as much demand as larger units. A unit that offers usage dates during the resort's off-season is not as likely to find a buyer as one that's available during peak season. A resort that hasn't been maintained is another price killer. Time-shares that are part of a chain, where credits can be used for airline tickets or other accommodations, often bring a higher return.

If you're in a hurry to sell, keep the price as low as possible. Weigh the pros and cons of keeping the unit or selling for a lower price. How much is your annual maintenance fee? Is it worth it to keep paying the fee instead of accepting a lower offer?

Hiring a Real-Estate Agency

There are hundreds of real-estate agencies that will list your time-share. Some of them charge an upfront fee and then a commission at the time of sale. Others work strictly on commission. Fees and commissions vary, but they are usually much higher than fees charged for selling a house or other property. The agency should tell you, in writing, how they plan to market your time-share. Be sure to investigate the agency before you sign a contract.

Paying an upfront fee is rarely a good idea. Some states do not allow agencies to charge upfront fees. Some agencies hide the truth by calling an upfront fee an "appraisal fee." Don't believe it. No one needs to appraise your unit before it's listed for sale.

Check with state real-estate commissions to verify that the agency and its sales staff are licensed to practice real estate in the states in which they operate. Check the agency's complaint records with the Better Business Bureau and with their state attorney general's office.

Agencies who are members of the American Resort Development Association (ARDA) are expected to abide by certain ethical guidelines when selling time-shares.

Other Resale Options

Some resort developers offer resale programs. Salespeople working there have the advantage of easy access to buyers who are interested in that resort or chain, but their first focus is probably to sell new units. Compare their fees and marketing practices with those of other agencies.

Run, don't walk, away from anyone who promises you a quick sale. No one can guarantee that that your time-share will sell quickly unless they are offering to purchase it.

Time-Share Auctions

You can sell your time-share on an online auction service such as eBay. Search the term "timeshare," with no hyphens, to find the most listings. Pay attention to sales prices and to write-ups. Which ones sound the most appealing? Work those marketing techniques into your own ad.

User Groups Classifieds

User groups offer several member services, including "For Sale" and "Wanted to Buy" ads. This type of classified reaches the right target audience for your time-share.

Write to Other Owners

If you have a fixed unit and time, find out who owns the time-share for the weeks just before and just after you. They might be interested in increasing their time.

Chapter 16

Being a Landlord for Your Properties

Are you ready to be a landlord? It can be frustrating to deal with tenants and the inevitable repair and maintenance problems. You must understand local and federal laws that affect your properties and tenants. You have to be prepared for market changes that can leave your properties untenanted. But if you have the ability to stay focused, real-estate rentals can provide an ongoing income.

The Fair Housing Act

One of the first things every landlord must do is become familiar with the federal fair housing regulations, laws enacted to discourage discrimination against groups of people. There's no need to be paranoid about every word you write in an ad or say to a potential tenant, but it's important to know what the law states and to comply with it.

The Fair Housing Act prohibits housing discrimination based on race, color, religion, sex, national origin, familial status, or disability. The act affects landlords as well as other entities, including banks and insurance companies.

The entire Fair Housing Act can be viewed online at the HUD Web site, *www.hud.gov*. The agency offers booklets to help you understand and comply with these laws. Be sure to find out if your local or state laws include additional fair housing guidelines.

ALERT!

The government uses testers to make sure that landlords are operating under fair housing guidelines. Learn the laws and follow them, because you never know when a potential tenant is actually a federal employee who's been sent to check out your rental practices.

What's Considered Illegal

Whether you are renting or selling, you cannot take any of the following actions simply because someone is a member of one of the groups protected against discrimination:

- Refuse to negotiate, rent, or sell housing
- Make housing unavailable
- Deny someone a dwelling
- Set different terms, conditions, or privileges for different groups of people
- Provide different services or facilities to different groups of people
- Falsely deny that housing is available for sale or rent
- Profit by persuading owners to sell or rent based on news of changes to neighborhood demographics, the overall makeup of people who live there

FACT

The U.S. Department of Housing and Urban Development (HUD) investigates complaints made about discriminatory practices. The Department of Justice can initiate a lawsuit if they believe the accused offender has shown a pattern of discriminatory behavior.

Exemptions to the Federal Law

Most housing is covered by the Fair Housing Act, but some dwellings are exempt. Exemptions include an owner-occupied building that contains no more than four units when units are being sold or rented without employing a real-estate broker. A single-family residence is exempt if it is rented or sold by an owner who does not own more than three such homes. Only one such sale is exempt during a twenty-four month period if the residence is not owner occupied. Rental rooms are exempt in an owner-occupied dwelling of four or fewer units.

Religious organizations can require that prospects be a member of their religion as long as they do not exclude people from the religion based on their belonging to the other protected classes.

Even when exemptions are allowed, owners cannot use discriminatory advertising to find tenants and buyers.

Some buildings and communities qualify as housing intended strictly for older persons. If yours does not, you cannot discriminate against families with children. Refer to current fair housing laws to find out what steps you must take to qualify a development as senior housing.

Language Appropriate to Housing Ads

One of the best things to remember when writing your ads is to talk about the property, *not* about the people you envision living there. Ads should not contain any statement that indicates you have a preference about the type of person who should occupy the property.

Statements such as "perfect for senior citizens," "nice apartment for young professionals," and "family-oriented housing development" should be avoided. Don't put yourself in a position where any group could question your motives.

Section 8 Housing

You also have the option of getting involved with the Section 8 housing program. The Department of Housing and Urban Development (HUD) oversees the program, which offers rental assistance to low-income families. Approved tenants pay a portion of their housing costs, with the balance paid through the program's housing choice voucher.

From the landlord's point of view, there are pros and cons to the program. You are assured payment of the guaranteed portion of the rent, but not the tenant's share. The government will not pay for repairs if the tenant damages the property. There are sometimes delays in processing your payment, and allowed rents can be low. Talk with your local housing authority about Section 8 to help you determine if the program is one you wish to be involved with.

Finding Good Tenants

You'll have fewer problems with tenants if you screen them carefully before you allow them to rent your properties. Remember, you cannot turn away applicants simply because they are members of a protected group, but you can and should obtain a current credit report for each adult who signs the lease, and you should have written standards that *all* tenants must pass. Here are some tips for your tenant-search process:

- Establish requirements regarding creditworthiness and minimum income.
- Set requirements that eliminate tenants with poor rental references— although many landlords will not give you specific information about past performance as a protection against liability issues.
- Require that a tenant be employed and have a consistent employment record.
- Require that tenants purchase an insurance policy to cover their personal belongings. An uninsured tenant is more likely to sue you if something happens to his possessions.
  Requirements must be applied consistently to all applicants. You

cannot make exceptions for one person and then turn down another person with similar problems. Inconsistency leaves you open to a lawsuit.

ALERT!

When you put your policies regarding rental rules and acceptable property use in writing, it's obvious from the beginning that everyone who rents from you is subject to the same rules and regulations. Print out your guidelines and give a copy to every prospective tenant.

Existing Tenants

When you buy a property that's already occupied by a tenant, you will likely be bound to the lease signed by the tenant and former owner. Review all leases carefully before you make an offer on a property, getting input from an experienced real-estate attorney if you aren't sure what actions to take when the lease expires. If you decide to buy the property, the attorney can help you draft changes and guide you through the process of updating all leases as they expire if that is necessary.

Leasing Options

A lease gives a tenant a temporary right to possess a property for a stated purpose. The document usually states how long the lease period lasts, how much the tenant must pay for use of the property, when payments are to be made, and how the property will be used, along with an outline of the duties and obligations of all parties who sign it. In a lease document, the landlord is called the lessor and the tenant is called the lessee.

Fixed-Rent Lease

In a fixed-rent lease, also called a gross lease, the tenant pays a fixed amount for the rental and the landlord is responsible for hazard insurance premiums, mortgage payments, repair costs, property taxes, and other costs required to maintain and protect the building. Either the tenant or landlord can be responsible for utilities. A fixed lease is normally used for residential rental agreements.

Net Lease

A net lease is used when the tenant will be responsible for some or all of the costs of maintaining the property, such as taxes and other specific expenses. Net leases are typically used for commercial and industrial buildings and land.

Percentage Lease

A percentage lease bases rent on a percentage of the tenant's gross or net income. This type of lease is most often used for retail stores. It usually states a minimum amount of rent that's due from the tenant, no matter what the tenant's income is.

Graduated Lease

A graduated lease calls for increases in rent at some future date. Graduated leases are most often used for the rental of office space. An index lease bases rent on the rise or fall of an economic index, in much the same way as an adjustable-rate mortgage fluctuates. A reappraisal lease allows rents to change based on changes in the property's value. There are other types of leases drafted to apply to specific circumstances.

The Residential Lease

Residential leases can be negotiated for any lawful purpose. You must ensure that the lease you use conforms to state and local laws, but there are some typical elements to consider no matter where you live. Even though they won't all apply to every situation, all are items you should consider when determining elements you want to incorporate into your rental agreements. Specific details can be included as addenda, separate pages that outline additional elements of the lease that are signed by all parties.

Leases should contain the names of all persons who will live in the structure and the signatures of those who are responsible for paying rent. Inserting a special statement, called a *joint and several liability clause*, makes every person who signs the contract responsible for rent and compliance with other clauses, not just the amount they feel is their "share." An attorney can help you draft the clause.

The lease should state its beginning and end dates, and it should address what happens at its expiration. Some types of leases allow a tenant to remain on a month-to-month basis without signing a new lease. Some leases automatically renew upon expiration unless a notice to vacate is given by one of the parties. Make sure your lease contracts include details that outline exactly what each party must do at expiration.

It's a good idea to insert a clause that states you must approve the addition of any new tenants before they are allowed to move in with current renters. If you allow additional tenants, the adults should sign the rental agreement.

Common Lease Provisions

Details should include instructions on how tenants must give you written notice of the intent to vacate. The lead time for tenants to notify you if they plan to vacate is up to you and should be chosen for best results in your market. Thirty days is typical, but it's not appropriate for every situation. If experience shows that it takes sixty days to find a tenant, you might want to increase the notification date.

Property Use

The lease should state how the property is to be used. Can the tenant operate a home-based business that requires walk-in customers? If the rental is in a development that bans such businesses, the decision isn't yours. In some cases, the decision is up to you. With more and more people working out of their homes, you should consider the types of businesses you will and will not allow.

Detailed Property Description

The lease should include information that describes any portion of the property in need of repairs when the tenant moves in. This is normally accomplished by using a checklist to help tenants inspect items and list problems, such as scuffed paint, cracked or burned countertops, or a hole in the carpet. If you fix the items, the tenant should acknowledge the repairs in writing.

The lease should also contain an inventory of personal property included with the rental, things like appliances, curtains and blinds, and furniture. The list should include specific information about the brands and age of items, including serial numbers when possible.

ALERT!

The preprinted leases available at office supply stores are a good starting point, but they rarely include the clauses necessary to protect your interests. Before using them, seek advice from a real-estate attorney or another investor who has experience managing similar properties.

You might wish to take photos of the property's condition before tenants move in, asking them to sign off that the condition depicted is accurate. When they move, you can compare the photos to the property's current condition to determine if changes are due to damage or normal wear and tear.

Rents, Late Fees, and Security Deposit

The lease should state how much rent is to be paid, when it is due, and to whom it must be given. You can insert clauses regarding late payments and associated fees for them and defining the charges the tenant must pay for a bounced check.

You must also determine how much security deposit to charge your tenants. To be competitive, call landlords with similar properties to see what the going rate is, then decide if it works for you. You'll have to decide when the deposit is due and whether or not tenants will earn interest on the amount. You should describe in writing what a tenant must do to be eligible for a deposit refund at the end of the lease, including details about the length of time you will take to make the refund.

Deposits must often be held in trust accounts during the time of the lease, and many states regulate maximum amounts that you can charge a tenant for a deposit. Check your state and local regulations to make sure your decisions comply with laws in your area.

Pet Provisions

It's up to you to decide whether pets should be allowed on the property. The only exception is that fair housing laws do not allow you to turn away people who live with service animals, such as seeing eye dogs for the blind.

Many landlords do not allow pets under any circumstances. If pet restrictions are typical in your area, allowing pets—with a nonrefundable pet fee—will give your units an additional set of tenants to draw from.

Restrictions and Laws

The lease should require tenants to abide by all deed restrictions for the property and to all federal, state, and local laws. That topic covers everything from assigned parking spaces to the use or sale of illegal drugs. Properties can be seized and sold if illegal drugs are found on the premises, even if the owners have no idea drugs are present.

Keeping It Clean

Do you provide a place for tenants to dispose of trash? Do you offer regular pest control treatments? How are repairs handled, and can tenants contact you quickly if a problem emerges? You want the tenants to keep the property clean and in good condition, and good tenants want a landlord who cares enough about the property to help them do it.

Make sure the lease contains wording that gives you and your agents a right to enter the dwelling at a reasonable time with reasonable notice. A twenty-four-hour notice is common.

On the other hand, the landlord should not have to pay for repairs to fixtures or the structure if they were caused by tenant abuse. Cover the what-ifs of repairs in your lease, stating who pays for what under different circumstances.

Eviction Provisions

A carefully worded lease that protects your rights is essential, but it isn't a guarantee that tenants will vacate when they should. It's important to become familiar with tenant rights in your area so that you can work to remove tenants as quickly as possible by lawful means if eviction becomes necessary.

A lease could include hefty per-day costs for tenants who stay in the residence without permission after the lease expires. The clause doesn't guarantee you'll ever collect the funds, but the threat of it is enough to discourage some tenants from staying.

Do You Need Help?

Unless you have the time and feel comfortable making repairs yourself, you will probably need one or more people you can depend on to step in when problems arise. You might even decide to hire a property management firm to handle the daily operations of your rental business. The choices you make affect the character of your rentals *and* your bottom line.

All but the handiest of us need occasional help with maintenance issues, especially those that involve plumbing and electrical repairs. You may already know someone you can turn to for help. If you don't, talk to some of your local real-estate agents—particularly agents who handle rentals. Most agents are willing to share their sources.

The number of rentals you manage will dictate how you work with repairpersons. Do you want them to be on call, or will you need them only during regular business hours? You know which will be more affordable, but sometimes emergencies happen. Finding someone who you know can come quickly if necessary is a plus.

What types of repairs can you foresee? Plumbers, electricians, roofers, heating and air-conditioning repairpersons, locksmiths—brainstorm the what-ifs, and try to line up people who can step in to help with problems.

Outside property management might be a necessity if you have a job that demands a great deal of your time, or if the property you are renting is not located near your home. Don't hire an individual or management firm without interviewing several potential candidates. Pay attention to the following:

- What are the fees and the services you can expect to receive for those fees?
- How much does the firm want up front for a repair fund?
- What type of training have management personnel had? How many years of property management experience do they have?
- Can they supply references from other clients?
- What is the opinion of tenants who live in properties managed by the firm?
- How are funds held, and when you can expect payments for monthly rents?
- How is the company's credit rating? Make sure the management company has no unresolved complaints with the Better Business Bureau.
- Get evidence that the company's brokerage license is active. (You can get this information from your state real-estate commission.)

Using a property management firm isn't the best choice for everyone, but sometimes it is necessary. Make the best choice you can, and avoid signing lengthy contracts so that you can move on if the relationship does not work out.

You will give your tenants and your properties more care than anyone else will. It's your venture—you care about it. This isn't just a job, it's the thing you *want* to do. That gives you an edge that no management firm can provide. Your tenants will see your dedication, and if you've chosen tenants wisely, they will appreciate your desire to keep the property in tip-top condition.

Chapter 17

Like-Kind Exchanges and REITs

Internal Revenue Code §1031 allows investors to exchange like-kind properties by trading a property held for business or investment purposes for another one also held for investment purposes. Taxes on the gains received from the sale are deferred. Real estate investment trusts (REITs) allow investors to buy shares in large groupings of properties in the same way they invest in stock market offerings. Purchasing REIT shares is one way to invest in real estate without taking on the burden of buying and selling properties.

Like-Kind Exchange Basics

A like-kind exchange is possible when you buy and sell properties that are held for investment or business purposes. The technique cannot be used when selling your personal residence. Although personal property such as cars and airplanes can be exchanged, this chapter will stick to reviewing the exchange of real-estate properties. The advice offered here is a good start, and it is not intended to replace legal advice. You should contact a real-estate or tax attorney before you initiate any paperwork that involves buying and selling investment property you wish to include in a like-kind exchange.

FACT

During an exchange, you'll become familiar with two terms. The *relinquished* property is the property you sell, and the *replacement* property is the new investment property.

Tax Deference

The first thing you need to understand about §1031 like-kind exchange is that it does not eliminate the gains tax due on the sale—it only postpones it. If you ever decide to cash out of your investments, your taxes will be computed on the final, accumulated basis and sales amount. The deferment is like getting an interest-free loan on the tax dollars you would have owed on a cash sale.

You should talk with a tax professional to determine the amount of gain that will be deferred in a transaction, but there are a few basic guidelines to keep in mind:

- The fair market value of the replacement property must be equal to or greater than the fair market value of the relinquished property.
- The equity you have in the replacement property should be equal to or greater than the equity you had in the relinquished property.
- If you trade down in equity or fair market value, you will be taxed on the difference.

ALERT!

If, in addition to like-kind property, you receive money or unlike property in an exchange on which you realize a gain, you have a partially taxable exchange. You are taxed on the gain you realize, but only to the extent of the money and the fair market value of the unlike property you receive.

What Are Like-Kind Properties?

Another requirement is that the exchanged properties must be like-kind. That term is a little confusing because it doesn't mean you have to exchange an office building for another office building, a duplex for a duplex, or a piece of land for another piece of land. Any real property is considered like-kind when compared with another real-estate property.

To be eligible, the relinquished and replacement properties must be properties held for investment purposes or for use in a trade or business. This includes the following:

- Rental houses and buildings, raw land, industrial property, farms, and office buildings
- A vacation home used as a rental
- A real-estate lease that runs for longer than thirty years

Real estate held as inventory for sale is not eligible for exchange. Neither does your personal residence or a vacation home that you personally use more than two weeks each year.

Real property in the United States and real property outside of the United States are not like-kind properties. The IRS defines foreign property as any property not located in a state or the District of Columbia.

Avoiding Receipt of Funds

If you actually or constructively receive money or unlike property in payment for the property you transfer, the IRS will treat the transaction as a sale, not a deferred exchange. Constructive receipt occurs when money or unlike property is either credited to you or available to you.

When you do a like-kind exchange, the proceeds from the sale are never in your possession and not available—you must sign away that right. The funds are held by a neutral party, called a *qualified intermediary*, *facilitator*, or *accommodator*, until a replacement property is acquired. The intermediary uses the money to purchase the replacement property, arranging for the title to be in your name.

The Qualified Intermediary

For an exchange to be successful, you cannot take possession of the funds from the sale of the relinquished property or the title to the replacement property until the end of the transaction. You must give up your rights to access the proceeds until after the exchange is complete. Those rules are impossible to follow for an individual working alone. The solution is to hire a qualified intermediary, a person or firm that acts as a buffer between you, the proceeds, and the other parties involved in the sale.

The qualified intermediary cannot be related to you. The intermediary cannot be someone who has been your employee, attorney, accountant, investment banker or broker, or real-estate agent or broker within the two-year period before the transfer of the property you give up.

FACT

It is permissible for you to earn interest on the funds held by the intermediary. Discuss interest-bearing accounts with the intermediary before signing a contract.

A real-estate or tax attorney can usually help you find a qualified intermediary. Title insurance companies sometimes provide the service or will help you locate a company that does. The intermediary will charge a fee for its services, so be sure to get the facts about costs before you sign a contract.

It's a good idea to compare the services, costs, and references of several qualified intermediaries before selecting one to handle your 1031 exchange. Be sure to ask potential intermediaries for references and find out who audits their work. Also ask how disbursements are handled—

funds should not leave your account without your approval or the approval of your attorney.

Be sure to request a step-by-step explanation of the entire exchange process and ask as many questions as it takes for you to feel comfortable with the company's ability to complete a successful transaction and handle your proceeds with care.

The Written Agreement

You must have a written agreement with an intermediary before you close on the relinquished property. The agreement will cover many topics and give the intermediary the power to do the following:

- Sell the relinquished property and deed it to the buyer.
- Take possession of the proceeds from the sale.
- Hold the proceeds until it's time to close on the replacement property.
- Use the proceeds to purchase the replacement property and arrange for it to be deeded to you.

Get the Paperwork Right the First Time

Part of a successful transaction involves ensuring that every bit of paperwork associated with it meets the approval of the IRS. You must make sure that all documentation the IRS wants to see in a transaction has been handled correctly. That includes the wording of your sales and purchase agreements.

The listing agreement you sign with a real-estate agency should include a statement that discloses your intent to use the proceeds from the sale of the property to perform a like-kind exchange. An offer to purchase must also contain wording that notifies the seller of the replacement property that you intend to do an exchange. Before you sign any contract, ask your attorney or intermediary to suggest disclosure wording that is acceptable to the IRS.

Give your intermediary copies of all documents associated with your exchange. Your attorney or CPA can tell you which tax forms you must file with the IRS.

There are special rules that govern exchanging property with a relative. Ask your attorney or intermediary to explain how that type of exchange transaction is handled.

Purchasing the Replacement Property

The IRS has very specific guidelines for identifying and closing on your replacement property. The rules are not flexible, so it's important to understand the customs of the real-estate market you are working in before you commit to closing dates on either the sales or purchase transaction. You want to be sure you can handle both transactions in the allowed time.

You must identify a replacement property within forty-five days of closing on the relinquished property. This time is called the identification period. The identification must be submitted in writing to your qualified intermediary. Be sure to identify the property as accurately as possible. Including a legal description leaves no doubt which property you are identifying.

You are allowed to identify up to three replacement properties without calculating their total fair market value to determine how that value compares to the fair market value of your relinquished property. If you identify more than three properties, their total fair market value cannot be more than double the value of the relinquished property's fair market value.

Identifying multiple properties helps ensure that you can work out a contract and closing on at least one of them. You don't have to buy all of the identified properties, but you can if you wish.

The Closing Process

You must close on a replacement property within 180 days of the relinquished property's closing or by the due date of your tax return for the year the relinquished property was sold, including extensions. This period is called the receipt period.

Here's an example. If you close on the relinquished property in late December, you have until April 15 of the next year to acquire the replacement property. If you file for an extension, you can extend the closing date, but not past the 180 day limit.

If you close on the relinquished property in January, you automatically have the full 180 days to acquire its replacement, since your tax return for the acquisition will not be due until the following year.

FACT

A like-kind exchange is sometimes called a *Starker* exchange, after *Starker v. United States*, the case that resulted in the U.S. Supreme Court's first approval of deferred exchanges.

If an Exchange Doesn't Work

If you have not identified a property by the end of the forty-five-day identification period, the intermediary can return your funds to you. If you have identified a property, but you do not acquire it within the 180-day receipt period, the intermediary will give you your proceeds.

The intermediary will not give you any excess proceeds that are held in your account until after the replacement property is purchased. Proceeds not used to purchase the replacement property are taxed as they would be for a cash sale.

Buying First, Selling Later

Reverse exchanges became possible in 2002. In order to make a reverse exchange work, the title to your replacement property must held by an exchange accommodation titleholder (EAT) until you sell the relinquished property. A qualified intermediary is then used to complete the exchange.

Some of the steps in a reverse exchange are the opposite of those in a regular like-kind exchange. Instead of identifying a replacement property, you'll identify the relinquished property within the forty-five-day identification period and close on it within the 180-day replacement period.

You will sign a written agreement with the EAT that's similar to the contract you sign with a qualified intermediary. Ask your attorney and intermediary to explain the specifics of working with a qualified EAT to perform a reverse exchange. Be sure to get recommendations for the wording that should be inserted in purchase and sales contracts.

Not Always the Best Solution

Like-kind transfers aren't always the best choice for transactions that involve investment properties. To avoid tax, you must use all of your proceeds from the relinquished property to buy its replacement. That probably isn't an option if you need the funds for other purposes. If the gain you expect to realize is minimal, it might not make sense to pay an intermediary's fees.

You might know that it will be difficult to identify and close on replacement properties within the allotted time. You'll still owe the intermediary a fee, even if you can't follow through on the exchange. You're the only one who can decide if it's worthwhile to attempt an exchange under those conditions.

What Is a REIT?

A REIT is an investment company that owns and operates income-producing real estate and sometimes finances real-estate transactions, profiting from the interest received during the borrower's payback. REIT shares are a good choice for anyone with a desire to invest in real estate, but they are especially useful for investors who do not have the cash, desire, or time to deal with the purchase of individual properties. Investors can buy shares anytime they have additional cash to invest and then watch their investment grow as the funds are managed by professionals with expertise in the field of real-estate investments.

A REIT is a pass-through entity, which means its profits are passed on to its shareholders. The Internal Revenue Service requires each REIT to pay out at least 90 percent of its taxable income and capital gains to shareholders every year. Individual investors pay taxes on their gains, but the REIT itself is not taxed. A REIT must satisfy several IRS rules before it is granted this tax-exempt status.

At least 75 percent of a REIT's assets must be in the form of real estate, cash, or mortgages, and there are strict IRS rules regarding the source of each trust's income and the control of its shares. There must be at least 100 shareholders, and shares must be transferable. No more than 50 percent of a REIT's shares may be held by five or fewer individuals during the last half of a taxable year. These and other IRS rules were put in place to help ensure that a REIT is governed by its shareholders and not by the wishes of a few individuals.

What about UPREITs?
These are REITs that own a controlling interest in another company that owns real estate, rather than directly owning the real estate in the name of the REIT.

QUESTION?

Types of REITs

There are three broad categories of REITs—the equity trust, the mortgage trust, and trusts that are a blend of the two, called hybrid trusts. Equity trusts acquire and manage many kinds of income-producing properties. Mortgage trusts make loans or purchase mortgages that are backed by real-estate liens. Hybrid trusts invest in both areas. REITs can further specialize by focusing on properties in a specific geographical location.

The National Association of Real-Estate Investment Trusts categorizes equity trusts by the type of properties they specialize in, as follows:

- Industrial and office trusts specialize in either industrial or office properties, or both.
- Retail REITs specialize in strip centers, larger malls, and other types of retail properties.
- Residential REITs might own multifamily apartments or developments for manufactured housing.
- Some REITs specialize in lodging and resorts, holding ownership in hotels, motels, and resort properties.

- Some REIT's specialize in ownership and management of self-storage units.
- Health-care REITs own hospitals and other health-care facilities.
- Other equity trusts are classified as specialty REITs, owning properties such as golf courses, timberland, prisons, and many other specific types of real-estate that don't fall into another category.

A diversified REIT invests in more than one type of property.

How REITs Work

Individuals buy shares in real-estate investment trusts, and so do other investors, such as pension funds, insurance companies, banks, and mutual funds. Shares in most REITs can be purchased on the major stock exchanges, and financial planners help investors select a company just as they would other investments that are held for current income and long-term appreciation.

REITs offer an annual report and prospectus to help current and potential investors evaluate their income and growth potential. Some of the things you should consider when evaluating a trust are its management, its source of current funding, its potential for future funding, and its earnings.

Different types of REITs perform differently in various economic conditions. Since a REIT's property investments are sometimes focused in specific geographical locations, a potential investor should research the supply and demand for the type of property held within the trust's portfolio. For instance, a REIT that specializes in apartment buildings in college towns with growing student populations might be in a position to keep the majority of its units rented.

A REIT's shareholders elect trustees or a board of directors, who in turn appoint management personnel. Some of the current management teams were past owners of private corporations that have become today's publicly traded REITs, shifting their ownership into the company's stock at the switch, while staying on to continue managing the new public corporation as they had when it was a private enterprise.

REITs distribute the majority of their income to investors each year, so in order to grow they must be in a position to obtain additional capital to continue making investments.

How Do I Evaluate a REIT?

REIT performance is judged using net income as defined by generally accepted accounting principles (GAAP). Another important factor is funds from operations (FFO). It looks at GAAP net income but excludes gains or losses from the sales of most properties and the depreciation of the trust's real-estate holdings. Depreciation is excluded from the calculations because real estate maintains more value than other items that type of calculation is used to assess, such as personal property or machinery.

Investors can compare a REIT's stock price to its net asset value (NAV), a per-share calculation that analyzes the market value of the company's assets. The NAV is only one aspect of the trust that you should consider. You can research specific REITs by using the tools at one of the online sources listed in Appendix C.

FACT

REITs are required to send IRS Form 1099-DIV to each of their shareholders. That form shows investors the total of their prior year's dividends and indicates how dividends should be allocated on the investor's current tax return.

Most experts recommend that you consider the management team's experience and the length of time they have worked together. Do they have a good track record for choosing worthwhile investments and managing them effectively? Has the team remained stable for a long period of time, or have members been replaced frequently in an effort to improve the trust's operations and income? An investment professional can help you find answers to those questions.

Look at a REIT's past acquisitions. Have they steadily increased over the years, or are they stagnant? Where is new funding coming from? What about paid dividends and investment growth—has the REIT produced good results in both areas? Your investment planner can walk you through all of the specifics you must consider when evaluating a trust's past, present, and future potential.

It's important to research a REIT just as carefully as you would any other stock. Get started by finding an investment planner whose opinion you trust, and ask that person as many questions as it takes to feel comfortable that you understand the basics of REIT evaluation. For reading materials, visit your local library and browse the online REIT resources in Appendix C.

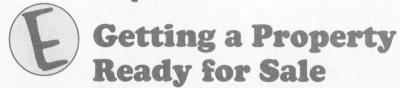

Chapter 18

Getting a Property Ready for Sale

When it's time to sell your property, you want to be able to make a good profit. To maximize your chances for a quick and profitable sale, consider doing some renovations and updating. Some quick improvements can bring significantly higher returns. Follow the guidelines presented in this chapter to make sure potential buyers or renters see your property's best features from the very first day because you won't have a second chance to impress them.

Updates That Bring Results

Structural repairs, such as replacing old roof components and fixing foundation issues, are a necessity, but cosmetics and remodeling projects should be chosen in their order of importance. Some updates yield more return on the dollar spent when it's time to rent or sell.

What's important in one part of the country might not be as critical in another—one more reason to know your real-estate market. Well-planned repairs and updates will result in an investment that you can turn around for a profit.

There's an old saying that you should not try to own the most expensive house on the block. It's true—averages rule the market. The eventual list price or rental fee of the house you're refurbishing should be at or slightly less than the majority of homes in the neighborhood. Don't get so carried away with updates that you end up with a structure that must be priced above the neighborhood's average selling price.

Curb Appeal Is Essential

For a quicker sale and more showings, you'll want to attract attention from the moment potential buyers or renters see your property, and that means enhancing its curb appeal. Stand back and view the property as if you were seeing it for the first time. If you were a home-buyer, would you want to take a closer look? If not, it's time to get to work on curb appeal.

Get started with curb appeal basics:

- Repaint exteriors, using neutral colors.
- Clean windows so they sparkle.
- Make sure the roof is in good condition and free of leaves and other debris.
- Keep lawns freshly trimmed and weed-free.
- Edge sidewalks and driveways to remove overgrown grass.
- Rake up and dispose of fallen leaves.
- Put away tools and equipment in a storage shed or garage instead of leaving them in the yard.
- Make sure porches and decks are in good condition.

What's the most popular exterior color?
Although your specific area might vary, the National Association of Realtors reports that the most popular house color is white. Driving through your favorite neighborhoods is a good way to preview exterior colors and exterior features. Which houses make you say "Wow!"?

Landscaping Changes

Nice landscaping always enhances a property's curb appeal. You might not recover all of your landscaping investment, but it can help a house sell in a much quicker time. Before you begin, do some research to find out if the majority of buyers in your area prefer a manicured look or a lot that doesn't take as much effort to maintain.

You don't always have to do extensive landscaping to improve curb appeal. Sometimes removing an unattractive bush or tree is exactly what a property needs to improve its appearance, especially when the planting is hiding an attractive feature. Take a close look at the lot to see if some elements should be removed.

Evening Appeal Is Important

Don't forget to give the house nighttime appeal. Many buyers do drive-bys in the evenings after work. The soft glow of outside lighting can do wonders to enhance the property's appearance.

Here are a few ways to perk up the property's nighttime appeal:

- String low-voltage lights along the edges of the driveway.
- Install a decorative, freestanding yard lamp.
- Update porch lighting.
- Use soft spotlights to enhance plantings.

Think *soft* and *subdued* to make the property a nighttime winner. If the house looks well lit and welcoming, the buyers' interest will be piqued.

ALERT! Don't opt for outdoor solar lighting if your lot is in the shade. Solar lights are quick and easy to install, but they need to be in full sunlight for most of the day in order to operate efficiently at night.

Enhance the Front Door

A new front door can do wonders for a home's curb appeal. Doors with leaded or frosted glass panels are attractive during the day, when details can be seen, and also at night, when interior lights are on to make them shine. If you can't justify the expense of a new door, give the old door a fresh finish and update its hardware.

Interior Face-Lifts

Fresh paint is nearly always a must if you want the property to show well. Steer clear of wallpaper, because it rarely suits the tastes of individual buyers. Instead, show buyers and renters a somewhat neutral palette that makes it easy for them to imagine how their own decorating styles will fit into the house.

If existing carpeting can't be cleaned thoroughly, consider ripping it out and starting fresh, but decide first if hardwood flooring or tile would be a better choice for some rooms.

Finally, don't neglect your closets. Make them neat and tidy, removing overflow to other areas if necessary.

Kitchen and Bathroom Updates

Refreshing the kitchen and bathrooms is always high on the list of remodeling jobs that pay off when it's time to sell or rent. Even people who don't cook seem to want a well-planned, stylish kitchen with feature-packed appliances.

New flooring always boosts the appearance of a kitchen or bath. If you use vinyl, be sure it's of a high quality. Ceramic tile or laminate flooring offers a richer appearance. New sinks with new faucet hardware can help modernize both kitchens and baths, and so can revamped lighting.

Some kitchen cabinets can be updated nicely by refinishing or painting them and adding new hardware. In other cases, you'll need to start fresh with new cabinetry. Baths that can be turned into comfortable, spa-like retreats can help sell a property, especially when they're part of a larger master suite.

New countertops are a good way to enhance a kitchen or bath. Corian and granite are popular, but their price may be prohibitive for the type of home you are refurbishing. Fresh laminate counter-tops are affordable, durable, and available in hundreds of styles and colors.

Insulated Windows and High-Efficiency Furnaces

No matter what type of climate you're located in, buyers want a home that's energy efficient. Insulated windows and high-efficiency furnaces can pay for themselves when it's time to sell. Making sure the structure has adequate insulation in walls and attics is another must.

Replace plastic, dated skylights with more energy-efficient glass models, if possible. Newer skylight versions offer other benefits—they are more attractive and less likely to crack and leak.

Perks and Extras

Spend some time thinking about your property and the market. What extra features would be a good investment, enhancing the value of the property and making it more enticing to potential buyers? Think of features that will help you compete with other sellers and that will raise the property value by more than the amount it would take to add the feature.

Fireplace Maintenance and Additions

If the house has a fireplace, make sure it's in good working order. Consider adding gas logs or a freestanding decorative gas stove to homes without a fireplace if they're popular in your area. Both types of units are available as vented and vent-free appliances.

Vented gas logs burn with a realistic-looking yellow flame. They require a chimney that's in good working order so that deadly carbon monoxide gas and other byproducts of combustion are whisked to the outside.

Vent-free gas logs do not require a chimney. They burn with a hot blue flame that is designed to eliminate carbon monoxide gas. They should be burned for short periods and closely monitored for safety. Vent-free gas logs are illegal in some areas. Consider installing carbon monoxide detectors if the house has any type of fireplace, especially if the property will be a rental.

Gas logs are not a solution for a problem chimney. If the chimney isn't safe for burning wood, it isn't safe for burning gas. Always make needed repairs and thoroughly clean the chimney before you switch to gas logs.

Sunrooms and Decks

A new sunroom or decking that overlooks a nice view or tranquil setting can pay for itself. Existing porches that are in good condition can sometimes be turned into sunrooms with less expense than starting from scratch. If the view from a new sunroom or deck wouldn't be desirable, consider putting your money into other areas where view doesn't matter, such as a well-designed family room.

Laminate Flooring

Laminate flooring is a popular, machine-made product that is attractive, durable, and less expensive than wood flooring. Laminate is an excellent alternative for locations where you want the look of wood but where the price or location prohibits it. It can be installed on top of concrete, even in a basement where high humidity prevents wood from being used.

Final Preparations

The property should be spotless—clean and fresh. Be sure to pick up loose paint chips, sawdust, and anything else left over from repairs. Clean the windows and skylights, inside and out. Make sure there are no odors. A freshly remodeled house might not have the same odors you'll sniff in a lived-in home, but there can be traces of chemicals hanging in the air. Open the windows to air out the house before you show it to prospective buyers.

Clean the gutters and make sure drainage spouts point into tubing that leads away from the foundation. Buyers always notice gutters that are full of leaves or twigs, and it makes them wonder what else hasn't been taken care of. If there's a lawn, keep it freshly mowed.

Have you ever noticed that in the wintertime, the inside of an unheated house often feels colder than the outside temperature? Buyers can't wait to leave houses like that—it's an immediate turn-off. If you can afford it, run the heat or air conditioning so that the interior is at least somewhat comfortable.

Take a cue from professional home stagers, and bring in furnishings to make the house looked lived in. Avoid clutter—choose simple, tasteful furniture and supporting accessories. You might even consider hiring a professional stager to prepare an upscale home. In larger cities, stagers often have a warehouse of furnishings to draw from.

ALERT!

Vacant houses with no utilities on are prime candidates for the development of mildew and mold accumulation, especially in damp climates. Allowing the heating or air conditioning to remain on will help keep your property in better condition.

The property you are marketing and the area it's located in will dictate many of the preparations you should make. How does the property compare to other similar real-estate properties on the market? When you see something that sells quickly, determine why, and try to duplicate those factors in your own properties. You won't become an expert overnight, but in time, you'll know instinctively what to do to enhance each of your new properties. For more information on staging, visit *www.stagedhomes.com.*

Chapter 19

E For Sale by Owner (FSBO)

I f you sell your properties yourself, you will be responsible for every issue connected to the transaction, from marketing to negotiating contracts to getting the sale to closing. If you've read earlier chapters, you're already familiar with some of the issues you'll encounter, such as required disclosures, fair housing laws, and contract negotiations, but there are many other issues sellers must deal with to ensure a successful sale.

Dealing with Buyers

Not everyone is cut out to sell real estate, even when it's their own. Dealing with potential buyers can be time consuming and frustrating. Do you have the time? Can you ignore your personal feelings during negotiations and keep from getting excited or upset if the buyers are less than tactful about your property? Are you able to keep track of small details? If you answered "yes" to these questions, give the FSBO option a try. After a few attempts, you'll know if it's the right route for your property sales.

> The majority of home-buyers use a real-estate agent to find them a home. Selling by owner will cut out many of those buyers. One solution is to let agents know you will work with them, offering half of the normal commission if they bring you a buyer.

Most sellers decide to sell by owner in order to save a commission fee, but that mindset only makes sense if you know exactly how to proceed with marketing and selling the property. Statistics show that a high percentage of FSBO real estate is sold for less than market value, usually because sellers aren't savvy about the local real-estate market or don't know how to negotiate a contract that looks out for their interests.

As a real-estate investor, you can't let that scenario describe you. You won't become an expert overnight, but continued hands-on experience will eventually make you one. There's no better time to get started.

Don't Take It Personally

Since you'll deal directly with potential buyers, get prepared to hear complaints about the property. They hate the carpeting. Who would have ever chosen those awful paint colors! The house is way overpriced. You'll hear it all. Toughen up and don't take it personally. You have to remain calm and detached in order to negotiate successfully with less-than-tactful buyers.

ALERT!

Most buyers who contact FSBO sellers are looking for a deal. After all, you're not paying a commission, so you can let them have it for far less than other properties. Stay aware of that attitude when you start to negotiate the contract—the property has the same market value, no matter who is selling it.

Do You Understand the Paperwork?

If you are providing forms for the buyer, do you have access to preprinted, standard forms that are specific to your state's laws? Don't rely on generic forms that do not cover the real-estate laws in your state. The offer to purchase and its addenda are critical, since they determine how every aspect of the contract moves forward. If the buyer presents you with a signed offer, be sure to have them reviewed by an experienced real-estate attorney.

Handling the Buyer's Deposit

The buyer's good faith deposit is not yours until closing, and it should be held in trust by a neutral third party. Your contract should contain wording that describes what happens to the deposit if the contract falls through. If buyers cannot get financing, the deposit is normally refunded to them. If they back out for no reason, the deposit can go either way. Address the what-ifs in your contract, and make sure the buyers understand how their deposits will be handled.

FACT

If a contract states that *time is of the essence*, it means that the event scheduled for that date must occur then unless both parties approve of the change. Not all states use that clause in standard contracts, so check local customs to find out if it applies to you.

Making Sure Your Buyers Are Preapproved

You'd be surprised how many buyers don't go to a real-estate agent because they know they aren't qualified to buy a house. For some reason, they think that FSBO sellers can always help them get into a house with owner financing. Don't waste your time negotiating with unqualified buyers. Ask to see a preapproval letter right away, and never sign a contract without one. Do not settle for a prequalification letter, which is not an in-depth look at the buyer's finances.

How Much Space Are You Selling?

Every year, incorrectly measured square footage results in numerous lawsuits against sellers and real-estate agents. If you are working with a real-estate agent, it's the agent's responsibility to get the correct square footage number; FSBO sellers must make sure to do this themselves.

It's critical to understand how residential living space is calculated. Never depend on the square footage statements found on a previous multiple listing sheet or county tax records. You can't use blueprints to figure square footage, because last-minute changes might have been made during the home's construction. Don't use appraisals, either, because even appraisers make mistakes. Your reputation and finances are both on the line, so measure square footage yourself using accepted techniques, then cross check the results with previous calculations, if they are available.

ALERT!

It's a good idea to calculate a home's *total* square footage, which includes finished and unfinished spaces, and even the area occupied by decks and patios. You never know when a prospective buyer will want both figures, so be prepared to answer their questions before you advertise the property.

Your state's real-estate commission might have already established square footage guidelines that you can follow. Call your state real-estate commission or look on its Web site to determine if measuring standards are in place.

The methods described here are based on widely accepted square footage guidelines, so they will help you learn the basic do's and don'ts of calculating residential square footage. No matter which measuring method you decide to use, hang on to your drawings and all other paperwork associated with the procedures you used to measure the residence. You'll be in a much better position to defend your calculations if you can show how the results were obtained.

Measure the Exterior

Square footage calculations are always based on exterior measurements. Use the following techniques to measure the exterior of a single-family residence:

1. Start measuring at one corner of the house and continue to measure the remaining exterior walls. Round measurements up to the next inch (or tenth of an inch for greater accuracy).
2. Record your measurements, and use them to make a sketch of the perimeter of the house.
3. Sketch in the position of unfinished areas, such as garages and utility areas.
4. If all areas of the structure qualify as living areas, you will use your sketch and measurements to calculate the square footage of the entire shape.

Sometimes you must determine a portion of a home's dimensions by measuring from the interior. When that happens, add six inches for each exterior wall and four inches for each interior wall you encounter during the measuring process and then sketch the area in to your exterior drawing.

QUESTION?

What qualifies as finished living space?
Finished square footage must be space intended for human occupancy. It must be heated by a conventional, permanent heating system. It must be finished, with walls, floors, and ceilings that are constructed from materials generally accepted for interior construction. It must also be directly accessible from another portion of the living area.

Unfinished areas must be deducted from the total square footage. Garages and unfinished utility areas are examples of rooms that must often be subtracted to obtain the total for the living space. Sketch them in, and deduct their square footage when you make calculations.

Other Measurements

If you've got sloped ceilings, as in A-frame homes or in the attic where ceilings are usually sloped at a sharp angle, you can't just measure room dimensions where sloped walls meet the floor. Include only the square footage for the portion of the room where the ceiling height is at least five feet. To be included at all, a minimum of one half of the finished area of the room must have ceilings at least seven feet high.

Bay Windows

The area occupied by a bay window may be counted in your total square footage if it has a floor, a ceiling height of at least seven feet, and meets other criteria for finished living area.

Furnace Rooms

If the furnace, water heater, or other similar item is located in a small closet within the living area, the area should be included in the total square footage.

Hallways and Closets

Hallways and closets are counted as part of the total square footage if they are a functional part of the living space. For instance, they are included if they are in a bedroom or within another room that's heated and finished. A closet in an unfinished basement should not be counted.

Stairways

If the upper opening for the stairway is larger than its length and width, you must deduct the excess open space from the upper level's square footage.

Open Foyers and Other Open Spaces

Be careful not to include open areas on the first level as part of the square footage for a home's upper level. This may seem obvious, but you'd be surprised how many people forget to deduct that space when totaling their figures.

Rooms Accessed Through an Unfinished Area

You should not count the square footage of a room that is finished and heated if it is accessed through an unfinished area—for instance, a laundry room that you enter by walking through an unfinished basement or garage. You can describe the space in your advertising, but be sure to mention that it is not included in the home's square footage.

Commonly Used Mathematical Formulas

You'll encounter several common shapes when you measure a home's square footage, and the area of each shape is calculated using a specific formula. Here are several formulas and graphics that will help you complete your square footage calculations.

Rectangles and Squares

Calculating the area of rectangles is easy. All you need to do multiply length by width. For example, if a room is ten feet in length and eight feet in width, the area is eighty square feet.

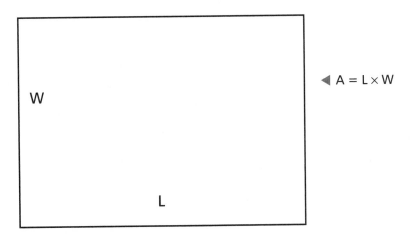

$$\blacktriangleleft\ A = L \times W$$

Triangles

If you've got a triangular area to measure, figure out the length of the base and the height, then multiply the two figures and divide the result in half. For example, if the base is ten feet and the height is fifteen feet, you'll need to do the following calculations: $10 \times 15 \div 2 = 75$.

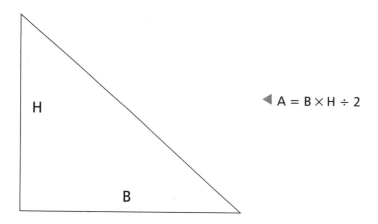

$\blacktriangleleft A = B \times H \div 2$

Circles and Semicircles

To calculate a circular area, you'll need to calculate the radius (the distance from anywhere in the circle to the center), square the result, and multiply it by Π (roughly 3.14). For a circle with a ten-foot radius, you'll need to do the following: $3.14 \times 10^2 = 314$ square feet.

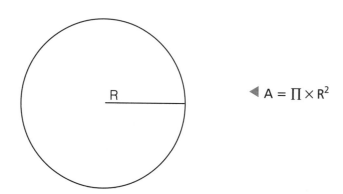

$\blacktriangleleft A = \Pi \times R^2$

If you have half of a circle, divide that number by two. If you have a quarter of a circle, divide the total by four.

Take a second look at your sketch before you leave the house, making corrections if necessary. Once you are accustomed to doing it, measuring square footage isn't difficult at all.

Combined Shapes

If you've got oddly shaped spaces, try to break them down into simple geometric figures like rectangles and triangles, then calculate the smaller areas and add them up.

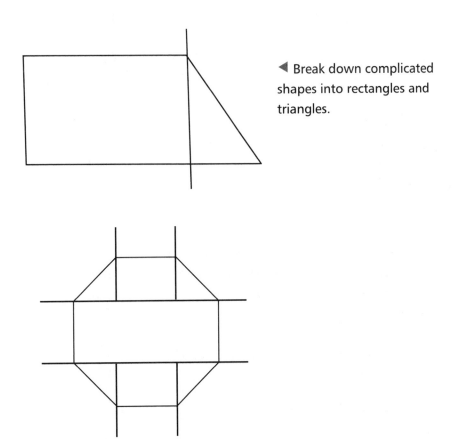

◀ Break down complicated shapes into rectangles and triangles.

First Marketing Steps

Properties in high-traffic, high-demand locations can sometimes be sold by simply placing a "For Sale" sign in the front yard, but that scenario is not typical of successful real-estate transactions throughout the United States. Get motivated, and take your first steps toward marketing the property to potential buyers.

Your first step is to create an attractive "For Sale" sign, making sure your contact information is legible and can be seen from a distance. Talk to an advertising specialty company—you know, the people who sell personalized pens, pencils, calendars, and other items. They often sell personalized yard signs, too. Ask local political candidates where they had signs made, or contact a sign-making shop.

You can order personalized signs from the same companies that real-estate agencies use. That's somewhat expensive, but if you plan to market many properties, these durable signs might be your best choice. You'll find a list of sign companies in Appendix C.

If your property is not located in a high-traffic area, you might want to use small directional signs. Place them at the corners of busier streets, using as many signs as necessary to lead people to the property. Place directional signs up against a street sign or other permanent item to help keep them from blowing away or being mowed down by highway maintenance crews. Always ask for permission before placing a directional sign on private property.

Consider purchasing a brochure box for the front yard. Put promotional flyers in it for prospective buyers to pick up during times you might not be available. Make sure the information includes your phone number.

Notify Nearby Neighbors

Visit your county courthouse and study local tax maps to find the names and addresses of nearby neighbors, branching out as far as you feel is practical. Send each one a letter or postcard with details about the property, because they might have friends or family who would like to live in the neighborhood. If you're looking for more real estate, mention it, because you might find someone who wants to sell. Address your postcards and envelopes by hand, rather than using printed labels. Recipients are more likely to open and look at a personalized note than what appears to be a mass-produced piece of advertising.

QUESTION?

How should I determine the price of my property?
You can use the same techniques to price the refurbished property that you used to evaluate it when you bought it. Refer back to Chapter 7 for tips that will help you determine value.

Brainstorm Advertising Possibilities

Have you researched your local newspapers and other potential sources of advertising? Look into using some of the following sources:

- Classified ads in your regular local newspaper
- Classified ads in specialty ad papers (if they exist)
- Text advertising on your cable company's local information channel
- Online ads for local newspapers
- Printed magazines that specialize in FSBO listings

It's also a good idea to list your property with an online FSBO search engine. Study each site carefully to determine which one offers the best marketing package. Search for listings in your area to see how owners are promoting their properties. Some FSBO Web sites offer signs at reduced rates and can help connect you with other services you'll need during the transaction; *www.forsalebyowner.com* and *www.owners.com* are two good options.

Writing Your Ads

There's no magic formula for writing ads about your properties. Successful advertising is sometimes a matter of trial and error as you determine what works best in your market. There are many tips that will help you get started, but tweak the techniques as needed to get the best results with your target audience.

Classified ads usually produce excellent results for home-sellers. Read as many ads as possible to see which ones stand out the most. Are certain features mentioned repeatedly, such as views, quiet street, a specific school district, or one-level living? If agents repeatedly talk up a feature, you know it's something buyers are looking for. If your property falls into a popular category, make use of it.

Don't give away too much information. Tease buyers a little, giving them enough details to ask for a showing, but not so many that they feel they already know everything about the property. Short, targeted statements are more likely to be read than a long description, and short and sweet is especially true with Internet advertising, where readers always seem to be in a hurry.

Use bold text at the beginning of your ad or buy a classified display ad and start it with a white text header on a black background. Don't forget to include your contact information.

ALERT!

When you get ready to write your ads, remember the fair housing laws discussed in Chapter 16. The golden rule is to talk about the property, not about the people you envision living there.

Include Interior and Exterior Photos

Photograph the property inside and out. Photos used in flyers or online must capture a buyer's attention from the first glance, so choose the best time of day to record the property from different angles. For example, don't photograph the front of the house if the sun is behind it and glaring into your lens unless you can manipulate the settings to compensate for backlighting. A digital camera with both a wide-angle lens and zoom lens is a good choice for many photographic tasks. A wide angle helps you include the entire structure, and a zoom lets you move in for close-ups.

Interior shots can be difficult. They must be well lit but with a minimum of the glare that can be caused by incandescent bulbs and light streaming through windows. Use a powerful flash unit if possible, and experiment to find the best lighting combinations.

Get Your Disclosures Ready

Some FSBO sellers don't realize that they are required to give prospective buyers one or more disclosure statements that describe elements of the property. Disclosure laws vary in each state, so you must be familiar with your local regulations in order to comply. Don't neglect this important step in the sales process, because it could come back to haunt you in the form of a lawsuit after the sale if you neglect to disclose faulty components.

Federal laws require that you provide buyers with lead paint information about any residence built prior to 1978. Hefty fines can be levied for noncompliance. Refer to Chapter 9 for more information about lead paint disclosures.

Call your state real-estate commission to find out which disclosures you are required to give buyers when they make an offer on the property. Staff at your local board of Realtors can give you the phone number for your state's real-estate commission.

FACT

Most real-estate commissions have a Web site where you can find disclosure forms to print out or download to your computer. You'll find a links at *www.homebuying.about.com/od/licenselaw/index.htm.*

There might be instances in which you can avoid filling out disclosures about the condition of the property. Some states do not require disclosure from sellers who have never lived in the residence. Ask your real-estate commission about exceptions that apply in your area.

Special disclosures are required for many areas, such as flood zones and regions at risk to frequent earthquakes. The real-estate commission can tell you which disclosures you are required to provide potential buyers. You can learn more about property disclosures in Chapter 8.

Showing the Property

You've made repairs and thoroughly cleaned the property. You've spiffed up its curb appeal. Now it's time to show it to prospective buyers. Put your people skills to work, and get ready to deal with all sorts of individuals.

Real-estate agents ask owners to leave the property when it's being shown. You obviously cannot do that, but you'll be more effective if you are aware of the reasons that agents require it.

• **Sellers make buyers uncomfortable.** Buyers usually hesitate to open cabinet and closet doors or look into other closed areas when a seller is present. Invite them to do that, or do it for them.
• **Sellers tend to hover.** They want to stay right with buyers so that they can answer every question. Unfortunately, this doesn't give buyers the freedom to explore the property.
• **Sellers chit-chat too much.** It's good to get a feel for who the buyers are and why they are interested in the property, but give them some space to look around without constant conversation.

Give your buyers some space—and that includes a bit of privacy to compare notes if they are couples.

Try to show the property when it's convenient for your buyers, but don't let them intrude into your life *too* much. You can be accommodating without being pushed around. You have a schedule, too.

Be courteous. Answer the buyers' questions openly and honestly, because buyers know when you are trying to avoid the facts. Have packets of information ready to offer as handouts. Brochures and flyers should include at least a few photos of the property and some basic information about it. You can add items such as required disclosures, copies of surveys or tax maps if available, and any other information you would like to convey.

You've already read about negotiations and contracts in Chapter 10. Those same techniques will help you when it's time to sell. Refer back to other chapters for details about all aspects of your real-estate transaction.

Hold an Open House

Real-estate agents know that an open house rarely sells the house on display, but it's a great way to get buyer and seller leads. Many of the people who show up at open houses are curious neighbors and home-sellers who want to see how the property compares with theirs.

If you have several properties for sale, holding open-house showings is a worthwhile investment of your time. Prepare handouts about everything you have for sale, and show them to prospective buyers. Get names and phone numbers from everyone who attends so that you can follow up to show them your other properties.

Even if you only have one property for sale, it's not a bad idea to hold an open house. Just don't be too disappointed if it doesn't result in an offer.

Chapter 20

Selling with a Real-Estate Agent

You might not have time to market your resales—or maybe you simply don't like to deal directly with buyers. Don't let the thought of paying a commission stop you from working with a real-estate agency when it suits your needs, because listing doesn't necessarily mean you'll make less of a profit when you sell the property.

Choosing an Agent and Agency

Choosing an agent to sell your property requires a different approach than the one you used to find someone to help you buy. Nevertheless, it's ideal if the same person can help you with both jobs, because developing a business relationship with an excellent agent can help you in many ways.

First, your listing agent must be a *full-time* real-estate agent. If buyers and other agents have questions about the property, they want the answers now, not when the listing agent can manage to get away from his full-time job. Successful listing agents are not part-timers.

ALERT!

Agents don't want you to know they work part-time—they know it's a negative. Ask the agent directly how many hours a week they spend working real estate and if they have any other jobs. If the agent sidesteps your response, it might be a good idea to move on. It's not a good idea to begin a business relationship with someone who is evasive.

Does the agent have a professional appearance and manner? The agent you choose is a reflection of your property. An unprofessional appearance and attitude is a buyer turnoff. How long has the agent been involved with real-estate sales? It's a valid question, but don't get too hung up on it. Hard-working new agents can be as effective as established agents, especially if they are part of an aggressive office.

Does the agent belong to all area multiple listing services? The more places your listing shows up, the better coverage it gets. Your agent's first choice will be to sell the property himself, but promoting it to every agent within reach must be done from the very first day. Think of it like this. A single agent might be working with twenty qualified buyers at any given time, but your property won't be suitable to all—if any—of those buyers. Listing the property in a multiple listing service brings in every member agent, drastically increasing the buyer pool.

There are many other questions you should ask an agent during an interview, including the following:

- How many of your recent listings have sold during their contract period? How many listings expired without a sale?
- Do you have special real-estate training that goes above and beyond what's required to be licensed?
- What type of advertising do you have in mind for the property?
- Will you hold an open house for other agents or for the public?
- Will you prepare marketing materials to leave in the house for agents and buyers to pick up?
- Will you send flyers or postcards to agents within the MLS? Can you show me examples of previous marketing materials?
- Which components of my property do you feel are the best features to promote?
- How often will you call me with showing reports and feedback?

Ask as many questions as possible that cannot be answered with a "yes" or "no" response. That type of open-ended question forces the agent to talk about her plans for your property, and many of the responses will no doubt trigger more questions from you.

Always ask an agent for referrals from satisfied sellers. If the agent cannot provide them, something is wrong. Ask your friends if they can recommend a good selling agent. If they've had any type of real-estate sales experience, they won't just mention the good agents—they'll give you feedback for agents they do *not* recommend.

The Marketing Plan

The agent must be able to show you a reasonable marketing plan. Does the agent or firm have a good Internet presence? Will the agent do a virtual tour of your property to allow online buyers the opportunity to take an online walk-through? How does the agency stack up against other agencies that are advertising on a local level? You should have a good feel for the answers to all of those questions based on the agent search you did when you bought the property.

After you choose an agent, monitor the plan carefully to make sure that promises turn into actions. If the plan isn't implemented, ask the agent to make corrections. If no corrections are made, ask to be released from the contract. Remember that the broker in charge is your agent too, and he should be notified if the listing agent does not follow through on promises.

Open Houses

Most open houses held for buyers do not sell the house being shown. A better type of open house is one held for real-estate agents— the people who are in control of showing your property to buyers. At the very least, your agent should have a showing for all other agents within his office, but holding a second open house for all agents within the MLS is also highly recommended. They won't all attend, but everyone who does will tend to remember your property when a suitable buyer comes around.

Ask as many questions as you need to determine which agent is best for your needs, but keep in mind that final agent selection will require some gut instinct on your part. Personalities come into play, so you'll no doubt choose an agent based in part on the knowledge that you can get along with that agent during the listing period. There are plenty of good agents out there. Don't choose someone who you cannot stand dealing with, because there's surely someone who can offer good services *and* a good working relationship.

Many agencies will negotiate the duration of a listing agreement. If there's a reason why you would like to change the suggested timeframe, discuss it with your agent before signing. Chances are good that the agency will comply with your request.

Types of Listing Contracts

Agents use three basic types of listing agreements, and each one comes with a different set of pros and cons. Real-estate agencies might only offer you one choice when you decide to list, but if you understand the variations, you can negotiate for an alternate agreement when it seems more appropriate for the property you are selling.

Exclusive Right-to-Sell Agreement

This is the type of contract that nearly every agency offers its sellers. The agreement states that the agency will receive a commission no matter who buys the property. It's up to the agency to actively market the property and work to get a sales contract to the closing table. In a multiple listing situation, the listing agency shares its commission with another member agency that produces a buyer.

Exclusive Agency Agreement

This agreement is similar because it gives a specific real-estate agency the right to sell the property. If another agency has a buyer, it must come through the listing agency for its share of the commission. This listing differs from an exclusive right-to-sell because it allows the seller to sell the property without paying a commission if he finds a buyer who has not been introduced to the property by the agency.

Open Listing Agreement

A seller can sign this type of agreement with multiple agencies. No individual agency has an exclusive on selling the property, and the seller can sell it himself without paying a commission to anyone. The agreement says that the seller will pay an agency a specified commission at closing if they find a buyer.

QUESTION?

Why do some properties for sale have advertising signs from many agencies in their yards?
They're probably open listings, and each sign represents one of the agencies that has a contract with the seller. You can call any of those agencies—or the seller—for information about the property.

Which Listing Agreement Is Best?

Agencies prefer to use an exclusive right-to-sell agreement because it protects their interests. Good real-estate agencies spend a great deal of time and money to market each of their listed properties. It isn't worthwhile for them to sign an exclusive agency agreement—and then move forward with their regular marketing plan—if you retain the right to sell the property without paying a commission.

Many agencies will sign open listings, but that's often the end of their true involvement with the property. If a buyer wants to see it, they'll comply, but they certainly won't spend dollars to promote a property that's listed with multiple agencies.

Getting Out of the Listing Agreement

Some agencies provide sellers with a written promise that says you can cancel the contract if they do not follow through on their marketing plan. If they do not offer such a promise, ask for it. This addition to your contract should outline the actions or omissions that would allow you to cancel the contract. It should be signed by you, the agent, and the agency's broker in charge.

Filling Out the Listing Contract

Most agencies use preprinted listing contracts that are part of forms created by software packages. Preprinted forms are usually developed by attorneys working under contract for the company that sells the software to real-estate agencies. They are based on the laws for the state they are used in, and they might be endorsed or approved by real-estate licensing commissions and agent trade associations.

The forms are a fill-in-the-blanks type of contract covering the most common topics that must be negotiated between a seller and an agency. The forms should include at least one area where special provisions can be inserted—topics that might not be common but are important to your specific listing agreement.

Your listing contract should include the length of time it will remain in force, with specific beginning and ending dates. Automatic extensions are illegal in some states, and they should *always* be avoided. There's no way that you know going into a relationship that the agent will remain your agent of choice after six months of unsuccessful marketing.

Most agencies have an office policy that concerns the duration of listing agreements. A three-month listing is normal in some areas, but in others you'll find that listings for six months or even a year are not out of line. What's the average time it takes to sell and close a property similar to the one you are selling? Knowing the answer to that questions will help you understand why an agency might ask for a specific length of time to market your property.

The agency's commission rate should be stated on the listing. You might be asked to initial a paragraph that gives the agency your permission to share a portion of the total commission with another agency if that agency produces a buyer. Commissions are sometimes negotiable, but you'll have to decide if it's worth a possible reduction in services to pay a lesser commission.

Another important item that must be entered is the listing price, the price you hope to receive for the property. The contract will probably say that you agree to pay a commission based on the price the property sells for, not the listing price, with the wording written to ensure that both parties are protected—you get an acceptable price, the agency is paid a commission based on that amount.

FACT

Buyers like to feel they are getting a deal. Unless your real-estate market is very competitive, it isn't likely you will have buyers lined up to offer you full price for the property. The list price should always contain some *wiggle* room—a little extra that allows you to negotiate with a buyer.

You'll be asked to give the agency permission to advertise the property and permission to include it in any multiple listing service the agency belongs to. There will probably be a place for you to say it's okay for your agency to place a "For Sale" sign in the yard and a lockbox on the front door. Your agent will explain any other permissions you are asked to give.

Many other important topics must be outlined in the listing agreement, including these:

- The property address and a short legal description that makes it clear which property is for sale
- The names of all owners and a signature from each
- A list of items that will—or will not—convey with the property
- Special showing instructions, such as pet warnings or a requirement for advance notice to show
- Details about owner financing, if you plan to offer it
- Details about the types of financing that are acceptable to the seller. For instance, will you accept a buyer looking for a VA loan?

The contract should cover every aspect of your agreement with the listing agency.

If You Have a Potential Buyer Before You List

Sometimes sellers have a friend or relative who has expressed an interest in buying the property but who cannot move forward for some reason. The seller needs to get the property listed but doesn't want to pay the agency a commission if the interested person decides to buy at a later time.

If that happens to you, ask the agency to exclude the buyer from your listing contract by inserting wording that states you can sell to that specific person without paying a commission. It isn't realistic to expect the agency to exclude the buyer for the entire length of the contract—that would be similar to taking an open listing. What's more likely is that the agency will agree to exclude the potential buyer for up to thirty days or so to give him time to decide whether or not he can buy the property.

Don't forget that most state laws require that you fill out and sign a property disclosure that gives potential buyers details about the structure and its components. Your state or local laws might require that you make additional disclosures. Disclosures are explained in Chapter 8.

Determine the Listing Price

You learned about comparative market analysis and other methods of real-estate valuation in Chapter 7, but now you have to approach pricing from a seller's standpoint. You'll have an agent to help you make comparisons—pay attention to the agent's recommendations. That doesn't mean you let the agent dictate the price, but do listen to the reasons given for pricing strategies. There are always unique properties that will sell for more than market value, but that scenario is not the norm. Your property is worth what it's worth—period. Pricing it too high results in fewer showings, especially after word gets around the agent community that it's overpriced. Why would a buyer pay you more for the property than it's worth when she can get more features in a home that's realistically priced? It rarely happens.

Even if you do find a buyer at the inflated price, the property will probably have to appraise for at least the sales amount. Banks require it, and cash buyers typically insert an addendum in their offer that states the property must appraise for at least the amount they are paying for it. You'll have to negotiate downwards at that point to make the sale, so don't waste your time marketing the property at a seriously inflated price.

Buyers often submit extremely low offers for overpriced properties. The mindset seems to be that if the seller is so clueless about pricing, it's okay to make an offer that goes in the other direction, as a sort of "So there!" response. Be realistic, and price the home right to begin with. It will sell in a shorter amount of time, and your cash flow will flourish, allowing you to move on to the next project.

ALERT!

Some sellers like to negotiate, so they prefer to keep the price way up there to allow for that. Don't! It just doesn't work. When buyers and their agents start comparing prices to features, the MLS sheet for your property will go in the trash can. Don't try to compete with properties that have a higher market value—yours will come up short by comparison.

How Much Do You Really Need?

You probably planned a target sales price when you purchased the property, but now that it's time to sell, you should evaluate the situation again to determine the least amount you would accept from a buyer. Use a software program or a plain sheet of paper to list the expenses related to your investment and to closing a sale.

1. Existing mortgages
2. Commission expense
3. Projected fees for attorneys, title work, excise tax, recording, and other seller expenses specific to your area
4. Taxes and assessments, property association dues, and other fees associated with your ownership for the year

Total your projected expenses. How does the market value of the property compare to your costs of selling it? If it's not as much of a profit as you'd like, are there ways to increase market value without spending a great deal of time and money? Ask each agent you interview that question to see if they have recommendations.

Your Duties to Your Agent

Yes, sellers have duties too. A successful real-estate transaction takes cooperation between the agent and the seller. There are many things you can do to help—and things you can do that hinder the sale of the property. Once you understand how important your actions are, it's not difficult to understand why agents expect certain commitments from you.

One good way to slow down the number of times your property is shown is to require that your selling agent be present for all showings. Why? Agents who want to show your property don't have time to coordinate a showing at a time when your own agent can be present, and they often don't like another agent hanging around when they are trying to interact with their buyers.

Is there truly a reason why your agent must be present? If you think only your own agent can point out special features, think again. It isn't that difficult. Your agent can leave brochures at the property that describe features in detail. Your agent will talk up every important feature in the MLS. Your agent can speak personally to every agent who wishes to show the property. In most cases, it is not necessary for a selling agent to be there for showings.

If you are afraid that items will be stolen, put them away. Even you and your own agent can't keep track of multiple buyers at every moment. Small items that are easy to slip into a pocket or purse should always be removed before you start showing the property.

Sometimes sellers want to be present for showings. That's usually not a good idea either. Let the agents deal with their clients without any inter-ference. Your property will book more showings and potential buyers will feel far more comfortable viewing the property if you are absent.

Showing vacant investment properties is somewhat different than showing real estate that's occupied. Vacant properties should be ready to show all the time, day or night, with little advance notice. No one's there to make a mess, but you should still stop by periodically to make sure the place is dust-free and ready for prospective buyers. Keep the lawn mowed, and do a spot check of other areas as often as needed.

Prepare Your Tenants for Showings

If the property you're showing is a rental, your agent will have to coordinate showings with the tenants. That often means allowing a twenty-four-hour advance notice to show. You'll occasionally encounter tenants who are not thrilled that you're selling the property because it leaves their future in doubt. The new owners must honor the current lease, but after its expiration, anything goes.

Tenants who are upset about the prospect of moving sometimes make a property difficult to show. They might stall a showing or insist on being present to "make sure their belongings aren't disturbed." They sometimes make negative statements to prospective buyers and their agents.

Get familiar with your state laws before you list a rented property to make sure you understand your tenant's rights to privacy and your rights as an owner. Talk with your tenants, giving them some notice before you list the property. Answer any questions they might have about the sales process and how it will affect their tenancy. Find out if they might want to buy the property.

Work closely with your agent to make sure the agency is respectful of tenant rights.

Be Honest with Your Agent

You expect honesty from your agent. Understand that the agent requires honesty from you, too. That begins with the property disclosure. If you know a system within the property has a problem, disclose it. If you don't disclose, it will come back to haunt you later. An undisclosed problem that's found during inspection can kill a contract—buyers wonder what else you haven't told them. An undisclosed problem discovered after closing could be serious enough to make the new owners pursue you for damages. It's not worth the damage to your reputation. Be honest, and work through problems from the very beginning.

Can You Offer Extras?

What sets your property apart from others? In a hot market, it might not matter, but in a typical real-estate market, adding an extra bonus can get a buyer's attention. Your agent can help you decide if extra perks are a good idea.

A home warranty can help put buyers at ease, especially for an older house with older appliances. Most home warranties don't have to be paid for until closing, and the price is minimal compared to the benefits you'll receive from offering it. You can choose to cover yourself while the property is under contract and usually for the same fee. Seller coverage differs slightly from the coverage offered to the buyers, so study each policy carefully before you commit to one. You can read more about home warranties in Chapter 8.

You might consider offering money back to the buyers at closing. That's a great method for properties priced in lower ranges, where buyers are sometimes short of cash even though they have excellent credit to obtain a loan.

In some areas, sellers offer a bonus to the selling real-estate agent. That method seems to work best for properties with higher market values, where buyers don't need as many incentives to purchase.

Are you willing to owner finance all or a portion of the property? How about a lease option agreement? Both of those methods can attract buyers, but be sure to discuss your plans with an experienced real-estate attorney before proceeding. Get all of the pros and cons, and let the attorney review your paperwork before you sign a listing agreement or sales contract.

Brainstorm with your agent to determine if you can offer any extras to attract more of the buying pool to your property.

When the Offer Comes In

Not having a personal attachment to the property can help you when offers come in, especially if they are low. Your agent is there to negotiate for you, so at least you don't have to worry about dealing directly with tactless buyers. Vent to your agent if necessary, but keep cool. Think back—have you ever submitted a low offer to a seller? Did you mean it as an insult? Probably not. You just wanted to get the best deal possible. Being in the seller's shoes gives you a better understanding of how a low offer is received. Some people take it personally, and they don't want to have any further dealings with the buyer. Avoid that type of reaction. Work with your agent to make a reasonable counter offer back to the buyer.

FACT

Offers sometimes go back and forth many times, with each party changing offer components before sending it back to the other for consideration. You'll hear the back-and-forth exchange called a *counteroffer,* or simply a *counter*.

Your counteroffer will probably involve more than just the price of the property. There are many other contract issues that are every bit as important to resolve.

- Is the buyer preapproved by a lender? If so, you want to see a copy of the preapproval letter before you sign the contract.
- Does the buyer have to sell a house before closing on yours? The contract should include a kick-out clause, an agreement that allows you to ask the buyer to either speed up the closing process or back out if another buyer is found.
- What about the other contingencies—are they reasonable? That includes planned inspections, the type of financing the buyer is looking for, and other issues.

The contract you are offered contains a full set of complex issues that must be considered before you agree to it. Most buyers don't expect you to agree to every one of their demands, so come up with a realistic counter to present to their agent. The offer might go back and forth several times before all parties are satisfied, and there will be many times that you cannot come to an agreement at all.

If too many negotiations end without a contract, you must ask yourself why. Is the same reason over and over? Perhaps the pricing is too high? How about repair issues—are there some aspects of the property that seem to bother every potential buyer? If you see a trend, take steps to correct the problem so that the next offer has a better chance of making it. When you do get a contract, refer back to Chapter 10 to help you get it to the closing table.

Every chapter of this book is as important to you as a seller as it was to you as a buyer. You must have a thorough understanding of both sides of a real-estate transaction in order to make the most of your investment career. Go back and review those chapters now, looking at them from a seller's standpoint. That exercise will help you remember what it was like to be a buyer, an important feeling that can make the negotiating process a little easier to get through.

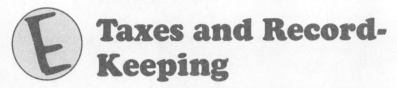

Chapter 21

Taxes and Record-Keeping

Investors must keep thorough records of the income and expenses associated with their investment properties. Good records make it easier to prepare reports when it's time to submit returns to the Internal Revenue Service, and they also help you monitor trends in order to develop a plan to reduce ongoing expenses. An accountant is your best source of information about methods for accurate record-keeping and the types of expenses you can expect to deduct from your income taxes.

Keep Track of Your Expenses

Keep records of every penny you spend on an investment property, entering the dollar amount and its purpose in a handwritten ledger or software accounting program. Retain your receipts for at least the number of years recommended by the Internal Revenue Service, but hold on to your written records for as long as possible so that you can refer back to them whenever you must answer a question about a property.

Typical expenses for an investment property might include the following:

- Repair and maintenance
- Property taxes
- Mortgage interest
- Utility service and garbage pickup fees
- Hazard insurance
- Fees charged by attorneys or property management personnel
- Advertising costs
- Depreciation

If you have more than one investment property, make sure you keep separate income and expense records for each one. Try to make your records as thorough as possible. When you make a payment, write the check number on the receipt, then do the reverse, listing the invoice number or other identifying information for the bill on the face of the check.

If the receipt isn't detailed, make it more complete by jotting down specifics on a piece of paper and attaching the note to the receipt. For example, a small home improvement store might give you a receipt that simply says "hardware." Make a note that the sale was for a towel rack or a toilet seat—whatever you actually purchased, because in six months you might not remember exactly what the receipt was for.

Capital Improvements

Some items are considered capital improvements rather than expenses, and these are treated differently on your tax return. Capital improvements are items that increase the value of the structure, and they are handled differently than expenses in a tax return.

If you replace the gravel in a driveway, it's an expense. If you turn the same gravel driveway into a paved drive, it might be classified as a capital improvement. Replacing a broken window is an expense, but updating all of the windows in a house to energy-efficient versions is probably a capital improvement. Capital improvements raise the tax basis of the structure—the total amount of your investment you can claim.

Depreciation Basics

You are probably familiar with depreciation (loss of value over time) from filing past tax returns. Depreciation is used to claim an expense for an item over a number of years, rather than all at once. The number of years used depends on the type of item involved. Real-estate agents and other businesspeople typically use depreciation methods to claim allowable expenses for automobiles, computer equipment, cameras, and other items required to perform their jobs.

Each type of equipment depreciates at a different rate. Some items are considered to have a useful life of five years. That means that one-fifth of the item's value is allowed as an expense during a calendar year. If the item is purchased mid year, the amount you can claim as an expense is based on the months and days it was owned, not the entire year.

Real estate can be depreciated too—not the land, but improvements to the land. The IRS has set a time of 27.5 years as the useful life for structures, so each year you are allowed a depreciation deduction of $1/27.5$ of a structure's value.

Depreciation is a paperwork figure only, and it's often enough to make an income-producing property appear to be losing money, even though its cash flow exceeds other annual expenses. Your real estate probably isn't losing value at the depreciated rate—it's more likely increasing in value, but in time, the structure will indeed need significant work or it will eventually fall down. Depreciation allowances help offset those costs.

What's the Basis?

The tax basis of some items are often their original cost, but real estate is one type of property where the tax basis changes over time. Basis is a changing amount that indicates how much an owner has invested in a property. It affects the amount of tax you must pay when you sell the real estate.

The original tax basis equals the cost of the property plus the closing costs to acquire it. Capital improvements are one item that increase the original tax basis, but the amount of depreciation you take each year decreases it. The ongoing figure after all additions and subtractions is called the adjusted tax basis.

FACT

The adjusted tax basis is important, because when you sell the property, your proceeds are subtracted from the basis to calculate your profits, called gains, and that's the amount you must pay taxes on. Higher gains mean higher taxes.

A Few Words About Taxes

The amount of capital gains tax you must pay depends on several factors, including how long you owned the property and if it has been fully depreciated. The sale of a personal residence might be exempt if you have lived in it for two out of the past five years. Even your vacation home may be exempt if you meet certain occupancy requirements.

The two-year rule can be taken over and over, and is an excellent tax tool for investors who buy fixer-uppers, live in them while they are refurbished, then sell. The taxes you save will add up nicely, allowing you to acquire more desirable properties—or to depend less on financing dollars.

The IRS considers income from real-estate investments to be passive income, while salaries, commissions, and compensation for other services are classified as active income. The reasons are best explained by an accountant, but the important fact about the difference is the way the two categories are treated on a tax return: passive losses cannot be deducted from active income.

The tax laws were created to keep large investors from using real-estate investments as tax shelters, but smaller investors get a break. If you meet certain qualifications, the IRS allows you a $25,000 allowance for passive loss write-offs against your active income.

If your gross adjusted income is less than $100,000, you qualify for the entire allowance. If your income falls between $100,000 and $150,000, you lose fifty cents of the allowance for every dollar your income exceeds $100,000.

The IRS requires that you actively participate in the management of the property. If you handle all management issues yourself, then it's a given that you are actively participating. If you hire a management firm, you probably don't qualify. A tax professional can help you determine your status and, if you do not qualify, can point out changes that might help you next year.

Other Ways to Reduce or Eliminate Taxes

There are several tax credit program and other methods you can use to help you lower or avoid capital gains and other taxes, described here.

Federal Historic Designations
If your property has been designated a historic building, you might be entitled to a federal investment tax credit. You must follow the guidelines carefully in order to receive the deduction, so consult with experts before attempting renovations.

Special Property Tax Deductions
Some areas offer property tax deductions for elderly homeowners, veterans, and the disabled. Special deductions on farm taxes might also be available.

Enterprise Zones

An area that's economically challenged might be designated as an enterprise zone, offering tax benefits for purchasing equipment and hiring employees.

Empowerment Zones

HUD allows some repair expenses for some areas to be written off all at once, rather than requiring the property owner to use depreciation methods. The goal of this program is to encourage investors to invest and refurbish residences in inner-city neighborhoods.

Tax-Deferred Exchanges

The 1031 exchange is an IRS tool that allows investors to defer payment of capital gains tax if they swap one property for another. This method is described in Chapter 17.

Owner Financing

Receiving money for a sale over a long period of time, rather than taking a lump-sum payment, reduces the amount of tax you must pay in any given year.

Tax laws are ever-changing, and a tax professional is one of your best sources of information for short- and long-term planning for your investment properties.

Finding an Accountant

An accountant can help you make the most of your real-estate acquisitions and sales by offering advice to help you understand how your business decisions affect your income and your tax obligations. The accountant you select must be someone who can do more than prepare your tax returns. Instead, he should be a person you can rely on to guide you through the process of structuring and operating your business in a manner that helps you retain as much of your profit as possible.

The best way to find an accountant is to ask for referrals from satisfied clients. Your friends, banker, financial planner, insurance agent, and real-estate agent might be able to suggest an accountant who they feel provides a quality service. If that doesn't work, gather names from your local telephone book.

Call the accountants on your list, and ask how long have they been in business. Do they have experience in helping clients plan and manage their real-estate investments? What type of educational background do they have? Make an appointment to meet in person with each firm you feel comfortable with after the initial phone call.

At the interview, talk with the accountant about their services. Will you work with the person you speak with during the interview, or will your account be assigned to another accountant? How easy is it to get an appointment—are they typically backed up for a month at a time, or can you anticipate a quicker appointment when you need help? What's the firm's fee structure, and how does it bill clients—after each appointment or service, or monthly? Will you be billed for phone calls or e-mails answered by your accountant? Ask any questions necessary to assure you that the firm can help with your specific needs.

Expertise is important, but it is not the only quality to consider when choosing an accountant. You must find someone you feel comfortable working with, especially if you are a beginning investor who will have many questions about your new business. Find someone who listens carefully to your questions and answers them using everyday language that you understand. Your accountant will play an important part in the success of your real-estate business, so take some time to find someone whom you trust and can depend on.

Glossary of Terms

1031 Exchange:
An Internal Revenue Service–endorsed transaction that allows a person to sell investment property and replace it with another property while deferring payment of capital gains taxes. IRS rules must be followed carefully to achieve an allowed transaction.

acceleration clause:
A clause in most home-loan contracts that allows the lender to demand full payment of your outstanding loan balance if you default on the loan or if you transfer title to another individual without lender approval.

adjustable-rate mortgage:
A loan with an interest rate that can go up or down. Rates are usually tied to an economic index.

amortized loan:
A loan where the periodic payments include both principal and interest.

appraisal:
In real estate, a report that estimates the value of a property or the inspection process that takes place before the report is compiled.

balloon mortgage:
A loan that requires the full remaining principal balance to be paid at a specific time.

biweekly mortgage payment:
A repayment plan in which you make a half payment every two weeks rather than a full payment each month and resulting in thirteen payments per year instead of twelve. Biweekly payments reduce the total interest paid and the time it takes to pay a mortgage.

buyer's agent:
A real-estate agent who has signed a contract to work for a buyer. The agent's loyalty and fiduciary responsibilities are to the buyer.

comparative market analysis:
Also called a CMA, an opinion of a property's value based on past sales of similar properties. CMAs are often calculated by real-estate agents prior to listing a property for sale.

condominium:
Also called condo. A unit in a multiunit building where the owner holds full title to the unit and its air space, but not the land beneath it or above it. The owner has an interest in common elements of the development that are held jointly with other unit owners.

contingency:
A contact provision that requires a specific event to occur before the contract becomes binding.

contract for deed:
A type of seller financing in which the seller retains title to a property until the buyer has made payment in full.

cooperative:
A unit in a multiunit building where each owner occupant owns stock in a corporation rather than possessing a deed to real property.

deed of trust:
A security instrument that's used to transfer partial title to a trustee until an associated lien is paid in full. The trustee is a neutral party who has the power to foreclose if loan payments are not made as stated in the contract.

deed restrictions:
Limits placed on the use of a property. Recorded on the deed.

discount points:
Fees paid to a lender to lower the interest rate. The cost of one point equals 1 percent of the loan amount.

dual agent:
A real-estate buyer's agent who is working with a client who views or buys a listing held by the agent's firm.

due-on-sale clause:
A clause in a mortgage contract that allows the lender to demand the loan be paid in full if the borrower transfers ownership of the property that secures the lien.

easement:
The right to use another party's land for a specific purpose.

encroachment:
A building, fence, or other structure that touches or crosses the boundary line of an adjacent property.

equity:
An owner's financial interests in a piece of real estate, calculated by subtracting the dollar amount of liens against the property from its fair market value.

escrow:
Valuable items that are held by a neutral third party until provisions of the contract controlling them are met. In real estate, it often applies to your earnest money, also called a good faith deposit.

escrow account:
An account that holds funds for another for a specific purpose. For instance, a lender collects monthly tax and insurance payments, placing them in an escrow fund and paying the borrower's related bills when they are due.

exclusive agency listing agreement:
A real-estate listing contract in which the seller gives a specific real-estate agency the right to sell the property, but retains the right to sell it herself without paying a commission if she finds a buyer who has not be introduced to the property by the agency.

exclusive right-to-sell listing agreement:
A real-estate listing contract in which the seller agrees to pay the agency a commission no matter who finds a buyer for the listed property.

facilitator:
A term used to describe real-estate agents who do not have a legal obligation to represent either a buyer or seller. The agent's job is to act as a neutral assistant to help the parties close a transaction. Not applicable to every state.

Fair Housing Act:
A federal law that prohibits housing discrimination on the basis of race, color, religion, sex, national origin, familial status, or disability.

fair market value:
The highest price a property would sell for in a reasonable length of time, provided both buyer and seller are knowledgeable and not under duress to buy or sell.

Fannie Mae:
Formerly a government agency called Federal National Mortgage Association, this corporation purchases mortgage loans on the secondary market, which helps keep funds available for real-estate loans.

first mortgage:
The mortgage-related lien that will be paid first when a piece of real-estate is sold or foreclosed.

fixed-rate loan:
A loan where the interest rates stays the same during the entire length of the loan.

foreclosure:
A legal procedure in which property used to secure a debt is recovered and sold by the lienholder in order to satisfy the debt. Also used to describe a home that's been through the foreclosure process.

Freddie Mac:
Formerly a government agency designed to provide secondary market services for low-income loans. Freddie Mac is now involved with all types of loans on the secondary market.

Ginnie Mae:
Ginnie Mae was created when Fannie Mae became a private corporation. It provides a secondary market for low-income and other special-assistance loans, and guarantees principal and interest payments to investors who buy mortgage-backed securities.

grantor:
The person who transfers real-estate title or to a grantee.

grantee:
The person who receives real estate from a grantor.

gross rent multiplier (GRM):
A method used to estimate value for income-producing properties by looking at the amount of rents collected versus sales prices of similar properties.

hazard insurance:
A policy that protects a property owner against loss from listed hazards such as fire, wind damage, and vandalism.

homeowner's association:
An association that manages the common areas of a condominium, planned unit development, or townhouse complex; an association made up and managed by owners who live in a specific housing development, overseeing issues such as road upkeep, deed restriction compliance, and other issues important to all owners.

HUD:
The Department of Housing and Urban Development, a government agency that oversees fair housing issues and numerous other mortgage and rent-related programs.

HUD-1 settlement statement:
The standard settlement statement that must be used for federally related mortgage loans.

HUD code:
A uniform code developed and overseen by the federal government that stipulates building codes that must be used for manufactured housing sold in the United States.

income capitalization:
A type of appraisal that uses income and expenses to estimate the value of an income-producing property.

lease:
A written contract between a property owner and a tenant that outlines the time period, required payments, and all other conditions under which the tenant has legal possession of the real estate.

lease option:
A type of lease in which a portion of each month's payment includes an additional amount that is applied toward a down payment if the tenant chooses to purchase the property during the specified time period.

lessee:
The tenant named in a lease document.

lessor:
The landlord named in a lease document.

lien:
A document granting a creditor the right to sell property that secures a debt if the borrower defaults on the loan.

life estate:
An interest in real estate that is limited in duration to the lifetime of the person designated on the deed.

manufactured home:
Housing that is built to conform to a federal code and transported to a building site on its own wheels.

material fact:
Factual details about a property, such as the age of its roof and details about the age and condition of its components.

mitigation:
An action that's taken to permanently eliminate or reduce a potential hazard; commonly heard in the home-buying community to describe the installation of radon reduction systems.

modular home:
Housing that is built in modules at a factory to conform to building codes at its ultimate designation. Transported to the building site on flatbed trucks and assembled.

mortgage:
A document that pledges real estate as security for a debt.

mortgage broker:
A businessperson who earns a fee by bringing together a borrower and a lender. Mortgage brokers typically work as agents for numerous lenders.

open listing:
A type of real-estate listing contract in which the seller agrees to pay a commission to an agency

who finds a buyer for a property, but retains the right to sell the property himself without owing a commission. Unlike exclusive agency listings, open listings can be signed with multiple agencies.

PITI:
The term used to describe the combination of principal, interest, taxes, and insurance due for a loan.

pre-foreclosure:
A property that is on the verge of foreclosure; formal foreclosure may not have taken place, but warnings may have been issued by lenders.

primary mortgage market:
The market in which mortgage loans are originated by banks, savings and loans, and other similar lenders.

private mortgage insurance:
Insurance coverage that most lenders require when making a real-estate loan for which the buyer makes less than a 20-percent down payment,

quitclaim deed:
A deed that allows the grantor to convey whatever interest he or she has in a property without guaranteeing that others have relinquished title.

REIT:
An investment company that owns and operates income-producing real estate and sometimes finances real-estate transactions. REITs sell shares of stock to individual investors.

REO:
Real-estate owned properties are foreclosed

properties that have been acquired by the lender at auction.

RESPA:
Real Estate Settlement Procedures Act is a law that attempts to ensure that buyers are given disclosures and estimates of closing costs by their lenders. It standardizes some of the forms used during real-estate closings.

restrictive covenants:
Restrictions to land use that usually apply to all properties within a specific development.

right-of-way:
A type of easement that conveys the right to pass over a tract of land.

second mortgage:
A mortgage that includes a recorded lien against a property, but in line to be paid after the first mortgage. Second mortgages are usually paid in order by the date they were recorded—first recorded, first paid. Also called a junior mortgage.

secondary mortgage market:
A market where existing mortgages are purchased from originators and resold to investors. The secondary mortgage market was created to keep funds flowing back to originating lenders so that they can continue to make new home loans.

seller's agent:
A real-estate agent whose loyalty and duty is to the seller of a property.

site-built home:
A house built entirely on-site, with no sections preassembled in a factory.

survey, boundary survey:
A measurement of a tract of land that shows its size, its boundaries, and the presence of all buildings associated with it. Surveys are performed by licensed surveyors.

time-share:
A vacation unit that can be owned by many individuals. For a traditional time-share, each owner holds title to the unit for a specific time each year.

title examination:
The process of examining public records associated with a property in order to determine facts about its ownership during a specific period of time.

title insurance:
An insurance policy that insures against loss due to defects in a real-estate title. Excluded losses are explained in each policy.

townhouse:
A unit in a multiunit complex that's normally attached to its neighbors along side walls. Each owner holds title to the unit and the land beneath the unit, and shares ownership of common areas with other owners. Also called a town home.

Monthly Payment Estimator

Y ou can use the following tables to estimate your monthly mortgage payments. All you need to know is the amount borrowed and the length of the mortgage (from five to thirty years). Don't forget that mortgage payments don't include property taxes and hazard insurance.

Interest Rate: 5.00%

Amount Borrowed	Length of Loan (in Years)					
	5	10	15	20	25	30
$50,000	$943.56	$530.33	$395.40	$329.98	$292.30	$268.41
$60,000	$1,132.27	$636.39	$474.48	$395.97	$350.75	$322.09
$70,000	$1,320.99	$742.46	$553.56	$461.97	$409.21	$375.78
$80,000	$1,509.70	$848.52	$632.63	$527.96	$467.67	$429.46
$90,000	$1,698.41	$954.59	$711.71	$593.96	$526.13	$483.14
$100,000	$1,887.12	$1,060.66	$790.79	$659.96	$584.59	$536.82
$110,000	$2,075.84	$1,166.72	$869.87	$725.95	$643.05	$590.50
$120,000	$2,264.55	$1,272.79	$948.95	$791.95	$701.51	$644.19
$130,000	$2,453.26	$1,378.85	$1,028.03	$857.94	$759.97	$697.87
$140,000	$2,641.97	$1,484.92	$1,107.11	$923.94	$818.43	$751.55
$150,000	$2,830.69	$1,590.98	$1,186.19	$989.93	$876.89	$805.23
$160,000	$3,019.40	$1,697.05	$1,265.27	$1,055.93	$935.34	$858.91
$170,000	$3,208.11	$1,803.11	$1,344.35	$1,121.92	$993.80	$912.60
$180,000	$3,396.82	$1,909.18	$1,423.43	$1,187.92	$1,052.26	$966.28
$190,000	$3,585.53	$2,015.24	$1,502.51	$1,253.92	$1,110.72	$1,019.96
$200,000	$3,774.25	$2,121.31	$1,581.59	$1,319.91	$1,169.18	$1,073.64
$210,000	$3,962.96	$2,227.38	$1,660.67	$1,385.91	$1,227.64	$1,127.33
$220,000	$4,151.67	$2,333.44	$1,739.75	$1,451.90	$1,286.10	$1,181.01
$230,000	$4,340.38	$2,439.51	$1,818.83	$1,517.90	$1,344.56	$1,234.69
$240,000	$4,529.10	$2,545.57	$1,897.90	$1,583.89	$1,403.02	$1,288.37
$250,000	$4,717.81	$2,651.64	$1,976.98	$1,649.89	$1,461.48	$1,342.05
$260,000	$4,906.52	$2,757.70	$2,056.06	$1,715.88	$1,519.93	$1,395.74
$270,000	$5,095.23	$2,863.77	$2,135.14	$1,781.88	$1,578.39	$1,449.42
$280,000	$5,283.95	$2,969.83	$2,214.22	$1,847.88	$1,636.85	$1,503.10
$290,000	$5,472.66	$3,075.90	$2,293.30	$1,913.87	$1,695.31	$1,556.78
$300,000	$5,661.37	$3,181.97	$2,372.38	$1,979.87	$1,753.77	$1,610.46
$310,000	$5,850.08	$3,288.03	$2,451.46	$2,045.86	$1,812.23	$1,664.15

Interest Rate: 5.50%

Amount Borrowed	Length of Loan (in Years)					
	5	10	15	20	25	30
$50,000	$955.06	$542.63	$408.54	$343.94	$307.04	$283.89
$60,000	$1,146.07	$651.16	$490.25	$412.73	$368.45	$340.67
$70,000	$1,337.08	$759.68	$571.96	$481.52	$429.86	$397.45
$80,000	$1,528.09	$868.21	$653.67	$550.31	$491.27	$454.23
$90,000	$1,719.10	$976.74	$735.38	$619.10	$552.68	$511.01
$100,000	$1,910.12	$1,085.26	$817.08	$687.89	$614.09	$567.79
$110,000	$2,101.13	$1,193.79	$898.79	$756.68	$675.50	$624.57
$120,000	$2,292.14	$1,302.32	$980.50	$825.46	$736.90	$681.35
$130,000	$2,483.15	$1,410.84	$1,062.21	$894.25	$798.31	$738.13
$140,000	$2,674.16	$1,519.37	$1,143.92	$963.04	$859.72	$794.90
$150,000	$2,865.17	$1,627.89	$1,225.63	$1,031.83	$921.13	$851.68
$160,000	$3,056.19	$1,736.42	$1,307.33	$1,100.62	$982.54	$908.46
$170,000	$3,247.20	$1,844.95	$1,389.04	$1,169.41	$1,043.95	$965.24
$180,000	$3,438.21	$1,953.47	$1,470.75	$1,238.20	$1,105.36	$1,022.02
$190,000	$3,629.22	$2,062.00	$1,552.46	$1,306.99	$1,166.77	$1,078.80
$200,000	$3,820.23	$2,170.53	$1,634.17	$1,375.77	$1,228.17	$1,135.58
$210,000	$4,011.24	$2,279.05	$1,715.88	$1,444.56	$1,289.58	$1,192.36
$220,000	$4,202.26	$2,387.58	$1,797.58	$1,513.35	$1,350.99	$1,249.14
$230,000	$4,393.27	$2,496.10	$1,879.29	$1,582.14	$1,412.40	$1,305.91
$240,000	$4,584.28	$2,604.63	$1,961.00	$1,650.93	$1,473.81	$1,362.69
$250,000	$4,775.29	$2,713.16	$2,042.71	$1,719.72	$1,535.22	$1,419.47
$260,000	$4,966.30	$2,821.68	$2,124.42	$1,788.51	$1,596.63	$1,476.25
$270,000	$5,157.31	$2,930.21	$2,206.13	$1,857.30	$1,658.04	$1,533.03
$280,000	$5,348.33	$3,038.74	$2,287.83	$1,926.08	$1,719.44	$1,589.81
$290,000	$5,539.34	$3,147.26	$2,369.54	$1,994.87	$1,780.85	$1,646.59
$300,000	$5,730.35	$3,255.79	$2,451.25	$2,063.66	$1,842.26	$1,703.37
$310,000	$5,921.36	$3,364.31	$2,532.96	$2,132.45	$1,903.67	$1,760.15

Interest Rate: 6.00%

Amount Borrowed	Length of Loan (in Years)					
	5	10	15	20	25	30
$50,000	$966.64	$555.10	$421.93	$358.22	$322.15	$299.78
$60,000	$1,159.97	$666.12	$506.31	$429.86	$386.58	$359.73
$70,000	$1,353.30	$777.14	$590.70	$501.50	$451.01	$419.69
$80,000	$1,546.62	$888.16	$675.09	$573.14	$515.44	$479.64
$90,000	$1,739.95	$999.18	$759.47	$644.79	$579.87	$539.60
$100,000	$1,933.28	$1,110.21	$843.86	$716.43	$644.30	$599.55
$110,000	$2,126.61	$1,221.23	$928.24	$788.07	$708.73	$659.51
$120,000	$2,319.94	$1,332.25	$1,012.63	$859.72	$773.16	$719.46
$130,000	$2,513.26	$1,443.27	$1,097.01	$931.36	$837.59	$779.42
$140,000	$2,706.59	$1,554.29	$1,181.40	$1,003.00	$902.02	$839.37
$150,000	$2,899.92	$1,665.31	$1,265.79	$1,074.65	$966.45	$899.33
$160,000	$3,093.25	$1,776.33	$1,350.17	$1,146.29	$1,030.88	$959.28
$170,000	$3,286.58	$1,887.35	$1,434.56	$1,217.93	$1,095.31	$1,019.24
$180,000	$3,479.90	$1,998.37	$1,518.94	$1,289.58	$1,159.74	$1,079.19
$190,000	$3,673.23	$2,109.39	$1,603.33	$1,361.22	$1,224.17	$1,139.15
$200,000	$3,866.56	$2,220.41	$1,687.71	$1,432.86	$1,288.60	$1,199.10
$210,000	$4,059.89	$2,331.43	$1,772.10	$1,504.51	$1,353.03	$1,259.06
$220,000	$4,253.22	$2,442.45	$1,856.49	$1,576.15	$1,417.46	$1,319.01
$230,000	$4,446.54	$2,553.47	$1,940.87	$1,647.79	$1,481.89	$1,378.97
$240,000	$4,639.87	$2,664.49	$2,025.26	$1,719.43	$1,546.32	$1,438.92
$250,000	$4,833.20	$2,775.51	$2,109.64	$1,791.08	$1,610.75	$1,498.88
$260,000	$5,026.53	$2,886.53	$2,194.03	$1,862.72	$1,675.18	$1,558.83
$270,000	$5,219.86	$2,997.55	$2,278.41	$1,934.36	$1,739.61	$1,618.79
$280,000	$5,413.18	$3,108.57	$2,362.80	$2,006.01	$1,804.04	$1,678.74
$290,000	$5,606.51	$3,219.59	$2,447.18	$2,077.65	$1,868.47	$1,738.70
$300,000	$5,799.84	$3,330.62	$2,531.57	$2,149.29	$1,932.90	$1,798.65
$310,000	$5,993.17	$3,441.64	$2,615.96	$2,220.94	$1,997.33	$1,858.61

Interest Rate: 6.50%

Amount Borrowed	Length of Loan (in Years)					
	5	10	15	20	25	30
$50,000	$978.31	$567.74	$435.55	$372.79	$337.60	$316.03
$60,000	$1,173.97	$681.29	$522.66	$447.34	$405.12	$379.24
$70,000	$1,369.63	$794.84	$609.78	$521.90	$472.65	$442.45
$80,000	$1,565.29	$908.38	$696.89	$596.46	$540.17	$505.65
$90,000	$1,760.95	$1,021.93	$784.00	$671.02	$607.69	$568.86
$100,000	$1,956.61	$1,135.48	$871.11	$745.57	$675.21	$632.07
$110,000	$2,152.28	$1,249.03	$958.22	$820.13	$742.73	$695.27
$120,000	$2,347.94	$1,362.58	$1,045.33	$894.69	$810.25	$758.48
$130,000	$2,543.60	$1,476.12	$1,132.44	$969.25	$877.77	$821.69
$140,000	$2,739.26	$1,589.67	$1,219.55	$1,043.80	$945.29	$884.90
$150,000	$2,934.92	$1,703.22	$1,306.66	$1,118.36	$1,012.81	$948.10
$160,000	$3,130.58	$1,816.77	$1,393.77	$1,192.92	$1,080.33	$1,011.31
$170,000	$3,326.25	$1,930.32	$1,480.88	$1,267.47	$1,147.85	$1,074.52
$180,000	$3,521.91	$2,043.86	$1,567.99	$1,342.03	$1,215.37	$1,137.72
$190,000	$3,717.57	$2,157.41	$1,655.10	$1,416.59	$1,282.89	$1,200.93
$200,000	$3,913.23	$2,270.96	$1,742.21	$1,491.15	$1,350.41	$1,264.14
$210,000	$4,108.89	$2,384.51	$1,829.33	$1,565.70	$1,417.94	$1,327.34
$220,000	$4,304.55	$2,498.06	$1,916.44	$1,640.26	$1,485.46	$1,390.55
$230,000	$4,500.21	$2,611.60	$2,003.55	$1,714.82	$1,552.98	$1,453.76
$240,000	$4,695.88	$2,725.15	$2,090.66	$1,789.38	$1,620.50	$1,516.96
$250,000	$4,891.54	$2,838.70	$2,177.77	$1,863.93	$1,688.02	$1,580.17
$260,000	$5,087.20	$2,952.25	$2,264.88	$1,938.49	$1,755.54	$1,643.38
$270,000	$5,282.86	$3,065.80	$2,351.99	$2,013.05	$1,823.06	$1,706.58
$280,000	$5,478.52	$3,179.34	$2,439.10	$2,087.60	$1,890.58	$1,769.79
$290,000	$5,674.18	$3,292.89	$2,526.21	$2,162.16	$1,958.10	$1,833.00
$300,000	$5,869.84	$3,406.44	$2,613.32	$2,236.72	$2,025.62	$1,896.20
$310,000	$6,065.51	$3,519.99	$2,700.43	$2,311.28	$2,093.14	$1,959.41

Interest Rate: 7.00%

Amount Borrowed	Length of Loan (in Years)					
	5	10	15	20	25	30
$50,000	$990.06	$580.54	$449.41	$387.65	$353.39	$332.65
$60,000	$1,188.07	$696.65	$539.30	$465.18	$424.07	$399.18
$70,000	$1,386.08	$812.76	$629.18	$542.71	$494.75	$465.71
$80,000	$1,584.10	$928.87	$719.06	$620.24	$565.42	$532.24
$90,000	$1,782.11	$1,044.98	$808.95	$697.77	$636.10	$598.77
$100,000	$1,980.12	$1,161.08	$898.83	$775.30	$706.78	$665.30
$110,000	$2,178.13	$1,277.19	$988.71	$852.83	$777.46	$731.83
$120,000	$2,376.14	$1,393.30	$1,078.59	$930.36	$848.14	$798.36
$130,000	$2,574.16	$1,509.41	$1,168.48	$1,007.89	$918.81	$864.89
$140,000	$2,772.17	$1,625.52	$1,258.36	$1,085.42	$989.49	$931.42
$150,000	$2,970.18	$1,741.63	$1,348.24	$1,162.95	$1,060.17	$997.95
$160,000	$3,168.19	$1,857.74	$1,438.13	$1,240.48	$1,130.85	$1,064.48
$170,000	$3,366.20	$1,973.84	$1,528.01	$1,318.01	$1,201.52	$1,131.01
$180,000	$3,564.22	$2,089.95	$1,617.89	$1,395.54	$1,272.20	$1,197.54
$190,000	$3,762.23	$2,206.06	$1,707.77	$1,473.07	$1,342.88	$1,264.07
$200,000	$3,960.24	$2,322.17	$1,797.66	$1,550.60	$1,413.56	$1,330.60
$210,000	$4,158.25	$2,438.28	$1,887.54	$1,628.13	$1,484.24	$1,397.14
$220,000	$4,356.26	$2,554.39	$1,977.42	$1,705.66	$1,554.91	$1,463.67
$230,000	$4,554.28	$2,670.50	$2,067.31	$1,783.19	$1,625.59	$1,530.20
$240,000	$4,752.29	$2,786.60	$2,157.19	$1,860.72	$1,696.27	$1,596.73
$250,000	$4,950.30	$2,902.71	$2,247.07	$1,938.25	$1,766.95	$1,663.26
$260,000	$5,148.31	$3,018.82	$2,336.95	$2,015.78	$1,837.63	$1,729.79
$270,000	$5,346.32	$3,134.93	$2,426.84	$2,093.31	$1,908.30	$1,796.32
$280,000	$5,544.34	$3,251.04	$2,516.72	$2,170.84	$1,978.98	$1,862.85
$290,000	$5,742.35	$3,367.15	$2,606.60	$2,248.37	$2,049.66	$1,929.38
$300,000	$5,940.36	$3,483.25	$2,696.48	$2,325.90	$2,120.34	$1,995.91
$310,000	$6,138.37	$3,599.36	$2,786.37	$2,403.43	$2,191.02	$2,062.44

Interest Rate: 7.50%

Amount Borrowed	Length of Loan (in Years)					
	5	10	15	20	25	30
$50,000	$1,001.90	$593.51	$463.51	$402.80	$369.50	$349.61
$60,000	$1,202.28	$712.21	$556.21	$483.36	$443.39	$419.53
$70,000	$1,402.66	$830.91	$648.91	$563.92	$517.29	$489.45
$80,000	$1,603.04	$949.61	$741.61	$644.47	$591.19	$559.37
$90,000	$1,803.42	$1,068.32	$834.31	$725.03	$665.09	$629.29
$100,000	$2,003.79	$1,187.02	$927.01	$805.59	$738.99	$699.21
$110,000	$2,204.17	$1,305.72	$1,019.71	$886.15	$812.89	$769.14
$120,000	$2,404.55	$1,424.42	$1,112.41	$966.71	$886.79	$839.06
$130,000	$2,604.93	$1,543.12	$1,205.12	$1,047.27	$960.69	$908.98
$140,000	$2,805.31	$1,661.82	$1,297.82	$1,127.83	$1,034.59	$978.90
$150,000	$3,005.69	$1,780.53	$1,390.52	$1,208.39	$1,108.49	$1,048.82
$160,000	$3,206.07	$1,899.23	$1,483.22	$1,288.95	$1,182.39	$1,118.74
$170,000	$3,406.45	$2,017.93	$1,575.92	$1,369.51	$1,256.29	$1,188.66
$180,000	$3,606.83	$2,136.63	$1,668.62	$1,450.07	$1,330.18	$1,258.59
$190,000	$3,807.21	$2,255.33	$1,761.32	$1,530.63	$1,404.08	$1,328.51
$200,000	$4,007.59	$2,374.04	$1,854.02	$1,611.19	$1,477.98	$1,398.43
$210,000	$4,207.97	$2,492.74	$1,946.73	$1,691.75	$1,551.88	$1,468.35
$220,000	$4,408.35	$2,611.44	$2,039.43	$1,772.31	$1,625.78	$1,538.27
$230,000	$4,608.73	$2,730.14	$2,132.13	$1,852.86	$1,699.68	$1,608.19
$240,000	$4,809.11	$2,848.84	$2,224.83	$1,933.42	$1,773.58	$1,678.11
$250,000	$5,009.49	$2,967.54	$2,317.53	$2,013.98	$1,847.48	$1,748.04
$260,000	$5,209.87	$3,086.25	$2,410.23	$2,094.54	$1,921.38	$1,817.96
$270,000	$5,410.25	$3,204.95	$2,502.93	$2,175.10	$1,995.28	$1,887.88
$280,000	$5,610.63	$3,323.65	$2,595.63	$2,255.66	$2,069.18	$1,957.80
$290,000	$5,811.01	$3,442.35	$2,688.34	$2,336.22	$2,143.07	$2,027.72
$300,000	$6,011.38	$3,561.05	$2,781.04	$2,416.78	$2,216.97	$2,097.64
$310,000	$6,211.76	$3,679.75	$2,873.74	$2,497.34	$2,290.87	$2,167.56

Interest Rate: 8.00%

Amount Borrowed	Length of Loan (in Years)					
	5	10	15	20	25	30
$50,000	$1,013.82	$606.64	$477.83	$418.22	$385.91	$366.88
$60,000	$1,216.58	$727.97	$573.39	$501.86	$463.09	$440.26
$70,000	$1,419.35	$849.29	$668.96	$585.51	$540.27	$513.64
$80,000	$1,622.11	$970.62	$764.52	$669.15	$617.45	$587.01
$90,000	$1,824.88	$1,091.95	$860.09	$752.80	$694.63	$660.39
$100,000	$2,027.64	$1,213.28	$955.65	$836.44	$771.82	$733.76
$110,000	$2,230.40	$1,334.60	$1,051.22	$920.08	$849.00	$807.14
$120,000	$2,433.17	$1,455.93	$1,146.78	$1,003.73	$926.18	$880.52
$130,000	$2,635.93	$1,577.26	$1,242.35	$1,087.37	$1,003.36	$953.89
$140,000	$2,838.70	$1,698.59	$1,337.91	$1,171.02	$1,080.54	$1,027.27
$150,000	$3,041.46	$1,819.91	$1,433.48	$1,254.66	$1,157.72	$1,100.65
$160,000	$3,244.22	$1,941.24	$1,529.04	$1,338.30	$1,234.91	$1,174.02
$170,000	$3,446.99	$2,062.57	$1,624.61	$1,421.95	$1,312.09	$1,247.40
$180,000	$3,649.75	$2,183.90	$1,720.17	$1,505.59	$1,389.27	$1,320.78
$190,000	$3,852.51	$2,305.22	$1,815.74	$1,589.24	$1,466.45	$1,394.15
$200,000	$4,055.28	$2,426.55	$1,911.30	$1,672.88	$1,543.63	$1,467.53
$210,000	$4,258.04	$2,547.88	$2,006.87	$1,756.52	$1,620.81	$1,540.91
$220,000	$4,460.81	$2,669.21	$2,102.43	$1,840.17	$1,698.00	$1,614.28
$230,000	$4,663.57	$2,790.53	$2,198.00	$1,923.81	$1,775.18	$1,687.66
$240,000	$4,866.33	$2,911.86	$2,293.57	$2,007.46	$1,852.36	$1,761.03
$250,000	$5,069.10	$3,033.19	$2,389.13	$2,091.10	$1,929.54	$1,834.41
$260,000	$5,271.86	$3,154.52	$2,484.70	$2,174.74	$2,006.72	$1,907.79
$270,000	$5,474.63	$3,275.85	$2,580.26	$2,258.39	$2,083.90	$1,981.16
$280,000	$5,677.39	$3,397.17	$2,675.83	$2,342.03	$2,161.09	$2,054.54
$290,000	$5,880.15	$3,518.50	$2,771.39	$2,425.68	$2,238.27	$2,127.92
$300,000	$6,082.92	$3,639.83	$2,866.96	$2,509.32	$2,315.45	$2,201.29
$310,000	$6,285.68	$3,761.16	$2,962.52	$2,592.96	$2,392.63	$2,274.67

Interest Rate: 8.50%

Amount Borrowed	Length of Loan (in Years)					
	5	10	15	20	25	30
$50,000	$1,025.83	$619.93	$492.37	$433.91	$402.61	$384.46
$60,000	$1,230.99	$743.91	$590.84	$520.69	$483.14	$461.35
$70,000	$1,436.16	$867.90	$689.32	$607.48	$563.66	$538.24
$80,000	$1,641.32	$991.89	$787.79	$694.26	$644.18	$615.13
$90,000	$1,846.49	$1,115.87	$886.27	$781.04	$724.70	$692.02
$100,000	$2,051.65	$1,239.86	$984.74	$867.82	$805.23	$768.91
$110,000	$2,256.82	$1,363.84	$1,083.21	$954.61	$885.75	$845.80
$120,000	$2,461.98	$1,487.83	$1,181.69	$1,041.39	$966.27	$922.70
$130,000	$2,667.15	$1,611.81	$1,280.16	$1,128.17	$1,046.80	$999.59
$140,000	$2,872.31	$1,735.80	$1,378.64	$1,214.95	$1,127.32	$1,076.48
$150,000	$3,077.48	$1,859.79	$1,477.11	$1,301.73	$1,207.84	$1,153.37
$160,000	$3,282.65	$1,983.77	$1,575.58	$1,388.52	$1,288.36	$1,230.26
$170,000	$3,487.81	$2,107.76	$1,674.06	$1,475.30	$1,368.89	$1,307.15
$180,000	$3,692.98	$2,231.74	$1,772.53	$1,562.08	$1,449.41	$1,384.04
$190,000	$3,898.14	$2,355.73	$1,871.01	$1,648.86	$1,529.93	$1,460.94
$200,000	$4,103.31	$2,479.71	$1,969.48	$1,735.65	$1,610.45	$1,537.83
$210,000	$4,308.47	$2,603.70	$2,067.95	$1,822.43	$1,690.98	$1,614.72
$220,000	$4,513.64	$2,727.69	$2,166.43	$1,909.21	$1,771.50	$1,691.61
$230,000	$4,718.80	$2,851.67	$2,264.90	$1,995.99	$1,852.02	$1,768.50
$240,000	$4,923.97	$2,975.66	$2,363.37	$2,082.78	$1,932.55	$1,845.39
$250,000	$5,129.13	$3,099.64	$2,461.85	$2,169.56	$2,013.07	$1,922.28
$260,000	$5,334.30	$3,223.63	$2,560.32	$2,256.34	$2,093.59	$1,999.18
$270,000	$5,539.46	$3,347.61	$2,658.80	$2,343.12	$2,174.11	$2,076.07
$280,000	$5,744.63	$3,471.60	$2,757.27	$2,429.91	$2,254.64	$2,152.96
$290,000	$5,949.79	$3,595.58	$2,855.74	$2,516.69	$2,335.16	$2,229.85
$300,000	$6,154.96	$3,719.57	$2,954.22	$2,603.47	$2,415.68	$2,306.74
$310,000	$6,360.12	$3,843.56	$3,052.69	$2,690.25	$2,496.20	$2,383.63

Interest Rate: 9.00%

Amount Borrowed	Length of Loan (in Years)					
	5	10	15	20	25	30
$50,000	$1,037.92	$633.38	$507.13	$449.86	$419.60	$402.31
$60,000	$1,245.50	$760.05	$608.56	$539.84	$503.52	$482.77
$70,000	$1,453.08	$886.73	$709.99	$629.81	$587.44	$563.24
$80,000	$1,660.67	$1,013.41	$811.41	$719.78	$671.36	$643.70
$90,000	$1,868.25	$1,140.08	$912.84	$809.75	$755.28	$724.16
$100,000	$2,075.84	$1,266.76	$1,014.27	$899.73	$839.20	$804.62
$110,000	$2,283.42	$1,393.43	$1,115.69	$989.70	$923.12	$885.08
$120,000	$2,491.00	$1,520.11	$1,217.12	$1,079.67	$1,007.04	$965.55
$130,000	$2,698.59	$1,646.79	$1,318.55	$1,169.64	$1,090.96	$1,046.01
$140,000	$2,906.17	$1,773.46	$1,419.97	$1,259.62	$1,174.87	$1,126.47
$150,000	$3,113.75	$1,900.14	$1,521.40	$1,349.59	$1,258.79	$1,206.93
$160,000	$3,321.34	$2,026.81	$1,622.83	$1,439.56	$1,342.71	$1,287.40
$170,000	$3,528.92	$2,153.49	$1,724.25	$1,529.53	$1,426.63	$1,367.86
$180,000	$3,736.50	$2,280.16	$1,825.68	$1,619.51	$1,510.55	$1,448.32
$190,000	$3,944.09	$2,406.84	$1,927.11	$1,709.48	$1,594.47	$1,528.78
$200,000	$4,151.67	$2,533.52	$2,028.53	$1,799.45	$1,678.39	$1,609.25
$210,000	$4,359.25	$2,660.19	$2,129.96	$1,889.42	$1,762.31	$1,689.71
$220,000	$4,566.84	$2,786.87	$2,231.39	$1,979.40	$1,846.23	$1,770.17
$230,000	$4,774.42	$2,913.54	$2,332.81	$2,069.37	$1,930.15	$1,850.63
$240,000	$4,982.01	$3,040.22	$2,434.24	$2,159.34	$2,014.07	$1,931.09
$250,000	$5,189.59	$3,166.89	$2,535.67	$2,249.31	$2,097.99	$2,011.56
$260,000	$5,397.17	$3,293.57	$2,637.09	$2,339.29	$2,181.91	$2,092.02
$270,000	$5,604.76	$3,420.25	$2,738.52	$2,429.26	$2,265.83	$2,172.48
$280,000	$5,812.34	$3,546.92	$2,839.95	$2,519.23	$2,349.75	$2,252.94
$290,000	$6,019.92	$3,673.60	$2,941.37	$2,609.21	$2,433.67	$2,333.41
$300,000	$6,227.51	$3,800.27	$3,042.80	$2,699.18	$2,517.59	$2,413.87
$310,000	$6,435.09	$3,926.95	$3,144.23	$2,789.15	$2,601.51	$2,494.33

Interest Rate: 9.50%

Amount Borrowed	Length of Loan (in Years)					
	5	10	15	20	25	30
$50,000	$1,050.09	$646.99	$522.11	$466.07	$436.85	$420.43
$60,000	$1,260.11	$776.39	$626.53	$559.28	$524.22	$504.51
$70,000	$1,470.13	$905.78	$730.96	$652.49	$611.59	$588.60
$80,000	$1,680.15	$1,035.18	$835.38	$745.70	$698.96	$672.68
$90,000	$1,890.17	$1,164.58	$939.80	$838.92	$786.33	$756.77
$100,000	$2,100.19	$1,293.98	$1,044.22	$932.13	$873.70	$840.85
$110,000	$2,310.20	$1,423.37	$1,148.65	$1,025.34	$961.07	$924.94
$120,000	$2,520.22	$1,552.77	$1,253.07	$1,118.56	$1,048.44	$1,009.03
$130,000	$2,730.24	$1,682.17	$1,357.49	$1,211.77	$1,135.81	$1,093.11
$140,000	$2,940.26	$1,811.57	$1,461.91	$1,304.98	$1,223.18	$1,177.20
$150,000	$3,150.28	$1,940.96	$1,566.34	$1,398.20	$1,310.54	$1,261.28
$160,000	$3,360.30	$2,070.36	$1,670.76	$1,491.41	$1,397.91	$1,345.37
$170,000	$3,570.32	$2,199.76	$1,775.18	$1,584.62	$1,485.28	$1,429.45
$180,000	$3,780.34	$2,329.16	$1,879.60	$1,677.84	$1,572.65	$1,513.54
$190,000	$3,990.35	$2,458.55	$1,984.03	$1,771.05	$1,660.02	$1,597.62
$200,000	$4,200.37	$2,587.95	$2,088.45	$1,864.26	$1,747.39	$1,681.71
$210,000	$4,410.39	$2,717.35	$2,192.87	$1,957.48	$1,834.76	$1,765.79
$220,000	$4,620.41	$2,846.75	$2,297.29	$2,050.69	$1,922.13	$1,849.88
$230,000	$4,830.43	$2,976.14	$2,401.72	$2,143.90	$2,009.50	$1,933.96
$240,000	$5,040.45	$3,105.54	$2,506.14	$2,237.11	$2,096.87	$2,018.05
$250,000	$5,250.47	$3,234.94	$2,610.56	$2,330.33	$2,184.24	$2,102.14
$260,000	$5,460.48	$3,364.34	$2,714.98	$2,423.54	$2,271.61	$2,186.22
$270,000	$5,670.50	$3,493.73	$2,819.41	$2,516.75	$2,358.98	$2,270.31
$280,000	$5,880.52	$3,623.13	$2,923.83	$2,609.97	$2,446.35	$2,354.39
$290,000	$6,090.54	$3,752.53	$3,028.25	$2,703.18	$2,533.72	$2,438.48
$300,000	$6,300.56	$3,881.93	$3,132.67	$2,796.39	$2,621.09	$2,522.56
$310,000	$6,510.58	$4,011.32	$3,237.10	$2,889.61	$2,708.46	$2,606.65

Interest Rate: 10.00%

Amount Borrowed	Length of Loan (in Years)					
	5	10	15	20	25	30
$50,000	$1,062.35	$660.75	$537.30	$482.51	$454.35	$438.79
$60,000	$1,274.82	$792.90	$644.76	$579.01	$545.22	$526.54
$70,000	$1,487.29	$925.06	$752.22	$675.52	$636.09	$614.30
$80,000	$1,699.76	$1,057.21	$859.68	$772.02	$726.96	$702.06
$90,000	$1,912.23	$1,189.36	$967.14	$868.52	$817.83	$789.81
$100,000	$2,124.70	$1,321.51	$1,074.61	$965.02	$908.70	$877.57
$110,000	$2,337.17	$1,453.66	$1,182.07	$1,061.52	$999.57	$965.33
$120,000	$2,549.65	$1,585.81	$1,289.53	$1,158.03	$1,090.44	$1,053.09
$130,000	$2,762.12	$1,717.96	$1,396.99	$1,254.53	$1,181.31	$1,140.84
$140,000	$2,974.59	$1,850.11	$1,504.45	$1,351.03	$1,272.18	$1,228.60
$150,000	$3,187.06	$1,982.26	$1,611.91	$1,447.53	$1,363.05	$1,316.36
$160,000	$3,399.53	$2,114.41	$1,719.37	$1,544.03	$1,453.92	$1,404.11
$170,000	$3,612.00	$2,246.56	$1,826.83	$1,640.54	$1,544.79	$1,491.87
$180,000	$3,824.47	$2,378.71	$1,934.29	$1,737.04	$1,635.66	$1,579.63
$190,000	$4,036.94	$2,510.86	$2,041.75	$1,833.54	$1,726.53	$1,667.39
$200,000	$4,249.41	$2,643.01	$2,149.21	$1,930.04	$1,817.40	$1,755.14
$210,000	$4,461.88	$2,775.17	$2,256.67	$2,026.55	$1,908.27	$1,842.90
$220,000	$4,674.35	$2,907.32	$2,364.13	$2,123.05	$1,999.14	$1,930.66
$230,000	$4,886.82	$3,039.47	$2,471.59	$2,219.55	$2,090.01	$2,018.41
$240,000	$5,099.29	$3,171.62	$2,579.05	$2,316.05	$2,180.88	$2,106.17
$250,000	$5,311.76	$3,303.77	$2,686.51	$2,412.55	$2,271.75	$2,193.93
$260,000	$5,524.23	$3,435.92	$2,793.97	$2,509.06	$2,362.62	$2,281.69
$270,000	$5,736.70	$3,568.07	$2,901.43	$2,605.56	$2,453.49	$2,369.44
$280,000	$5,949.17	$3,700.22	$3,008.89	$2,702.06	$2,544.36	$2,457.20
$290,000	$6,161.64	$3,832.37	$3,116.35	$2,798.56	$2,635.23	$2,544.96
$300,000	$6,374.11	$3,964.52	$3,223.82	$2,895.06	$2,726.10	$2,632.71
$310,000	$6,586.58	$4,096.67	$3,331.28	$2,991.57	$2,816.97	$2,720.47

Interest Rate: 10.50%

Amount Borrowed	Length of Loan (in Years)					
	5	10	15	20	25	30
$50,000	$1,074.70	$674.67	$552.70	$499.19	$472.09	$457.37
$60,000	$1,289.63	$809.61	$663.24	$599.03	$566.51	$548.84
$70,000	$1,504.57	$944.54	$773.78	$698.87	$660.93	$640.32
$80,000	$1,719.51	$1,079.48	$884.32	$798.70	$755.35	$731.79
$90,000	$1,934.45	$1,214.41	$994.86	$898.54	$849.76	$823.27
$100,000	$2,149.39	$1,349.35	$1,105.40	$998.38	$944.18	$914.74
$110,000	$2,364.33	$1,484.28	$1,215.94	$1,098.22	$1,038.60	$1,006.21
$120,000	$2,579.27	$1,619.22	$1,326.48	$1,198.06	$1,133.02	$1,097.69
$130,000	$2,794.21	$1,754.15	$1,437.02	$1,297.89	$1,227.44	$1,189.16
$140,000	$3,009.15	$1,889.09	$1,547.56	$1,397.73	$1,321.85	$1,280.64
$150,000	$3,224.09	$2,024.02	$1,658.10	$1,497.57	$1,416.27	$1,372.11
$160,000	$3,439.02	$2,158.96	$1,768.64	$1,597.41	$1,510.69	$1,463.58
$170,000	$3,653.96	$2,293.89	$1,879.18	$1,697.25	$1,605.11	$1,555.06
$180,000	$3,868.90	$2,428.83	$1,989.72	$1,797.08	$1,699.53	$1,646.53
$190,000	$4,083.84	$2,563.76	$2,100.26	$1,896.92	$1,793.95	$1,738.00
$200,000	$4,298.78	$2,698.70	$2,210.80	$1,996.76	$1,888.36	$1,829.48
$210,000	$4,513.72	$2,833.63	$2,321.34	$2,096.60	$1,982.78	$1,920.95
$220,000	$4,728.66	$2,968.57	$2,431.88	$2,196.44	$2,077.20	$2,012.43
$230,000	$4,943.60	$3,103.50	$2,542.42	$2,296.27	$2,171.62	$2,103.90
$240,000	$5,158.54	$3,238.44	$2,652.96	$2,396.11	$2,266.04	$2,195.37
$250,000	$5,373.48	$3,373.37	$2,763.50	$2,495.95	$2,360.45	$2,286.85
$260,000	$5,588.41	$3,508.31	$2,874.04	$2,595.79	$2,454.87	$2,378.32
$270,000	$5,803.35	$3,643.24	$2,984.58	$2,695.63	$2,549.29	$2,469.80
$280,000	$6,018.29	$3,778.18	$3,095.12	$2,795.46	$2,643.71	$2,561.27
$290,000	$6,233.23	$3,913.11	$3,205.66	$2,895.30	$2,738.13	$2,652.74
$300,000	$6,448.17	$4,048.05	$3,316.20	$2,995.14	$2,832.55	$2,744.22
$310,000	$6,663.11	$4,182.98	$3,426.74	$3,094.98	$2,926.96	$2,835.69

Interest Rate: 11.00%

Amount Borrowed	Length of Loan (in Years)					
	5	10	15	20	25	30
$50,000	$1,087.12	$688.75	$568.30	$516.09	$490.06	$476.16
$60,000	$1,304.55	$826.50	$681.96	$619.31	$588.07	$571.39
$70,000	$1,521.97	$964.25	$795.62	$722.53	$686.08	$666.63
$80,000	$1,739.39	$1,102.00	$909.28	$825.75	$784.09	$761.86
$90,000	$1,956.82	$1,239.75	$1,022.94	$928.97	$882.10	$857.09
$100,000	$2,174.24	$1,377.50	$1,136.60	$1,032.19	$980.11	$952.32
$110,000	$2,391.67	$1,515.25	$1,250.26	$1,135.41	$1,078.12	$1,047.56
$120,000	$2,609.09	$1,653.00	$1,363.92	$1,238.63	$1,176.14	$1,142.79
$130,000	$2,826.51	$1,790.75	$1,477.58	$1,341.84	$1,274.15	$1,238.02
$140,000	$3,043.94	$1,928.50	$1,591.24	$1,445.06	$1,372.16	$1,333.25
$150,000	$3,261.36	$2,066.25	$1,704.90	$1,548.28	$1,470.17	$1,428.49
$160,000	$3,478.79	$2,204.00	$1,818.56	$1,651.50	$1,568.18	$1,523.72
$170,000	$3,696.21	$2,341.75	$1,932.21	$1,754.72	$1,666.19	$1,618.95
$180,000	$3,913.64	$2,479.50	$2,045.87	$1,857.94	$1,764.20	$1,714.18
$190,000	$4,131.06	$2,617.25	$2,159.53	$1,961.16	$1,862.21	$1,809.41
$200,000	$4,348.48	$2,755.00	$2,273.19	$2,064.38	$1,960.23	$1,904.65
$210,000	$4,565.91	$2,892.75	$2,386.85	$2,167.60	$2,058.24	$1,999.88
$220,000	$4,783.33	$3,030.50	$2,500.51	$2,270.81	$2,156.25	$2,095.11
$230,000	$5,000.76	$3,168.25	$2,614.17	$2,374.03	$2,254.26	$2,190.34
$240,000	$5,218.18	$3,306.00	$2,727.83	$2,477.25	$2,352.27	$2,285.58
$250,000	$5,435.61	$3,443.75	$2,841.49	$2,580.47	$2,450.28	$2,380.81
$260,000	$5,653.03	$3,581.50	$2,955.15	$2,683.69	$2,548.29	$2,476.04
$270,000	$5,870.45	$3,719.25	$3,068.81	$2,786.91	$2,646.31	$2,571.27
$280,000	$6,087.88	$3,857.00	$3,182.47	$2,890.13	$2,744.32	$2,666.51
$290,000	$6,305.30	$3,994.75	$3,296.13	$2,993.35	$2,842.33	$2,761.74
$300,000	$6,522.73	$4,132.50	$3,409.79	$3,096.57	$2,940.34	$2,856.97
$310,000	$6,740.15	$4,270.25	$3,523.45	$3,199.78	$3,038.35	$2,952.20

Interest Rate: 11.50%

Amount Borrowed	Length of Loan (in Years)					
	5	10	15	20	25	30
$50,000	$1,099.63	$702.98	$584.09	$533.21	$508.23	$495.15
$60,000	$1,319.56	$843.57	$700.91	$639.86	$609.88	$594.17
$70,000	$1,539.48	$984.17	$817.73	$746.50	$711.53	$693.20
$80,000	$1,759.41	$1,124.76	$934.55	$853.14	$813.18	$792.23
$90,000	$1,979.33	$1,265.36	$1,051.37	$959.79	$914.82	$891.26
$100,000	$2,199.26	$1,405.95	$1,168.19	$1,066.43	$1,016.47	$990.29
$110,000	$2,419.19	$1,546.55	$1,285.01	$1,173.07	$1,118.12	$1,089.32
$120,000	$2,639.11	$1,687.15	$1,401.83	$1,279.72	$1,219.76	$1,188.35
$130,000	$2,859.04	$1,827.74	$1,518.65	$1,386.36	$1,321.41	$1,287.38
$140,000	$3,078.97	$1,968.34	$1,635.47	$1,493.00	$1,423.06	$1,386.41
$150,000	$3,298.89	$2,108.93	$1,752.28	$1,599.64	$1,524.70	$1,485.44
$160,000	$3,518.82	$2,249.53	$1,869.10	$1,706.29	$1,626.35	$1,584.47
$170,000	$3,738.74	$2,390.12	$1,985.92	$1,812.93	$1,728.00	$1,683.50
$180,000	$3,958.67	$2,530.72	$2,102.74	$1,919.57	$1,829.64	$1,782.52
$190,000	$4,178.60	$2,671.31	$2,219.56	$2,026.22	$1,931.29	$1,881.55
$200,000	$4,398.52	$2,811.91	$2,336.38	$2,132.86	$2,032.94	$1,980.58
$210,000	$4,618.45	$2,952.50	$2,453.20	$2,239.50	$2,134.58	$2,079.61
$220,000	$4,838.37	$3,093.10	$2,570.02	$2,346.15	$2,236.23	$2,178.64
$230,000	$5,058.30	$3,233.70	$2,686.84	$2,452.79	$2,337.88	$2,277.67
$240,000	$5,278.23	$3,374.29	$2,803.66	$2,559.43	$2,439.53	$2,376.70
$250,000	$5,498.15	$3,514.89	$2,920.47	$2,666.07	$2,541.17	$2,475.73
$260,000	$5,718.08	$3,655.48	$3,037.29	$2,772.72	$2,642.82	$2,574.76
$270,000	$5,938.00	$3,796.08	$3,154.11	$2,879.36	$2,744.47	$2,673.79
$280,000	$6,157.93	$3,936.67	$3,270.93	$2,986.00	$2,846.11	$2,772.82
$290,000	$6,377.86	$4,077.27	$3,387.75	$3,092.65	$2,947.76	$2,871.85
$300,000	$6,597.78	$4,217.86	$3,504.57	$3,199.29	$3,049.41	$2,970.87
$310,000	$6,817.71	$4,358.46	$3,621.39	$3,305.93	$3,151.05	$3,069.90

Interest Rate: 12.00%

Amount Borrowed	Length of Loan (in Years)					
	5	10	15	20	25	30
$50,000	$1,112.22	$717.35	$600.08	$550.54	$526.61	$514.31
$60,000	$1,334.67	$860.83	$720.10	$660.65	$631.93	$617.17
$70,000	$1,557.11	$1,004.30	$840.12	$770.76	$737.26	$720.03
$80,000	$1,779.56	$1,147.77	$960.13	$880.87	$842.58	$822.89
$90,000	$2,002.00	$1,291.24	$1,080.15	$990.98	$947.90	$925.75
$100,000	$2,224.44	$1,434.71	$1,200.17	$1,101.09	$1,053.22	$1,028.61
$110,000	$2,446.89	$1,578.18	$1,320.18	$1,211.19	$1,158.55	$1,131.47
$120,000	$2,669.33	$1,721.65	$1,440.20	$1,321.30	$1,263.87	$1,234.34
$130,000	$2,891.78	$1,865.12	$1,560.22	$1,431.41	$1,369.19	$1,337.20
$140,000	$3,114.22	$2,008.59	$1,680.24	$1,541.52	$1,474.51	$1,440.06
$150,000	$3,336.67	$2,152.06	$1,800.25	$1,651.63	$1,579.84	$1,542.92
$160,000	$3,559.11	$2,295.54	$1,920.27	$1,761.74	$1,685.16	$1,645.78
$170,000	$3,781.56	$2,439.01	$2,040.29	$1,871.85	$1,790.48	$1,748.64
$180,000	$4,004.00	$2,582.48	$2,160.30	$1,981.96	$1,895.80	$1,851.50
$190,000	$4,226.45	$2,725.95	$2,280.32	$2,092.06	$2,001.13	$1,954.36
$200,000	$4,448.89	$2,869.42	$2,400.34	$2,202.17	$2,106.45	$2,057.23
$210,000	$4,671.33	$3,012.89	$2,520.35	$2,312.28	$2,211.77	$2,160.09
$220,000	$4,893.78	$3,156.36	$2,640.37	$2,422.39	$2,317.09	$2,262.95
$230,000	$5,116.22	$3,299.83	$2,760.39	$2,532.50	$2,422.42	$2,365.81
$240,000	$5,338.67	$3,443.30	$2,880.40	$2,642.61	$2,527.74	$2,468.67
$250,000	$5,561.11	$3,586.77	$3,000.42	$2,752.72	$2,633.06	$2,571.53
$260,000	$5,783.56	$3,730.24	$3,120.44	$2,862.82	$2,738.38	$2,674.39
$270,000	$6,006.00	$3,873.72	$3,240.45	$2,972.93	$2,843.71	$2,777.25
$280,000	$6,228.45	$4,017.19	$3,360.47	$3,083.04	$2,949.03	$2,880.12
$290,000	$6,450.89	$4,160.66	$3,480.49	$3,193.15	$3,054.35	$2,982.98
$300,000	$6,673.33	$4,304.13	$3,600.50	$3,303.26	$3,159.67	$3,085.84
$310,000	$6,895.78	$4,447.60	$3,720.52	$3,413.37	$3,264.99	$3,188.70

Interest Rate: 12.50%

Amount Borrowed	Length of Loan (in Years)					
	5	10	15	20	25	30
$50,000	$1,124.90	$731.88	$616.26	$568.07	$545.18	$533.63
$60,000	$1,349.88	$878.26	$739.51	$681.68	$654.21	$640.35
$70,000	$1,574.86	$1,024.63	$862.77	$795.30	$763.25	$747.08
$80,000	$1,799.84	$1,171.01	$986.02	$908.91	$872.28	$853.81
$90,000	$2,024.81	$1,317.39	$1,109.27	$1,022.53	$981.32	$960.53
$100,000	$2,249.79	$1,463.76	$1,232.52	$1,136.14	$1,090.35	$1,067.26
$110,000	$2,474.77	$1,610.14	$1,355.77	$1,249.75	$1,199.39	$1,173.98
$120,000	$2,699.75	$1,756.51	$1,479.03	$1,363.37	$1,308.42	$1,280.71
$130,000	$2,924.73	$1,902.89	$1,602.28	$1,476.98	$1,417.46	$1,387.44
$140,000	$3,149.71	$2,049.27	$1,725.53	$1,590.60	$1,526.50	$1,494.16
$150,000	$3,374.69	$2,195.64	$1,848.78	$1,704.21	$1,635.53	$1,600.89
$160,000	$3,599.67	$2,342.02	$1,972.04	$1,817.82	$1,744.57	$1,707.61
$170,000	$3,824.65	$2,488.39	$2,095.29	$1,931.44	$1,853.60	$1,814.34
$180,000	$4,049.63	$2,634.77	$2,218.54	$2,045.05	$1,962.64	$1,921.06
$190,000	$4,274.61	$2,781.15	$2,341.79	$2,158.67	$2,071.67	$2,027.79
$200,000	$4,499.59	$2,927.52	$2,465.04	$2,272.28	$2,180.71	$2,134.52
$210,000	$4,724.57	$3,073.90	$2,588.30	$2,385.90	$2,289.74	$2,241.24
$220,000	$4,949.55	$3,220.28	$2,711.55	$2,499.51	$2,398.78	$2,347.97
$230,000	$5,174.53	$3,366.65	$2,834.80	$2,613.12	$2,507.81	$2,454.69
$240,000	$5,399.51	$3,513.03	$2,958.05	$2,726.74	$2,616.85	$2,561.42
$250,000	$5,624.48	$3,659.40	$3,081.31	$2,840.35	$2,725.89	$2,668.14
$260,000	$5,849.46	$3,805.78	$3,204.56	$2,953.97	$2,834.92	$2,774.87
$270,000	$6,074.44	$3,952.16	$3,327.81	$3,067.58	$2,943.96	$2,881.60
$280,000	$6,299.42	$4,098.53	$3,451.06	$3,181.19	$3,052.99	$2,988.32
$290,000	$6,524.40	$4,244.91	$3,574.31	$3,294.81	$3,162.03	$3,095.05
$300,000	$6,749.38	$4,391.29	$3,697.57	$3,408.42	$3,271.06	$3,201.77
$310,000	$6,974.36	$4,537.66	$3,820.82	$3,522.04	$3,380.10	$3,308.50

Interest Rate: 13.00%

Amount Borrowed	Length of Loan (in Years)					
	5	10	15	20	25	30
$50,000	$1,137.65	$746.55	$632.62	$585.79	$563.92	$553.10
$60,000	$1,365.18	$895.86	$759.15	$702.95	$676.70	$663.72
$70,000	$1,592.72	$1,045.18	$885.67	$820.10	$789.48	$774.34
$80,000	$1,820.25	$1,194.49	$1,012.19	$937.26	$902.27	$884.96
$90,000	$2,047.78	$1,343.80	$1,138.72	$1,054.42	$1,015.05	$995.58
$100,000	$2,275.31	$1,493.11	$1,265.24	$1,171.58	$1,127.84	$1,106.20
$110,000	$2,502.84	$1,642.42	$1,391.77	$1,288.73	$1,240.62	$1,216.82
$120,000	$2,730.37	$1,791.73	$1,518.29	$1,405.89	$1,353.40	$1,327.44
$130,000	$2,957.90	$1,941.04	$1,644.81	$1,523.05	$1,466.19	$1,438.06
$140,000	$3,185.43	$2,090.35	$1,771.34	$1,640.21	$1,578.97	$1,548.68
$150,000	$3,412.96	$2,239.66	$1,897.86	$1,757.36	$1,691.75	$1,659.30
$160,000	$3,640.49	$2,388.97	$2,024.39	$1,874.52	$1,804.54	$1,769.92
$170,000	$3,868.02	$2,538.28	$2,150.91	$1,991.68	$1,917.32	$1,880.54
$180,000	$4,095.55	$2,687.59	$2,277.44	$2,108.84	$2,030.10	$1,991.16
$190,000	$4,323.08	$2,836.90	$2,403.96	$2,225.99	$2,142.89	$2,101.78
$200,000	$4,550.61	$2,986.21	$2,530.48	$2,343.15	$2,255.67	$2,212.40
$210,000	$4,778.15	$3,135.53	$2,657.01	$2,460.31	$2,368.45	$2,323.02
$220,000	$5,005.68	$3,284.84	$2,783.53	$2,577.47	$2,481.24	$2,433.64
$230,000	$5,233.21	$3,434.15	$2,910.06	$2,694.62	$2,594.02	$2,544.26
$240,000	$5,460.74	$3,583.46	$3,036.58	$2,811.78	$2,706.80	$2,654.88
$250,000	$5,688.27	$3,732.77	$3,163.11	$2,928.94	$2,819.59	$2,765.50
$260,000	$5,915.80	$3,882.08	$3,289.63	$3,046.10	$2,932.37	$2,876.12
$270,000	$6,143.33	$4,031.39	$3,416.15	$3,163.25	$3,045.16	$2,986.74
$280,000	$6,370.86	$4,180.70	$3,542.68	$3,280.41	$3,157.94	$3,097.36
$290,000	$6,598.39	$4,330.01	$3,669.20	$3,397.57	$3,270.72	$3,207.98
$300,000	$6,825.92	$4,479.32	$3,795.73	$3,514.73	$3,383.51	$3,318.60
$310,000	$7,053.45	$4,628.63	$3,922.25	$3,631.88	$3,496.29	$3,429.22

Additional Resources

General References

About Home-Buying and Selling

Find tutorials to help you with every step of a real-estate transaction, free e-courses on many topics, and search engines to help you locate property world-wide. ☎ 828-862-6520, 🖢 *www.homebuying.about.com*

California Association of Realtors

The CAR offers in-depth coverage of California real estate, including the rules and regulations required within that state. This well-organized Web site includes general information that's helpful for real-estate transactions throughout the United States. ☎ 213-739-8200, 🖢 *www.car.org*

Department of Housing and Urban Development

HUD is a government regulatory agency that oversees lenders, manages fair housing issues, and provides resources for numerous other issues related to real estate. ☎ 202-708-1112, 🖢 *www.hud.gov*

Credit and Money Management

Equifax

Equifax is one of the three major credit-reporting agencies. It offers a service that allows you to check your credit reports and scores online or order copies by mail. ☎ 800-685-1111, 🖢 *www.equifax.com*

Experian

Another of the three major credit-reporting agencies. Check your credit reports and scores online or order copies by mail. ☎ 888-397-3742, 🖢 *www.experian.com*

MyFico.com

Developers of the scoring system used by many lenders to determine loan eligibility. The Web site offers a great deal of advice about managing your credit and improving your scores. 🖢 *www.myfico.com*

Quicken
Track stocks and other publicly traded investments, manage your money, and read informative articles that can help you buy and sell real estate. ✑ *www.quicken.com*

TransUnion
The third major credit-reporting agency. Check your credit reports and scores online or order copies by mail. ✆ 800-916-8800, ✑ *www.transunion.com*

Foreclosure Information

Foreclosures.com
A company that offers tools to help you locate and buy foreclosed properties throughout the United States. You'll also find advice to help you learn the differences between legitimate foreclosure deals and offerings that might be questionable. ✆ 800-310-7730, ✑ *www.foreclosures.com*

For Sale By Owner Resources

For Sale By Owner
FSBO sellers can advertise their properties here and find marketing advice and general information to help them get a contract and complete the sale. ✆ 888-933-8900, ✑ *www.forsalebyowner.com*

Owners.com
A Web site where you can advertise your properties to buyers worldwide. Resources include general information to help you sell your real estate. ✆ 866-797-5025, ✑ *www.owners.com*

Hazardous Substances

U.S. Centers for Disease Control
The CDC is a government agency that provides information to help you learn about radon gas, toxic molds, asbestos, and other similar topics that affect your health and your real-estate transactions. ✆ 800-311-3435, ✑ *www.cdc.gov*

Environmental Protection Agency

EPA is a U.S. government agency that monitors environmental hazards such as asbestos, radon gas, molds, buried storage tanks, and other toxic materials important to anyone who plans to buy or sell real estate. ✆ 202-272-0167, ✍ *www.epa.gov*

National Flood Insurance Program

FEMA offers details about the National Flood Insurance Program. ✆ 202-566-1600, ✍ *www.fema.gov/nfip*

Home Repair and Home Warranty

About Home Repair

A Web site devoted to providing repair and update how-to information for homeowners. ✆ 212-204-2710, ✍ *www.homerepair.about.com*

American Home Shield Warranties

A company that provides home warranty coverage to home-buyers, home-sellers, and current owners who plan to keep their homes. ✆ 800-827-4636, ✍ *www.americanhomeshield.com*

HMS Home Warranties

HMS sells home warranty policies throughout the United States. ✆ 800-941-9000, ✍ *www.hmsnet.com*

Advice on Being a Landlord

Apartment Living/Rental

A user-friendly Web site that offers insights into the world of rental living. Get help with leases and general tenant-landlord relations. ✆ 212-204-2710, ✍ *www.apartments.about.com*

Listings Online

Homes.com

Homes.com is a real-estate search engine for agencies and agents. You'll find properties for sale throughout the United States. ✆ 888.329.7576, ✍ *www.homes.com*

HomeAdvisor.com

Another real-estate search engine, it offers listings and also includes tutorials to help answer your questions about real-estate transactions. ✆ *www.homeadvisor.com*

National Association of Realtors

You will find real-estate listings and an assortment of advice to help you buy real estate and work with real-estate agents. ✆ 805-557-2300, ✆ *www.realtor.com*

Mapping Services

HazardMaps.gov

FEMA's online advisory maps cover areas at risk to various types of hazards, including earthquake, hurricane, and flood. ✆ 202-566-1600, ✆ *www.hazardmaps.gov/atlas.php*

TerraServer.com

Terra Server offers aerial maps for locations throughout the world. ✆ *www.terraserver.com*

TopoZone.com

Find topographical maps using a zip code and address or by entering longitude and latitude for the location you are seeking. ✆ 978-251-4242, ✆ *www.topozone.com*

Mortgage Lenders and Brokers Online

Ameriquest

Ameriquest is an online broker that maintains over 250 local offices throughout the United States. ✆ 888-436-7571, ✆ *www.ameriquestmortgage.com*

Bank of America

Bank of America is a lender with banks in many locations throughout the United States. Apply for a loan locally or online. ✆ *www.bankofamerica.com*

Countrywide Financial

Countrywide can help you with a real-estate loan, financial planning services, insurance, and many other services related to the real-estate and financial industries. ✆ 800-556-9568, ✆ *www.countrywide.com*

Wells Fargo

Wells Fargo is a full-service bank that offers its customers loans of all types, along with checking, credit cards and other financial services. ✆ 800-869-3557, ✐ www.wellsfargo.com

Real-Estate News

Inman News

A real-estate news portal offering advice for real-estate professionals as well as others who wish to buy and sell real estate. ✆ 800-775-4662, ✐ www.inman.com

Realty Times

Realty Times is a Web site that provides real-estate news and feature articles written by a variety of columnists. ✆ 214-353-6980, ✐ www.realtytimes.com

Real-Estate Signs and Brochure Boxes

Dee Sign

Dee Sign supplies personalized and stock signs to the real-estate trade. The company also sells transparent brochure boxes. ✆ 800-333-7446, ✐ www.dee-sign.com

For Sale By Owner Advertising Service

This company specializes in FSBO yard signs. ✆ 713-664-4115, ✐ www.fsboadvertisingservice.com

Innovative Plastics

Innovative Plastics sells durable plastic brochure boxes that you can leave marketing materials in for pickup by passersby. ✆ 714-891-8800, ✐ www.plasticfab.com

REITs

National Association of Real-Estate Investment Trusts

Find in-depth information about the history of REITs, plus advice to help you understand the REIT market and make investment decisions. ✆ 202-739-9400, ✐ www.nareit.com

RV Parks and Campgrounds

National Association of RV Parks and Campgrounds

Find information about RV parks, including facts to help you understand what's involved in park development and management.
✍ *www.gocampingamerica.com*

Secondary Mortgage Market Agencies

Fannie Mae

Fannie Mae's Web site offers many resources to help people who wish to buy and sell real estate. ☎ 800-732-6643, ✍ *www.fanniemae.com*

Freddie Mac

Freddie Mac is another secondary market agency that offers real-estate advice on its Web site. ✍ *www.freddiemac.com*

Ginnie Mae

Ginnie Mae is a government agency that oversees some types of loans insured on the secondary market. Its Web site offers buying advice, including information on investing in government backed securities. ✍ *www.ginniemae.gov*

Tax Advice

Internal Revenue Service (IRS)

Locate forms and instructions to help you understand and abide by income reporting laws within the United States. ☎ 800-829-1040, ✍ *www.irs.govk*

Index

THE EVERYTHING SERIES!

BUSINESS

Everything® Business Planning Book
Everything® Coaching and Mentoring Book
Everything® Fundraising Book
Everything® Home-Based Business Book
Everything® Landlording Book
Everything® Leadership Book
Everything® Managing People Book
Everything® Negotiating Book
Everything® Network Marketing Book
Everything® Online Business Book
Everything® Project Management Book
Everything® Robert's Rules Book,
    $7.95($11.95 CAN)
Everything® Selling Book
Everything® Start Your Own Business Book
Everything® Time Management Book

COMPUTERS

Everything® Build Your Own Home Page Book
Everything® Computer Book

COOKBOOKS

Everything® Barbecue Cookbook
Everything® Bartender's Book, $9.95
    ($15.95 CAN)
Everything® Chinese Cookbook
Everything® Chocolate Cookbook
Everything® Cookbook
Everything® Dessert Cookbook
Everything® Diabetes Cookbook
Everything® Fondue Cookbook
Everything® Grilling Cookbook
Everything® Holiday Cookbook
Everything® Indian Cookbook
Everything® Low-Carb Cookbook
Everything® Low-Fat High-Flavor Cookbook
Everything® Low-Salt Cookbook
Everything® Mediterranean Cookbook
Everything® Mexican Cookbook
Everything® One-Pot Cookbook

Everything® Pasta Cookbook
Everything® Quick Meals Cookbook
Everything® Slow Cooker Cookbook
Everything® Soup Cookbook
Everything® Thai Cookbook
Everything® Vegetarian Cookbook
Everything® Wine Book

HEALTH

Everything® Alzheimer's Book
Everything® Anti-Aging Book
Everything® Diabetes Book
Everything® Dieting Book
Everything® Hypnosis Book
Everything® Low Cholesterol Book
Everything® Massage Book
Everything® Menopause Book
Everything® Nutrition Book
Everything® Reflexology Book
Everything® Reiki Book
Everything® Stress Management Book
Everything® Vitamins, Minerals, and
    Nutritional Supplements Book

HISTORY

Everything® American Government Book
Everything® American History Book
Everything® Civil War Book
Everything® Irish History & Heritage Book
Everything® Mafia Book
Everything® Middle East Book

HOBBIES & GAMES

Everything® Bridge Book
Everything® Candlemaking Book
Everything® Card Games Book
Everything® Cartooning Book
Everything® Casino Gambling Book, 2nd Ed.
Everything® Chess Basics Book
Everything® Collectibles Book
Everything® Crossword and Puzzle Book

Everything® Crossword Challenge Book
Everything® Drawing Book
Everything® Digital Photography Book
Everything® Easy Crosswords Book
Everything® Family Tree Book
Everything® Games Book
Everything® Knitting Book
Everything® Magic Book
Everything® Motorcycle Book
Everything® Online Genealogy Book
Everything® Photography Book
Everything® Poker Strategy Book
Everything® Pool & Billiards Book
Everything® Quilting Book
Everything® Scrapbooking Book
Everything® Sewing Book
Everything® Soapmaking Book

HOME IMPROVEMENT

Everything® Feng Shui Book
Everything® Feng Shui Decluttering Book,
    $9.95 ($15.95 CAN)
Everything® Fix-It Book
Everything® Homebuilding Book
Everything® Home Decorating Book
Everything® Landscaping Book
Everything® Lawn Care Book
Everything® Organize Your Home Book

EVERYTHING® KIDS' BOOKS

All titles are $6.95 ($10.95 Canada)
unless otherwise noted
Everything® Kids' Baseball Book, 3rd Ed.
Everything® Kids' Bible Trivia Book
Everything® Kids' Bugs Book
Everything® Kids' Christmas Puzzle
    & Activity Book
Everything® Kids' Cookbook
Everything® Kids' Halloween Puzzle
    & Activity Book ($9.95 CAN)

All Everything® books are priced at $12.95 or $14.95, unless otherwise stated. Prices subject to change without notice.
Canadian prices range from $11.95–$31.95, and are subject to change without notice.

Everything® Kids' Hidden Pictures Book
($9.95 CAN)
Everything® Kids' Joke Book
Everything® Kids' Knock Knock Book
($9.95 CAN)
Everything® Kids' Math Puzzles Book
Everything® Kids' Mazes Book
Everything® Kids' Money Book ($11.95 CAN)
Everything® Kids' Monsters Book
Everything® Kids' Nature Book ($11.95 CAN)
Everything® Kids' Puzzle Book
Everything® Kids' Riddles & Brain Teasers Book
Everything® Kids' Science Experiments Book
Everything® Kids' Soccer Book
Everything® Kids' Travel Activity Book

KIDS' STORY BOOKS

Everything® Bedtime Story Book
Everything® Bible Stories Book
Everything® Fairy Tales Book
Everything® Mother Goose Book

LANGUAGE

Everything® Conversational Japanese Book
(with CD), $19.95 ($31.95 CAN)
Everything® Inglés Book
Everything® French Phrase Book, $9.95
($15.95 CAN)
Everything® Learning French Book
Everything® Learning German Book
Everything® Learning Italian Book
Everything® Learning Latin Book
Everything® Learning Spanish Book
Everything® Sign Language Book
Everything® Spanish Phrase Book,
$9.95 ($15.95 CAN)
Everything® Spanish Verb Book,
$9.95 ($15.95 CAN)

MUSIC

Everything® Drums Book (with CD),
$19.95 ($31.95 CAN)
Everything® Guitar Book
Everything® Home Recording Book
Everything® Playing Piano and Keyboards Book
Everything® Rock & Blues Guitar Book
(with CD), $19.95 ($31.95 CAN)
Everything® Songwriting Book

NEW AGE

Everything® Astrology Book
Everything® Divining the Future Book
Everything® Dreams Book
Everything® Ghost Book
Everything® Love Signs Book,
$9.95 ($15.95 CAN)
Everything® Meditation Book
Everything® Numerology Book
Everything® Paganism Book
Everything® Palmistry Book
Everything® Psychic Book
Everything® Spells & Charms Book
Everything® Tarot Book
Everything® Wicca and Witchcraft Book

PARENTING

Everything® Baby Names Book
Everything® Baby Shower Book
Everything® Baby's First Food Book
Everything® Baby's First Year Book
Everything® Birthing Book
Everything® Breastfeeding Book
Everything® Father-to-Be Book
Everything® Get Ready for Baby Book
Everything® Getting Pregnant Book
Everything® Homeschooling Book
Everything® Parent's Guide to Children
with Asperger's Syndrome
Everything® Parent's Guide to Children
with Autism
Everything® Parent's Guide to Children
with Dyslexia
Everything® Parent's Guide to Positive Discipline
Everything® Parent's Guide to Raising a
Successful Child
Everything® Parenting a Teenager Book
Everything® Potty Training Book,
$9.95 ($15.95 CAN)
Everything® Pregnancy Book, 2nd Ed.
Everything® Pregnancy Fitness Book
Everything® Pregnancy Nutrition Book
Everything® Pregnancy Organizer,
$15.00 ($22.95 CAN)
Everything® Toddler Book
Everything® Tween Book

PERSONAL FINANCE

Everything® Budgeting Book
Everything® Get Out of Debt Book

Everything® Get Rich Book
Everything® Homebuying Book, 2nd Ed.
Everything® Homeselling Book
Everything® Investing Book
Everything® Money Book
Everything® Mutual Funds Book
Everything® Online Business Book
Everything® Personal Finance Book
Everything® Personal Finance in Your
20s & 30s Book
Everything® Real Estate Investing Book
Everything® Wills & Estate Planning Book

PETS

Everything® Cat Book
Everything® Dog Book
Everything® Dog Training and Tricks Book
Everything® Golden Retriever Book
Everything® Horse Book
Everything® Labrador Retriever Book
Everything® Poodle Book
Everything® Puppy Book
Everything® Rottweiler Book
Everything® Tropical Fish Book

REFERENCE

Everything® Astronomy Book
Everything® Car Care Book
Everything® Christmas Book,
$15.00 ($21.95 CAN)
Everything® Classical Mythology Book
Everything® Einstein Book
Everything® Etiquette Book
Everything® Great Thinkers Book
Everything® Philosophy Book
Everything® Psychology Book
Everything® Shakespeare Book
Everything® Tall Tales, Legends, & Other
Outrageous Lies Book
Everything® Toasts Book
Everything® Trivia Book
Everything® Weather Book

RELIGION

Everything® Angels Book
Everything® Bible Book
Everything® Buddhism Book
Everything® Catholicism Book
Everything® Christianity Book
Everything® Jewish History & Heritage Book

All Everything® books are priced at $12.95 or $14.95, unless otherwise stated. Prices subject to change without notice.
Canadian prices range from $11.95–$31.95, and are subject to change without notice.

Everything® Judaism Book
Everything® Koran Book
Everything® Prayer Book
Everything® Saints Book
Everything® Understanding Islam Book
Everything® World's Religions Book
Everything® Zen Book

SCHOOL & CAREERS

Everything® After College Book
Everything® Alternative Careers Book
Everything® College Survival Book
Everything® Cover Letter Book
Everything® Get-a-Job Book
Everything® Hot Careers Book
Everything® Job Interview Book
Everything® New Teacher Book
Everything® Online Job Search Book
Everything® Personal Finance Book
Everything® Practice Interview Book
Everything® Resume Book, 2nd Ed.
Everything® Study Book

SELF-HELP/ RELATIONSHIPS

Everything® Dating Book
Everything® Divorce Book
Everything® Great Marriage Book
Everything® Great Sex Book
Everything® Kama Sutra Book
Everything® Romance Book
Everything® Self-Esteem Book
Everything® Success Book

SPORTS & FITNESS

Everything® Body Shaping Book
Everything® Fishing Book
Everything® Fly-Fishing Book
Everything® Golf Book
Everything® Golf Instruction Book
Everything® Knots Book
Everything® Pilates Book
Everything® Running Book
Everything® Sailing Book, 2nd Ed.
Everything® T'ai Chi and QiGong Book
Everything® Total Fitness Book
Everything® Weight Training Book
Everything® Yoga Book

TRAVEL

Everything® Family Guide to Hawaii
Everything® Family Guide to New York City, 2nd Ed.
Everything® Family Guide to Washington D.C., 2nd Ed.
Everything® Family Guide to the Walt Disney World Resort®, Universal Studios®, and Greater Orlando, 4th Ed.
Everything® Guide to Las Vegas
Everything® Guide to New England
Everything® Travel Guide to the Disneyland Resort®, California Adventure®, Universal Studios®, and the Anaheim Area

WEDDINGS

Everything® Bachelorette Party Book, $9.95 ($15.95 CAN)

Everything® Bridesmaid Book, $9.95 ($15.95 CAN)
Everything® Creative Wedding Ideas Book
Everything® Elopement Book, $9.95 ($15.95 CAN)
Everything® Father of the Bride Book, $9.95 ($15.95 CAN)
Everything® Groom Book, $9.95 ($15.95 CAN)
Everything® Jewish Wedding Book
Everything® Mother of the Bride Book, $9.95 ($15.95)
Everything® Wedding Book, 3rd Ed.
Everything® Wedding Checklist, $7.95 ($12.95 CAN)
Everything® Wedding Etiquette Book, $7.95 ($12.95 CAN)
Everything® Wedding Organizer, $15.00 ($22.95 CAN)
Everything® Wedding Shower Book, $7.95 ($12.95 CAN)
Everything® Wedding Vows Book, $7.95 ($12.95 CAN)
Everything® Weddings on a Budget Book, $9.95 ($15.95 CAN)

WRITING

Everything® Creative Writing Book
Everything® Get Published Book
Everything® Grammar and Style Book
Everything® Grant Writing Book
Everything® Guide to Writing a Novel
Everything® Guide to Writing Children's Books
Everything® Screenwriting Book
Everything® Writing Well Book